Why Go On

About the Author

Connecticut native Lisa Wright is the author of four books, including novels *The Invisible Visitor* and *Thunder Destroys Me*. Her inspiration for writing lies in knowing that just one sentence can change the entire course of a human life.

You may contact Lisa through Outfox Books at: info@outfoxbooks.com.

Also by Lisa Wright:

Instant Love Advice for Women: You Are Only Three Questions Away From an Answer

Why Go On

Connecticut Residents Bring Dark Days to Light

Lisa Wright

Why Go On:
Connecticut Residents Bring Dark Days to Light

Copyright © 2015 Lisa Wright
All rights reserved.

ISBN: 978-0692513071

First Edition, 2015
Printed in the U.S.A.

With the exception of short excerpts reprinted for the purposes of book reviews, no part of this publication may be reproduced, stored in a retrieval system, or transmitted, in any form or by any means, electronic, mechanical, photocopying, recording or otherwise, without the prior permission of the copyright owner.

Edited by: Elizabeth Bruno
Cover Photography from jaboo2foto/Shutterstock.com
Interior photographs by Lisa Wright with the exception of:
Fernando & Crystal, Stephanie, Christina ("Fire"), Stan and Cjet.

Note: Some of the names used within have been changed in order to protect the anonymity of those who have requested it.

Outfox Books
P.O. Box 1155
Southbury, CT 06488
outfoxbooks.com
info@outfoxbooks.com

Table of Contents

Introduction	i
Fernando	1
Amanda	17
Ann	29
Jenifer	41
Tod	53
Corrine	67
Chris	79
Stephanie	93
Angelique	105
Shannon	117
Christine	129
Jan	141
Ray	155
Patty	167
Salvatore	179
Christina	191
Stan	203
Tom	217
Gary	231
Cjet	245
Resources	259

Introduction

I wrote this book with one main goal: *to give hope*. I wanted to show those who are struggling with a crisis that they can, and will, survive. At the very least, I wanted to remind readers to recognize and be grateful for the abundance that surrounds them.

To understand what is at the core of surviving a crisis I considered the question: *What really matters in life?* Yes, our families, health and happiness matter, but so do many other aspects of life. *Who are we?* and *Why are we here*? What is the purpose of suffering? Why are some destined to be tested while others live easier lives? When people experience adversity, what sustains their spirit? Which practices best facilitate healing and why? And what is healing? Is it the act of becoming harder and stronger, or softer, more vulnerable, and more compassionate?

I wanted to talk to people who have been through major hardship and hear their thoughts on these questions. I felt compelled to guide readers out of the fog of crisis and into the light of understanding and acceptance. I had no idea where to start. While I was figuring it all out, I decided to make myself useful in a different way.

In 2013, I sought to help struggling youth, particularly those who had already committed a serious crime. When I see impressionable youths facing arraignment, I don't see souls fit for punishment; I see minds ripe for redemption. One day I came across an ad in the paper for a program called "Thresholds," a volunteer initiative that teaches decision-making skills to prison inmates.

I began volunteering at Manson Youth Institution (MYI), a prison for young adults in Cheshire, Connecticut. I joined the group along with two new friends, Ray and his lovely wife Cathy. Our group was led by Genevieve (we called her Geni), a vivacious woman in her 70s.

Geni's heart was so huge it had to pass separately through the metal detector. When our little group met, we enjoyed a warm, welcoming atmosphere despite being inside a level 4, high security facility.

One evening while I waited for my inmate Luis to arrive for class, I noticed Ray was sitting alone too. I decided to start up a conversation with him. As an introvert, this was not a usual practice for me. Nonetheless, I crept out of my comfort zone and began talking to him about our students.

"They're good kids," I said, referring to the majority of inmates we saw slogging down the halls of MYI. "Most of these guys probably just had a bad childhood – or maybe grew up in an environment of crime."

An empathetic soul, Ray nodded in agreement to everything I said.

"They didn't grow up like *we* did," I said, thrusting a thumb toward my chest.

"That may be true for you," he said, "but I had a horrible childhood." For the next five minutes he plunged into his tumultuous life story. In that brief period he spoke of his dysfunctional family, drug abuse, a near death experience, his vision of Jesus, brain damage and subsequent healing through meditation. I peppered his story with an occasional, "Really?" or "Wow!"

Moments later, Ray's student Ricky bounded in, so I shuffled aside. Afterwards, I was left reeling. *How had I not known any of this?* Somehow, I felt his story should have been written on his face through the cursive curls of his eyebrows. Or perhaps there should have been dimples on his scalp, reflecting the battle scars on his brain. At the very least there should have been more sadness in his eyes than the bright, happy blue they always flashed.

Introduction

There was something magical about Ray's story. It lit my mind on fire. It reminded me that we all have our own tale of triumph to tell. We have our own stories to fascinate, enliven, inspire and educate many. It is so important that we share our stories with others and listen to theirs in return. You'll find Ray's story included in *Why Go On*. In the months that followed, I found the 19 others you'll soon read about.

The answers to my original questions were not the answers I expected to find. I expected to hear a lot about God and positive thinking. These ideas were only secondary.

Perseverance superseded an optimistic attitude. I didn't hear, "Think positive" as much as I heard, "Keep going. Just keep going."

What surprised me was that the higher power most often invoked was *other people*.

"Reach out," was the advice I heard over and over. "Don't isolate. Talk to someone who understands. Find your people." People are what healing is all about.

Perhaps the most direct way to connect to a higher power, in whatever sense you interpret the words "higher power," is in connecting with others. Seek out those who understand you – and when you regain your strength, offer help in the same way you were helped.

I firmly believe that Everything is Connected. Every person, every dog, every tree, every microbe, every rock, every scrap of paper, every ray of sunshine. Everything is connected in this magnificent ball of existence. Good and bad do not exist independently and neither do you and I. Our souls are inextricably linked with every saint and sinner. If you look hard enough, you'll see yourself in the eyes of everyone you meet. You were there and they were here. Resisting this universal bond creates strife. Realizing this interconnectedness brings peace.

These stories serve as a reminder that each of us is special and we all have our own important story to tell. This includes you. Your parents. Your friends. Your spouse. Your co-workers. That guy you don't like. The girl you *do* like. Your neighbor. Your ex. Your arch-rival. Your idol. We are all extraordinary, magnificent creatures.

To those who are reading this book for an answer to the question, "Why go on?" I will answer it straight away.

Because you can.

I don't say this in a flippant sense, but in the spirit of

encouragement.

Many give up on projects, dreams, relationships, or even life itself – not because they want to, but because they believe they cannot continue. They feel weighted down, immobile and dark. It takes dedication to change these feelings to ones of expansion and light, but know that it is always possible.

I sat with each one of the people profiled in this book and heard their stories firsthand. I can attest that they are regular people. Some of their challenges have been immense and unthinkable, but they possess no superhuman strength. They are just like you and me. I do not want you to read their stories and think, "I could never cope with *that*." I want you to read with an open mind and learn how they managed to get through.

If you have not yet found a way to deal with your own problems, be gentle with yourself. There is always another way. If you have not found the way yet, that's okay. Simply keep trying. I guarantee you that every person in this book has wondered, "Will I be able to get through this?" It is natural to have these doubts. But just remember, you *can*. This bears repeating.

Go on, because you can.

Go on, because you can.

I hope you learn, enjoy, and expand from reading these true stories of healing and triumph. These twenty individuals have forever changed my life for the better, and I hope they do the same for you.

Lisa Wright

Fernando

*"Have the freedom to choose a positive attitude
wherever you find yourself –
and in whatever conditions."*

Fernando enters the room holding an extra large button-down shirt suspended from a clothes hanger. Sewn above the breast pocket is a rectangular tag with the identification number "92A8325". The forest green material feels abrasive, oppressive and cold.

"The actual prison shirt. That's it right there. I smuggled it out," he says.

Fernando and his wife Crystal moved to their new condo in Danbury about a month ago. It's a quiet, comfortable and relaxed abode. Fernando points to a framed photo taken a few years ago of him, his wife and three children, now aged 22, 12 and 8. It's their first family portrait.

The youthful faces of this attractive, charismatic couple hide the hell they've been through. Fernando's golden brown eyes reveal his sharp, intelligent soul. He speaks clearly and deliberately, enunciating his words for he knows what meaning they hold. Although he is college educated, he is largely self-educated as well. On the wall opposite the couch hangs Fernando's degree in Behavioral Science from Mercy College, from which he graduated summa cum laude.

Fernando grew up about 60 miles south of Connecticut. His

parents emigrated from the Dominican Republic to the United States in their mid-teens, driven by the dream of a prosperous future in the land of opportunity. They raised their five children in Inwood, a neighborhood just north of Washington Heights in upper Manhattan. Fernando, the oldest, was educated in private schools and enjoyed a happy, pleasant childhood.

"One thing for sure, I was a happy kid. I was a very sociable person," he recalls. He describes himself as a natural leader.

There was a bifurcation to his persona. On one hand he pursued academic interests in geology, science and nature, while on the other he engaged in street savvy pastimes like bodybuilding and graffiti.

He shows me a photo of himself from late July 1991. He'd fit in nicely on the cover of Muscle & Fitness magazine, flaunting his ripped physique and intense, steely gaze. At the time this photo was taken he was embarking upon some major life changes. "Fun time" was over and he intended to start focusing on his future. He enrolled in college to pursue a career in the medical field.

"I wanted a future, I wanted a career, and I wanted to feel like I was making a difference," he says.

It was August 3, 1991. Summer was winding down. He and his friends went out to celebrate one of their final nights together doing what they did best: cruise for ladies. That night they took Fernando's father's new car out for the first time.

"I was just so happy and enjoying my father's car. We were driving around Manhattan and the Bronx, doing what we normally did, which was meeting pretty young ladies. Damsels in distress," he jokes. "And just having fun. Nothing different than what we would do every weekend."

The men didn't make a love connection that night, but they did hit a pothole somewhere around 4 a.m. and returned home with a flat tire. On August 4th, the crew hung out and fixed his dad's tire. August 5th passed by without much ado.

August 6th was the night his mother screamed.

Without warning, police officers swarmed Fernando's home late that evening. He was arrested at gunpoint as his family watched. He remembers being led to the squad car as his family shrieked, his mother reaching out to him helplessly through the upstairs window. Fernando had no clue what was going on, but being the good, upstanding, honest man he was – he was certain it would all be straightened out.

Overnight Fernando endured a 10-hour interrogation. For hours, officers refused to tell him what he was being questioned for. When they finally revealed his alleged crime, he could not believe what he heard.

Murder.

In the wee hours of August 4, 1991, 16-year-old Efrain Lopez entered into a scuffle with another man named Raymond Blount at the Marc Ballroom in Manhattan. Blount punched Lopez because he didn't like the way he was looking at him. Lopez made a phone call to his friend Luis Muñoz and let him know what happened. Muñoz was known on the streets as "Wool Lou" because he sold "wools," slang for crack cocaine. Wool Lou intended to even the score.

A second altercation between Lopez and Blount happened outside the club. The fight had grown into two opposing groups of kids armed with broken bottles and ready to battle. Wool Lou arrived on the scene, jogged up to Blount and shot him in the abdomen with a .25 caliber pistol. Blount died later that morning.

About two dozen witnesses were hauled into the Police Department for questioning, including friends of both Lopez and Blount. Blount's friends were loaded into a room en masse and left to peruse a pile of photos of local Latino felons.

Among the photos was one of Fernando Bermudez, who had been arrested a year prior on a petty marijuana charge – a misdemeanor. His photo was erroneously included in the felony pile. This tiny error set off a string of events that would forever change his life.

Fernando's picture attracted the attention of a female witness who thought he resembled the killer. Left alone to collude, Blount's witnesses agreed Fernando was the man who shot their friend.

On the other side, during a grueling 27-hour interrogation, Efrain Lopez admitted the killer was Luis Muñoz, or Wool Lou. Wool Lou was a Puerto Rican friend and neighbor with whom Lopez had gone to school.

Fernando's face bore a slight resemblance to Wool Lou, but that was where the similarities ended.

Wool Lou stood 5'11" and weighed about 165 pounds.

Bodybuilding Fernando was 6'1" and a muscular 205 pounds. Lopez's assertion that he went to school with the perpetrator meant that the killer had attended public school, not a private school as Fernando had. Wool Lou lived in an area six miles from Fernando's home. Fernando's nickname was not "Wool Lou"; it was "Most", a self-made moniker he lifted from the brand of a high-fiber cereal.

Fernando's friends confirmed his alibi to police. It made no impression. He passed a lie detector test with flying colors. It made no difference.

Instead of examining this exculpatory evidence, police maintained that Fernando was the perpetrator. The "real" Wool Lou was never pursued. Muñoz fled to Kentucky and changed his name. Police coaxed, harassed and harangued their witnesses, forcing them to testify that Fernando was the shooter. Many who would testify against Fernando had pending criminal charges erased in exchange for their testimony.

Stop to imagine the classic police line-up. A suspect is brought in and asked to stand in a line next to four or five other individuals. Height markers segment their bodies for a clearer idea of their build.

Fernando's line-up wasn't like that. Instead, he was joined by four police officers dressed in plain clothes. All five sat down on a bench instead of standing, in order to detract from the obvious height and weight disparity between Fernando and the true killer.

The torch of corruption was passed from law enforcement to the district attorney's office. The D.A.'s office withheld thousands of pages of documents from Fernando's lawyer before finally turning a portion of them over three days before the trial began. The little evidence they released was in many cases incomplete, inaccurate or manipulated in some way. This included video testimony from Efrain Lopez. The portions of his interview in which he references "Wool Lou" as the killer were redacted.

At trial, the state's five witnesses knew they had made a mistake. When they saw Fernando's hulking physique, they immediately thought, *That's not the guy.* Unfortunately, they stuck with their story when questioned on the stand. Presumably, each feared the consequences of changing their statement and losing the benefits tied to their testimony.

Still, Fernando held out hope that this mind-boggling misunderstanding would be resolved. His trial played out in only 11 days. Not a single piece of DNA evidence was submitted.

Jurors believed the testimony of the state's witnesses and convicted an innocent man of murder. On February 6, 1992, a week before his 23rd birthday, Fernando was sentenced to 23 years to life in prison.

He spent his first year in Riker's Island, living alongside 14,000 violent inmates. It wasn't easy adjusting to the fetid squalor of one of the nation's most dangerous prisons. Stabbings were commonplace in this endlessly traumatic environment.

He grew hopeless and miserable, desperate for a way out. He wanted the pain to end, and he even considered a final way out.

"I kept thinking about it," Fernando says. "I was just scared. I was scared of the unknown. It was very intimidating and at the same time I wanted the pain to end, but – I just said, you know, I've still got a whole life, I have to still fight. People love me. I have to live for them. I decided to postpone. I just said, 'Stop that. Stop it.' I was being tortured in my cell, in my mind, with that idea."

He created a different kind of escape by educating himself. He devoured books by the dozens and reached out to anyone who would listen. He contacted lawyers, journalists, non-profit organizations and anyone else who could help.

"I started praying. I said, I've got to become proactive. I've got to write letters. And I've got to see who can help me. That gave me solace," he says.

Shortly thereafter, he witnessed the body of a nearby cellmate being taken out on a stretcher.

"It was a very sad situation. He was a young boy, 18 years old, who killed himself. It made me think, 'Wow, I'm glad I didn't do that.'"

The appeals process began. His lawyer made a motion to throw out the verdict. It was denied. Meanwhile, on the streets, Fernando's family was vying for support, too. They bent the ear of anyone who would listen.

Crystal says, "They went out to the streets and his dad talked to everybody." Fernando's father worked in a parking garage where powerful, wealthy people kept their cars. He tried every day to make new connections.

"His dad got the compassion of several journalists. There were a lot of folks who felt sorry for him, understood what happened and just became part of a team. And they all started working," she says.

At the helm of the operation, was Fernando. He describes himself as the "captain of the ship," spending endless days hunched over the typewriter, hunting and pecking at the keys.

"I would disperse letters to try to get people to help me. I was always using communication and anything that I could to inspire people from the outside. It wasn't just a matter of waiting around for it to come to me. I had to go to it. I wasn't waiting for my ship to come to shore. I had to swim to the ship."

One special woman became particularly inspired. She wasn't an attorney, journalist or celebrity. News about his case made it all the way down to the state of Oklahoma. A minister's daughter watched a segment about Fernando on the news and her heart skipped a beat. Her name was Crystal.

Crystal describes hearing of Fernando's plight and being immediately drawn to it. "You know how you just have this thing that turns you inside out and you don't even know why?"

She told her mother she felt compelled to help this man. Her mother responded, "Maybe God wants you to pray for this person."

So Crystal prayed. But the next day, she felt worse. She told her mother she felt sick to her stomach about the whole thing. Her mother suggested she contact Fernando.

"Write him a letter and encourage him to believe that God will save him," her mother advised.

Crystal wrote him a letter. "He had gotten a lot of letters," she says. Something stood out to him about hers. "I was the only one talking about faith."

Through the mail, their relationship grew. Crystal was impressed by Fernando's maturity and intelligence. Before long, she wanted to meet him.

She slipped away from her safe, small-town environment to meet the man she would fall in love with. She kept her journey secret from everyone but her mother, whom she told she was headed north to "witness," or share her faith, with Fernando.

"I snuck off. That's something out of my character. I was very sheltered as a preacher's daughter, and I was really scared."

Crystal left and never looked back. "After that, it turned into a love affair, but not before ministering to him. My purpose was to give him hope in the Lord."

When they met, there was instant chemistry. "We were just so attracted to each other. Now we seem to fit, but at that time it was just like oil and vinegar. Most people didn't understand the connection, because he was such a playboy and here was just an innocent church girl from Oklahoma."

Now, in addition to the loving support of his family, he had a woman by his side, too. Crystal helped Fernando cope during his imprisonment.

Fernando says, "I had a routine that involved exercise, education, spirituality and my relationship. Those four things all wove into the ability to make money while I was incarcerated, the ability to stay grounded, to stay out of trouble and to work for something that I felt was an investment for our future, which was our relationship.

"All of that was woven into the fight to prove my innocence – which was in itself a challenge and a motivation to keep me going. Every day there was a distraction with that. That helped kill the time in a good way, rather than waste it."

He and his family eventually formed a giant cadre of followers all resolute to "Free Fernando." He commissioned a private investigator and a new attorney to help pro bono. His attorney, Mary Ann Di Bari, was a plucky former nun who began practicing law in her late 40s. Fernando was her first case. She helped instill hope and faith in a man who, at any moment, could lose both.

In 1993, his team rounded up the state's witnesses and questioned them. All five witnesses who testified against Fernando signed sworn statements recanting their testimony. This included Efrain Lopez, the prosecution's star witness.

It was a boon for Fernando, but only time would tell if it was enough to set him free.

Crystal moved from Oklahoma to New York State, and then later to Waterbury, Connecticut. She squeezed prison visits in whenever she could, but had to keep her "other life" secret from almost everyone, including her coworkers. The couple eventually married in a no-frills prison wedding. Conjugal visits allowed the couple to have three beautiful children. This was their way of sharing their love and thumbing their nose at the system.

Crystal says, "They looked at him as a number and a property. His DNA made it outside of that place."

Still, Crystal struggled as a sort-of-single mom taking care of three kids. She didn't know if or when her husband would ever be vindicated. Meanwhile, Fernando devised a way to earn money for his family and pay off some of the mounting debt related to his case.

He started a clothing business in prison. It was a simple, but profitable idea. He bought wholesale clothing and resold it to other inmates at cheap prices.

"I was beating the prices of most other sources, including the magazines and the Internet – places that people were ordering from that their family members were using. So it was a great opportunity." Fernando became a trusted source for attire that followed the prison's strict rules and regulations regarding color, material and other considerations.

Inmates often exchanged commissary items for their purchases, which he would send to Crystal to resell at bodegas and other local shops. He amassed stamps by the thousands, which he used toward legal fees.

All the while, Fernando continued to educate himself. He enrolled in college and received an associate's degree in business. He taught classes at the prison in Latin American History and English. He even earned himself a new nickname: "The Professor."

His case gained the attention of media outlets far and wide. His story appeared on the front page of the New York Times. His case was featured on MSNBC and Court TV. His face was on the front cover of a book called *Innocent: Inside Wrongful Convictions*. He was also assisted by The Innocence Project, a non-profit organization dedicated to exonerating those who have been wrongfully convicted. It seemed as though the whole world knew he was innocent – except the courts.

In 1997, four years after obtaining the five witness recantations, he would finally learn whether or not his conviction would be overturned.

It wasn't. His appeal was denied, again. Appeal after appeal after appeal failed. He ran out of fingers on which to count the amount of times he'd been denied. As his 11th appeal began, Fernando was running out of steam.

His attorney, Mary Ann Di Bari, gave him not only counsel, but counseling. Day after day, she prayed, imploring Fernando to keep faith in God and assuring him everything would be all right in the end.

Her words of encouragement fell on deaf ears. He had heard it all before. He'd heard the prayers of his lawyer, the screams of his fellow inmates, the judge's denial of his freedom, even the rhythmic chant of "Free Fernando." It was all the same, just a meaningless blur of despair that never went anywhere. What difference would the next appeal make?

"I was very despondent. Mary Ann always remained and still remains a source of hope and inspiration, but after a while you become so cynical in prison that you get tired of hearing the same thing and you don't see the results. I had gotten to a point in my life, after losing my appeals, that I just felt like giving up on God."

He recalls this as a "pivotal moment." While on the phone with Mary Ann, a most curious flake of hope fell from the Heavens. His mind drifted as it started to snow.

"There was a snowflake that dropped on my shoulder and I looked at it. I saw how unique it was, and then I realized that the next one was just as unique. Every one after that had different shapes and forms – they were all different from each other. And it made me realize that whoever created these snowflakes had to have a purpose for that, and surely would have a purpose for my own incarceration." He knew right then, "that there was a God, judging by the uniqueness of each individual creation of that snowflake."

That one moment gave him the strength to keep fighting. "It made me realize that I still needed to trust and believe. And that's what I decided to do."

He continued to pray. "I was so desperate to get out. I really wanted to get out of there. I didn't even care anymore." He asked God, "Give me any way. *Any* way – to get out." Soon, he would receive his first opportunity to do just that.

Bolstered by a new vigor, his life began turning around. In the summer of 2009 he was offered a plea deal. Fernando could walk out a free man, but he would have to plead guilty to manslaughter. This meant the guarantee of gaining his freedom with no risk of another failed appeal. But, pleading guilty to a crime he did not commit was an unfair obligation.

At first, it was a difficult decision. "But when the situation manifested itself, I said 'no,'" Fernando says.

For the first time since his trial, his appeal was overseen by a different judge than the one who convicted him. Judge Jonathan Cataldo reviewed his case with utter and complete disdain for what had transpired for nearly two decades. On November 12, 2009, after 18 years in prison, Fernando heard Judge Cataldo say the words he longed to hear.

"Motion granted."

Fernando's conviction was overturned on the basis of "actual innocence." It was a groundbreaking ruling. His case helped change legislation to reverse other wrongful convictions devoid of DNA evidence.

He had intended to give a glorious speech at the moment of his exoneration, but in court he was too overcome with emotion – and instead quietly wept into the shoulder of his attorney.

On the day of his release, throngs of journalists and supporters waited outside the prison, hungry to hear from their local hero.

Crystal recalls Fernando's extemporaneous speech that day.

"He had so much media there that you would have thought the President was there. They said that he made history with the length of time that he stood out there and spoke. He gave a speech as if he had prepared it, and he hadn't. So that was really his first public platform. He went on a roll after that. That's when The Innocence Project realized they had a speaker – a real one."

On his first day of freedom, he told the New York Times [*November 20, 2009*]:

> *"I'm feeling great on this glorious day of justice. I greet you in the name of hope and redemption. What was going through my body was an exorbitant amount of palpitations, joy and happiness to a level that I've never known before in my life."*

After spending years of hard time in tough prisons like Riker's Island, Sing Sing and Shawangunk Correctional Facility, 40-year-old Fernando was finally free to go home and catch up with his family.

Re-entry was not easy. Times had changed. Technology had grown from "stagecoach to hovercraft," he quipped. Even the notion of freedom was an unfamiliar concept. Some days he preferred to stay in his son's small room, seeking the safe and familiar surroundings of his jail cell.

Even today, the once sociable man has trouble dealing with large groups of people. "Celebration almost feels taboo. You kind of carry that forward," he says.

However, he feels completely comfortable in front of a crowd. He transformed his experience into captivating lectures. He has booked over 200 lectures all over the globe, including Germany, Japan, Italy and France. He has spoken at countless universities, including Yale, Princeton and Harvard.

"I have worked to become the first exonerated man in legal history to speak in every Ivy League school, and I'm almost there." After he speaks at Brown University and the University of Pennsylvania, he will have accomplished that goal.

He glows when he talks about his lectures. He speaks about a talk he gave a couple of years ago at Canterbury School, a private school in New Milford, Connecticut.

"Afterward we had such a good get-together. The kids wanted to stay past the lecture. I stayed in contact with one or two of them, mentoring some, and it was just great that in some of these venues you leave a lasting impression. And that's the *goodness* of the talks," he says, smiling as he emotes the word "goodness."

"It gives you the sense that you are making a difference in the lives of these people, these kids. I feel like I'm exercising something higher than myself. I want to make a difference in the system. You have to have something that gives you meaning and purpose – and the speaking does that. It gives me a sense that I'm accomplishing something against the forces that hurt me so badly.

"It gives me also a sense of prestige. In that, wow... here I am going from a prison cell to speaking at some of the best schools in the nation, at times even in the world."

He continues, "When we spoke in Germany, we had some students write us letters and they were like, 'Up until I heard your story, I was thinking about quitting law school. But because of your story, I'm

Why Go On: Connecticut Residents Bring Dark Days to Light

gonna stay – I'm gonna stay!'" With a giant smile, bursting with hope and passion, he says, "That's the type of thing where you think: Wow, you're making a difference here. This person may stay in law school, or go to law school as the result of hearing the story. That's great. This is worth it."

Crystal says his talks help more than criminal justice students.

Fernando and Crystal

"Some of them didn't have hope in their own lives and he pushed them where they needed to go. He's motivated them towards their own goals, even if they didn't have to do with law."

She marvels at Fernando's natural ability to speak. "That environment is home. That's where he's at his best. Even if he hadn't been through this situation, he was still born to speak."

Fernando tailors each lecture to the particular venue he's speaking at. If he's in a foreign country, he learns a little of their language. If he speaks at a college, he learns about the school's culture.

"For me it's a self-imposed challenge to do an original lecture tailored to each venue. I fancy myself as a person who can use all the knowledge that he gained in prison from the countless books I read, and apply what I was envisioning in prison in real life.

"For me it's almost like a puzzle, putting what I'm going to say together. For this particular venue I'm going to tell *this* story. I'm going to connect with their history, I'm going to connect with their culture, and I'm going to speak their language. It just feels like an accomplishment. It's like a work of words. And to me, it's a pleasure."

Even his old prison shirt plays a role in his presentations.

"Sometimes the shirt takes form throughout the lecture as something that survived."

Crystal adds her own thoughts on the family's survival. "You can find freedom in yourself. As long as you are negative, you are not free. You are putting yourself in bondage. That's one thing that we've always worked on, is to have freedom. They couldn't break him and they didn't break us."

She explains how choosing a positive mindset has become a daily ritual in their household. "We work every day. Every day we go through some sort of counseling in this house with each other to try to be better people, to try to understand our lives and what direction we are going in."

This passion for personal progress has not gone unnoticed. Those who know Fernando speak highly of him. His former professor, Dr. R. Averell Manes, Professor of Political Science and Conflict Studies at Western Connecticut State University, noticed right away he was special.

"I first met him as a student in a rigorous research methodology class about 18 months after his exoneration," she says. "I was immediately struck by his intensity, which I share, and his commitment to the cause of wrongful imprisonment. Despite having his hands full with readjusting to society, recovering from the trauma of his experiences, and assuming the role of full-time parent, he continued to fight for the cause of justice. I cannot say enough good things about him on every front. I admire him and consider myself fortunate to have him as a friend."

Fernando easily could have allowed his experiences to ruin his newfound freedom. He emerged from imprisonment wounded, but resolute to reclaim the life he lost. In Dr. Manes' class, he was conscientious, hard-working, and analytical.

"He received top grades in both classes he took with me," she says. "Fernando is a strong, intelligent, personable, well-spoken, really nice and highly inspirational person, speaker and advocate for justice. I admire him deeply on every level, and I know no one stronger.

"As a speaker, he is masterful and mesmerizing. Both times he spoke at my school, the audience was rapt with attention – you could hear a pin drop, which is not the norm at events largely peopled with young adults with busy lives and pressing commitments. The question portion of the events went on and on, with the audience not wanting it to end.

"Fernando was generous with his time, energy and willingness to share even the most difficult details of his experiences. I wish everyone could hear him speak. His presentation is polished yet genuine and real."

In late 2014, WCSU awarded him with the college's Alumni Association Appreciation Award. The award was personally funded by Dr. Manes to "recognize Fernando's contribution by speaking twice at WCSU, and his inspirational story."

Dr. Manes herself is no stranger to the issue of wrongful convictions. Her father, attorney Sidney Manes, has spent over a decade working on the case of Hector Rivas, a man he believes was wrongfully convicted by New York State in 1993 for murdering his ex-girlfriend. Dr. Manes believes the primary cause for wrongful convictions is not laziness or incompetence, but something far more sinister.

"The prison industrial complex in America is riddled with injustice and morally questionable practices – a correctional system for profit is inherently flawed. Racial and economic inequality mar the system fatally. Ongoing issues with over-policing minority neighborhoods, the overuse of force, and disparities in the treatment of the poor and people of color are a travesty of justice in this country. It's shameful."

One of the most distressing aspects for innocent inmates is the damning effects of remaining truthful. Inmates are often forced to admit guilt in exchange for their freedom.

Dr. Manes explains, "The way parole works, even if an inmate has served their term, they are not granted parole unless they acknowledge their guilt and express remorse. In the case of Mr. Rivas, on whose case my father has worked for more than 16 years, he will not acknowledge his guilt and express remorse because he is innocent. Therefore, he will not be released even when his sentence is complete. This is wrong.

"Also, I think we need a special track in the legal system for wrongful imprisonment cases because the wheels of justice are immorally slow. Inmates are denied their constitutionally guaranteed right to a speedy trial and appeal by a system which is overburdened and unlawfully slow, while the lives of these innocent people drains away."

Wrongful convictions happen in every state of the United States. In fact, in a recent report by the National Registry of Exonerations, Connecticut had the seventh highest number of exonerations in the country in 2013. Eyewitness misidentification is the leading cause of wrongful convictions.

Reform, Fernando believes, begins with state prosecutors.

"What would help change the system would be holding prosecutors accountable," he says. "Prosecutors get immunity and aren't held accountable even when it's proven that they have something directly to do with a wrongful conviction. That's not fair to everyone involved who gets affected by this. That allows them to not feel a deterrent effect and continue to do whatever they want to do, knowing that they can't be held liable, criminally prosecuted, sued and so forth."

Now a free man for about five years, his goal is simple. "I just want to start enjoying life." He wants to pursue the martial arts, work on his writing and provide for his family. When he's not lecturing, he spends time with his children, sometimes acting as a chaperone on their field trips.

Crystal believes their story serves as a cautionary tale that can help change lives.

"Our story helps heal. We love to volunteer and help people in all walks of life. We would like to leave a great legacy that what happened didn't happen in vain, either. If we're going to be chosen to go through this situation, then we want to make sure we leave something behind that's not forgettable."

Fernando adds, "A person has to persevere no matter what circumstances they find themselves in and they shouldn't give up." He reminds people that one always has "the freedom to choose a positive attitude wherever you find yourself and in whatever conditions you find yourself undergoing."

Fernando has lived in some of the worst possible conditions, under the worst possible circumstances. Like the snowflake that fell upon his shoulder, Fernando is entirely unique. Whether it was faith, hard work, or luck that secured his freedom, none of it would have been possible if he had ever given up.

Why Go On: Connecticut Residents Bring Dark Days to Light

    Persistence can move mountains and determination will climb them. In a sense he had been free all along, as no one could take away his will to live or his determination to fight. Fernando's story shows that the key to true freedom resides within the human spirit, unable to be stolen or confined.

Amanda

*"Had I never lost my ability to walk,
I may never have truly learned how to live."*

I met with Amanda at her apartment in central Connecticut, tucked in the woods a few miles beyond the main retail drag in town. She was waiting for me outside as I pulled up on a chilly, drizzly day. Even from a distance, I could sense the inner strength and determination in her eyes.

Propped against the railing of her deck is the Serenity Prayer, which she has hand painted on a ceramic tile.

> *"God, grant me the serenity to accept the things I cannot change,*
> *The courage to change the things I can*
> *And the wisdom to know the difference."*

Amanda suggested we meet in the complex's library for a comfortable and quiet place to sit. As she led me through a few side walkways and a long corridor I lagged behind, letting Amanda lead. I could sense she would have preferred to move faster, but she maintained a slower pace for the sake of being polite.

When we were settled, Amanda told me about her childhood. Growing up, she says she was "a *big* troublemaker." Her pretty hazel eyes twinkle as she laughs. "I was the typical defiant child with every kind of imaginable issue that you could possibly have."

Her lifetime battle with health issues started early. Around age 9 she was diagnosed with ADHD and subsequently medicated. Unfortunately, the medicine caused or contributed to an abundance of escalating problems.

The ADHD medication triggered two side effects: epileptic seizures and depression – and so she was prescribed anti-depressants and anti-seizure drugs. At age 15 she was given lithium, which caused her to become so severely ill, she was hospitalized. Doctors found she had four times the toxic level of lithium in her system, so she began dialysis treatments. A biopsy detected that she had auto-immune kidney disease, which explained why her body was not processing the lithium properly.

The discovery of kidney disease necessitated additional treatments. She was prescribed steroids and temporarily received oral chemotherapy.

Amanda's health troubles sparked her interest in healthcare. Around this time she decided she wanted to become a nurse.

"I've always wanted to help people," she says.

Always unique and full of energy, she gravitated to one of the most intense jobs in the field. "I wanted to be a flight nurse. I wanted something very different and exciting. I've always loved the extremes in life. It's not as much the adrenaline junkie thing, because I don't like skydiving and that kind of stuff. I'd rather go to crazy trauma crime scenes and be with somebody's neck hanging off. Stuff like that interested me."

Amanda was in remission from kidney disease by age 18, at which time doctors weaned her off many of her medications. However, by keeping her on steroids she later developed Addison's Disease, which wasn't diagnosed till she was 21. The disease requires her to take some type of corticosteroid such as prednisone for the rest of her life.

Life at school was another challenge. Side effects from the chemo, steroids and other drugs, including weight gain and hair loss, made her a perfect target for bullying and harassment.

"I just didn't like school at all. I skipped a lot. I was pretty defiant to my teachers and I always felt picked on and behind, so I developed attitude problems and behavioral issues."

Amanda

Anger was her chief emotional issue. "I was expelled from middle school because I threw a desk across the room." As a result, she was forced to attend a special private school for students with social, emotional and behavioral problems.

She was accepted back into the public school system in 11th grade. However, despite her best efforts to improve herself, things were not about to get easier any time soon.

By age 17, Amanda was doing okay, but things at home had become tense. She started seeing a new therapist in an attempt to smooth things over. At first, his treatments seemed legitimate. He gave her the same types of exercises she had been given by other therapists.

One day the therapist took her to a secluded park, threatened her life and sexually assaulted her. He threatened to drown her in the river "like the last girl" if she told anyone what happened.

"And he did have rope, duct tape and cinderblocks in his back seat," she says.

She started self-medicating with alcohol to control the stress, nightmares and flashbacks she experienced. After this went on for a year, she finally had the courage to tell someone. She later went to the police, but the man was never arrested.

Amanda continued to abuse alcohol and was in and out of rehabs before she was even legally able to drink. By age 21, she had a tenuous handle on her alcoholism and was working on getting her life back.

She had been living in a sober house for a few months and was beaming with what she calls "just got out of rehab positivity." She had enrolled in a nursing program at a local community college and things were looking up.

About a week before her first day of nursing school, she woke up to the sound of her alarm. In that moment, everything changed.

"As soon as I opened my eyes I knew something was wrong. As I attempted to crawl out of bed, I fell flat on my face."

She could not figure out what was happening to her. "I could not feel or move my legs. It was as if someone had cut off and removed the entire lower half of my body."

She immediately called her mother, who told her to call 911. She arrived at the hospital about ten minutes later, met by her frantic mother and swarms of doctors.

Her time at the local hospital was brief. After performing a few routine tests and examinations, she was released.

Hospital staff told her mother, "We don't know what's wrong with her. Take her home and let her rest."

Dissatisfied with that advice, her mother sought a second opinion. Staff picked Amanda up and placed her in the car. She and her mother drove to a second hospital.

The next hospital visit brought more tests. Staff ran blood work, MRI's, x-rays and a litany of other procedures. Doctors still could not diagnose Amanda's sudden paralysis, but one thing was clear: she could no longer care for herself. She could not go home, even to her mother's house, because she simply needed too much care.

"That's when they decided to send me to a nursing home."

Like many nursing homes, this facility was divided into two distinct sections: one floor was for temporary rehabilitation patients, while the other floor housed long-term, elderly patients who would reside there for the remainder of their life. Amanda's lack of a diagnosis and insufficient state insurance prevented her from staying on the rehab floor. In the blink of an eye, she went from a bright, independent woman with a promising future to a despondent young adult with no quality of life.

"I was surrounded by people dying," she says.

Amanda's new environment was dismal at best. She was left to sit in dirty diapers for hours at a time. She was told when to eat – and what she did eat were pureed or otherwise unpalatable meals. She was allowed only one shower per week and was bathed by relative strangers.

"It was downright neglectful in the nursing home," she says.

At the very least, she expected the support of her friends during this bleak and difficult time. Sadly, many of her closest friends were notably absent.

"I realized that when a major life event happens and you need your friends the most, everyone just disappears. I thought I'd have a million visitors at the nursing home. I'm like, *Where is everybody?*"

At first, many friends couldn't cope with the reality of her sudden and tragic paralysis. Later, her friends could not deal with her anger.

"I was a very negative person. I was just downright vulgar. I had the worst trucker mouth. Everything made me mad. I had a knack for being able to turn someone's whole mood right around, and not in a good way. If I was hurting, then I wanted all those who were happier than me to feel my pain as well."

She had one loyal friend who stayed faithfully by her side. Throughout the years of ups and downs, her friend Eric was always there for her. "He has stayed by my side since we met in middle school. He took so much emotional abuse, yet continued to support me."

Languishing in the nursing home, Amanda grieved for her old life. She dreamt of camping trips, swimming in the ocean, and feeling sand between her toes.

"The simple pleasures in life had been eliminated, leaving me isolated. It was really hard not to fall into a depression and hate life, to be honest," she says.

She was determined to move out of the nursing home. "After eight months of being there, I couldn't take it anymore. I started doing research on how to get out, and I came across this place," she says, referring to where she lives now, a handicapped accessible apartment that accommodates her unique needs.

"I have an aide that comes in to help me with laundry, dishes and cooking." Other than the assistance from her aides, Amanda was now pretty much on her own.

Independent at last, she reveled in the private and spacious new abode she shares with her roommate Jessica. The apartment is fairly similar to any standard two-bedroom apartment, but with a few adjustments.

One distinction is its open floor plan and absence of standard furniture. Here you won't find a coffee table, kitchen island, couches, or other furnishings that would get in the way of a wheelchair. Her belongings are kept along the perimeter of each room, keeping the space open and uncluttered.

The apartment includes a few other modifications necessary for Amanda's special needs.

"We have roll-under sinks, so there are no cabinets in the way. I can roll under the sink and do my own dishes. I can roll under the stove and cook. In the bathroom there are bars by the toilet so we can use them to transfer. The shower is roll-in. It's specifically designed for wheelchairs, power chairs and medical equipment, so that we can have our independence and not have to worry."

For months after the move she endured hundreds of tests, exams and shrugs from medical personnel who still could not diagnose her condition. After two years of waiting, she finally received an answer.

"I was diagnosed with transverse myelitis [pronounced *my-LIGHT-us*]. TM is an autoimmune disease. My body attacked my spinal cord, leaving a scar across the L4 section, resulting in permanent paralysis." Incidence of TM is rare, with only about 1,400 new cases diagnosed each year in the U.S. In some cases, the disease can be reversible, but for about a third of those affected, it's untreatable and incurable – meaning the rest of their lives will be spent in a wheelchair.

Even today, four years after onset, her doctors aren't entirely convinced she has TM. "Half the tests show it's probably TM, but one of the tests that's usually positive, is negative."

Amanda wanted a diagnosis so badly, but learning she had TM made her feel worse. Her new apartment was far better than the nursing home, but she was still unhappy.

"I was extremely angry and bitter. I hated everybody. I was rude to everybody. I literally just tore people up to the point no one wanted to be around me. I was an angry, miserable girl who people avoided at all costs."

About a year after moving into her apartment, she suffered a stroke caused by the hormone pills she had been taking to regulate her menstrual period. The stroke led to premature ovarian failure.

During this time, she relied on a familiar fallback: alcohol. Now that she was living on her own, she could come and go as she pleased – and drink whenever she liked.

"As soon as I got my freedom, I just went full-blown alcoholic."

Sitting in a wheelchair for 16 hours a day, along with the strenuous use of her upper body, caused pain and swelling in her back, wrists, arms and shoulders. Her doctor gave her a prescription for opiates, opening the door to a brand new addiction.

The pills made her feel good – so good that she'd use up every bottle way before the scheduled refill. To keep up with her habit, she'd replenish her stash through street pill dealers at a price of $80 apiece. As costs accumulated, Amanda couldn't keep up. One day a friend suggested she switch to heroin, a far cheaper alternative. She resisted the temptation for a long time. Heroin was for drug addicts, and she was not a drug addict.

"But, you run out of money really quickly. Let's just say that one thing led to another and before I knew it I was a full-blown heroin addict."

Sadly, Amanda is not alone. According to the U.S. Department of Health & Human Services, disabled individuals suffer from alcohol and drug abuse at a rate of 2-4 times higher than the general populace. The combination of imposed isolation, higher unemployment rates and over-prescription of addictive pain medication creates a perfect climate for addiction.

Amanda was at risk of losing everything.

"My scenario of hitting bottom was begging my mother for drug money. I sold anything and everything I had in my house, including my flat screen TV. I had only the bare basics. I could see the emotional death in my own mom and the fear every time I called her. She would constantly tell me how sick I was looking. I became aware of the hell I put my own family through, the disgust I had in myself, and the bad choices I was making."

Another eye-opener was the end of her friendship with Eric. "He cut himself from my life to avoid any more hurt feelings, betrayal, and lies.

"I had gotten to a point where I said, 'Look, your life is not going to get any better. It's either going to get worse and you're going to end up six feet under, or you can change it.' That's when I really decided that I was going to go all out and change and do whatever I had to do. And I'm really glad I did."

Amanda was using heroin for nearly a year before checking into a rehab. Unfortunately, finding a rehab willing to accept a handicapped patient was an uphill battle.

"I had gone to treatment for my alcoholism when I was able-bodied with no problem. You call, you get in; maybe there's a one or two day wait list. It took a good six months to find a place because I'm disabled. I was calling New York, New Jersey... I mean everywhere. I called hundreds of places. I got to the point I wrote into television shows; I didn't know what to do."

She contacted a state advocate for help. The advocate notified one of the government-run facilities that could not deny a patient because of their disability. Finally, Amanda was able to get the help she needed.

"I started the methadone program. That's what really helped me." The rehab also helped her safely discontinue the anti-anxiety medications she'd been on since childhood.

For too long Amanda had directed her energy into destructive habits, but now she had learned that lifestyle would no longer work for her.

"I had to realize that I'm not a victim, I'm a survivor. I felt bad for myself when I was a victim. I don't really feel bad for myself anymore."

After returning home from rehab, she was determined to fill her life with positive pursuits.

"I looked for activities to do. I knew they did the wheelchair rugby here at the apartment complex. An outside sports team comes in and uses our gym, so I inquired about that. I tried adaptive water skiing and that was really fun. I loved it. I loved the freeing feeling of gliding through the open river, my hair blowing behind me."

By opening herself up to optimism and hope, she gained new friends and an improved outlook on life.

"I was overjoyed by all of the positive changes that were taking place in my life. Not only did I gain a large group of friends, but I now had dreams and aspirations as well. I found that instead of pulling others down to make myself feel better, I could use my experience to strengthen the lives of others."

She became involved with local groups to channel her energy into something positive. "I joined the advocacy coalition and started fighting for the rights of other disabled individuals. I also volunteered my time to help mentor other young adults and children who may be struggling with tragic events in their lives. As I was adapting to my new life and partaking in all of these new and exciting experiences, I discovered that my life and the lives of those I encountered were changing for the better."

TM negated the possibility of Amanda becoming a nurse, let alone a flight nurse. Instead, she changed her focus and re-enrolled in school with a new major: Psychology.

"It wasn't until my sobriety that I really started gaining an interest in psychology and how the brain works. What really causes one person to have an addiction and the other one to not? What causes one person to go through a trauma and commit suicide, but another one can come out stronger? I'm looking at specializing in forensic psychology or research psychology. They're both Ph.D.'s."

Amanda feels that what she's been through in life gives her a special advantage in the field. "I can almost relate to anybody going through anything because I've been a victim of abuse, I've been a drug addict and alcoholic, and I've had health issues, both physical and mental. If I can help even one person, then it makes everything I went through worth it. There's a positive reason that I went through this, and I'm going to find it and use it. The gift of sobriety has given me the clear head to think that way."

Moreover, she hasn't given up on getting up. She's looking into an experimental procedure called IVIG, or intravenous immunoglobulin therapy. It's most effective if performed within the first six months after

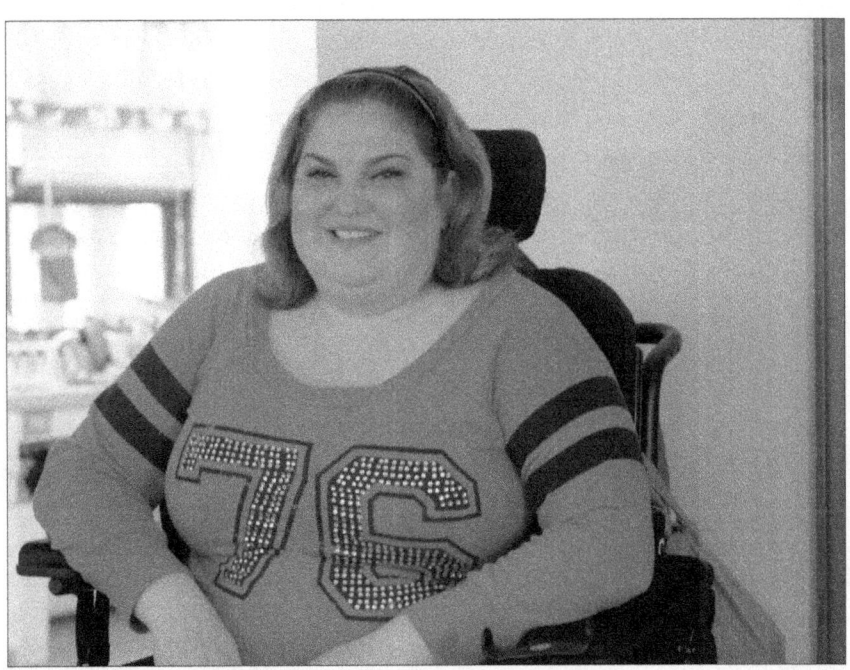

Amanda

onset of TM, but she hopes even at this point it could enable her to regain some ability to move her legs.

There's another way for her to start walking, too. Amanda has a pair of RGO's, or reciprocating gait orthosis.

"It's a giant chest piece and two giant leg pieces." The pieces connect, allowing her to walk by shifting her weight from one side to the other. "I use forearm crutches and my upper body to walk my legs. My mom can't fit my power chair in her car, so I put these on and I can go shopping."

The RGO's have been a godsend. "It's totally opened up my world." They are also great for the workout it gives her legs, keeping her muscles intact in case of a cure.

She's active in other ways, too. "I joined the YMCA to do Zumba and yoga. I just do the arms because that's all I can do, but I love it."

Of all the exercises Amanda could possibly do, it's the practice of positivity that's most important. Her motto is, "Had I never lost my ability to walk, I may never have truly learned how to live."

"Before all this I wanted to be a nurse, but I didn't want to do all the hard work to get there. I was constantly in and out of rehab because I felt like life had nothing to offer. It wasn't until I had this whole experience that I really woke up and was like, 'Your life can change in the blink of an eye – so either appreciate what you have because tomorrow it could be gone.' There are no guarantees. I want to make every single day count because I would have never dreamed that I would go to bed one night and woken up like this.

"I don't really see things so negatively anymore. When anything negative does happen, I always find a positive in it. I'm not guaranteed tomorrow or I'm not guaranteed a minute from now. If I could trade the life I have now for a set of legs, I wouldn't do it. If my choice was to have my old life back and my legs, or have the new insight I have and staying paralyzed – I'm all for staying this way. I was so trapped with my own emotional burdens and negativity, that now I truly feel free."

Amanda advises those who are struggling to stay on track, but be gentle about it. "It's okay to have bad days. I have days where I cry to my mom and say, 'This is really unfair. I can't do all that stuff I used to do.' But I can do other stuff," she says, her voice lilting upward. "And I have to remind myself of the other stuff I can do – or find a way to do it. Allow yourself to have a bad day, vent to someone you trust, scream and moan and then get over it. It's like someone who's newly diagnosed with cancer and it's unfair – *it is*. It is unfair. But you know what? You can come through it stronger and fight for your life or you can end up in a depression and let it kill you. Which are you gonna choose?"

By age 21, it seemed like the world had given up on her. By age 22, she had nearly given up on herself. She has experienced more adversity than most do in several lifetimes. Her message extends beyond advice for the disabled. Her story reminds able-bodied people that it is far more important to be able-minded. Amanda's inspiring life illustrates that no matter how bleak things appear, there is always a way to make life better. Happiness is not a spontaneous event, but a choice that is made. It may take hard work, resilience and patience, but to find happiness is to "truly learn how to live."

Ann

"I learned that I'm stronger than I thought I was."

Ann is a petite, gentle woman with an incredibly peaceful voice. Her serene aura conceals a focused, determined spirit that has survived devastatingly dark times. Five years ago she had no idea that one day she would unite these two traits for an important life journey.

Today, she wears a cheerful ensemble comprised of a light pink fleece jacket, dark pink t-shirt, athletic pants and a four-leaf clover pendant necklace. Her blue eyes and blonde hair sparkle in the light. We sat together in her kitchen in East Lyme, where she lives with her husband, sons, dogs and cats.

Ann and her husband Paul originally hail from Boston. Despite having left Massachusetts over two decades ago, one can still hear a Beantown accent in words like "year" and "hard." She went to college for retail management, before switching to marketing. "And now I'm a personal trainer," she says. She entered the world of fitness in the late '90s when she started working at a Curves for Women exercise center.

"I went in as an assistant manager and it kind of was a nice fit for me because I love fitness, nutrition and marketing. I got my personal training certificate and it started evolving from there. I like helping people get healthy and take care of themselves."

Ann has a typical all-American family. In past years, Paul

coached youth and high school football. Ann belongs to various networking and business organizations. Her three sons were active in school. She speaks highly of all her sons, but regards Brian, the youngest, with special esteem.

Growing up, she says, "He was a great kid; a lot of fun. He just had a great personality. He could talk to anybody, whether they were young or old. He was wise beyond his years."

As she begins to talk about Brian's childhood, her eyes crease and her throat tightens. She takes a moment to quietly plug back into an inner energy source before continuing.

Brian loved sports, music and socializing. Considering his bubbly, energetic personality, he would seem an unlikely candidate for a mood disorder. But in his mid-teens, Brian started showing signs of anxiety.

"He started having some panic attacks, and became depressed sometimes. We had him see a therapist. We did all the things we were supposed to do," Ann says. "For the most part he was okay. It would come and go – but he wouldn't talk about it a lot. He wouldn't share.

"He didn't sleep a lot. He would have panic attacks at school and would have to leave his classroom and gather himself. Or sometimes the teacher would dismiss him and he'd come home. He was a super sensitive kid. The littlest things really bothered him."

Whenever she would ask Brian how he was doing, he'd reassure her with the common teen brush-off, *I'm okay*.

"But he seemed okay. He still had good grades. He went to college."

Brian wanted to become a teacher and majored in education at Castleton State College in Castleton, Vermont.

The popularity he enjoyed in high school transferred to college, where he amassed dozens of new friends. His fun and friendly personality made him popular with the ladies, too. It wasn't just his enthusiasm and humor that drew people to him, but his kindness.

"Brian was always one to help people. He was always worried about everybody else and never really took the time to take care of himself. He had a lot of other friends who had depression issues, other friends who had drug issues, and so he was always going all over – he was everybody's best friend."

Ann

Ann provides important insight into the daunting question: *What do you say to someone who's lost a child?*

"The best thing people could say is, 'There are no words. I'm sorry, there are no words.' Because there *are* no words."

Ann's loved ones struggled to find a way to make her feel better as quickly as possible – but grief can't be rushed. "People want to fix it. That's what I found. And you can't fix it. This is something you can't fix. I learned it's just something you have to go with, and be with."

She detached herself from almost everyone. She avoided going to certain stores for fear of running into anyone Brian knew. Her despair was so great she entertained thoughts of joining her son on the other side to escape the pain.

When asked how she managed to get through those first few weeks, it's tough for her to put a finger on it.

You can sense the pressure in her chest as she says, "How do you survive? I have *no* idea. My other sons are one reason. I wouldn't want to hurt them anymore. Although there was a point where I thought, 'They'll be fine.' You justify in your head that everybody will be fine. They'll survive. They'll be hurt at first, but they'll be able to go on and be okay. The pain is just overwhelming. It was physically, emotionally… you feel like you're having a heart attack. You feel sick to your stomach."

She acknowledges a feeling of guilt that lingers – wondering if there was anything she could have done to prevent what happened.

"The 'woulda, coulda, shouldas' play in your head constantly. That's one thing that we can't stop: the guilt. What happens with grief is your heart says one thing and your mind says the other, and there's such a big difference between the two of them."

For Ann, her head says there is nothing she could have done to stop what happened, but her heart feels the opposite. She is not alone in these feelings. Suicide survivors often deal with complex emotions like guilt and anger. She's also not alone in her experience. Suicide is the second leading cause of death for young people aged 15-24, behind accidents.

Recovering from grief did not seem possible at first. She stopped working and spent most of her time at home. All she foresaw for her future was years of foggy depression.

"I didn't think I was ever going to go back to work," she says. "I couldn't teach yoga because it's about opening your heart and I'm like, 'I can't do that, my heart's broken.' I could never do anything again."

The loss of a child can break even the toughest family bonds. For Ann, her husband and her sons, they used their family bond to help them survive.

"You have to hold a unit together. I mean, the worst thing would be to add another loss to my children. You just do what you can, even though you're all grieving in your own way. Mothers, fathers, siblings, they all grieve in their own way. But just having the family together was important. It upsets them when I'm crying so much – but my boys have always really worried about me," she says, her voice cracking.

Her eldest son AJ moved back home the day Brian died, despite having a home of his own. He didn't move back alone. He brought along a new friend – a rescued pit bull puppy named Duffy.

"Duffy is what got me up every day."

Duffy today is an incredibly well-mannered pup with soulful eyes. He sweetly accepts affection before curling up in a remote area of the living room. Two or three years ago, he was a different dog.

Back then, she says, "He was a crazy, crazy guy, and he needed a lot of exercise." She was obliged to leave the safety of her bed to walk him. "Duffy would lie with me in bed and then I would take him and we would walk everywhere. Sometimes twice a day. He was a crazy guy. Look at him now over there," she says, admiring her unexpected therapist.

Duffy's personality starkly contrasts to Angel, the home's boisterous golden retriever. Trotting and wiggling throughout the kitchen, Angel desperately loves attention. She too, has been a source of comfort to Ann and her family – especially after the loss of the family's last retriever who passed away two months after Brian.

"I think Angel was a gift from him. I had been looking in the paper and online for goldens. Then I was at our house on Cape Cod, driving down the street and there was a big sign: *Golden Retriever Puppies*. So I went in and we got her.

"I think it was his way of making Christmas easier for us – because the holidays stink – and to have us be able to laugh about something."

In their own little way, the family pets helped fill the emptiness in her heart. "They provide unconditional love. They'll love you no matter what. They wag their tails no matter what. Duffy is why I got up every day, because he needed to be walked. He needed to be fed and taken care of. They are able to help you and they are able to comfort you in many ways. They know when you're upset. When I would go into my little episodes of tears, they would be right there with me, licking my face and just being loving."

What also helped was in learning how others endured the loss of a child. "What helped was reading stories similar to mine. You want to feel normal. When you're in the midst of your grief, you feel like you're the only person in the world that this happened to, that nobody else has experienced this."

She read the books of Elizabeth Edwards, Marie Osmond and Gloria Vanderbilt. All three had children who died prematurely. Edwards lost her child in a car accident, while Osmond and Vanderbilt lost a child to suicide.

"I just wanted to hear how they survived. How did you do it? I know there are no rules to this. Everybody's different. I just want to know that there's a little bit of hope."

Another book called *The Soul's Journey* gave her a different perspective on the meaning of life – and death.

"It claims that we all have a purpose in this life. Each soul has a purpose and we have a beginning and an end. Once our soul's purpose is done, we move on. So each experience we have in life is to learn and grow, and to help others. So when we move on, we go up to a higher level of our souls."

With the support of her family, friends, books and furry creatures, Ann began reaching out for help outside of the home. The only problem was, she couldn't find any.

Her doctor's solution came in the form of pieces of paper scrawled with the names of drugs and dosages.

"I think I left with three prescriptions," Ann says.

She had the prescriptions filled but didn't take any of them, mostly because of her sensitivity to medication. But, she admits, dangerous ideas crossed her mind. While lying in bed, she thought to herself, "I could take all of these pills right now if I wanted to."

Visits with grief counselors didn't help much, either. "It hard was finding a grief counselor that knows about loss. You need somebody who totally understands, and there's not that many out there who do." Ann continued her quest to find hope and normalcy. She eventually found it in other people who could understand what she was going through.

"When I was in my darkest days, I just wanted the slightest glimmer of hope. Tell me that things are going to be okay, that I will be able to survive this. The only way I was able to survive was talking with other people who totally understood, who had lost children. I had this huge group of amazing parents who have survived the losses of children from car accidents to drug overdoses to diseases. That's the only thing that helped me was being with other parents who 'got it.'"

Next, Ann found a bereavement center in Massachusetts called Hope Floats Healing and Wellness Center. Hope Floats offers daylong retreats utilizing all types of holistic tools to heal the mind and body. This includes meditation, acupuncture, counseling and support groups. She recognized the immediate need for these services back in Connecticut – and thus, her dream to start a foundation and healing center was born.

"I want to create something here in Connecticut to offer hope. Even for people who may be going through different life challenges, traumas and situations."

She has started the process by laying some groundwork. "I started a suicide support group in Old Lyme. I went to training with the American Foundation of Suicide Prevention to become a survivor facilitator – they call them 'survivors.' Then I have another support group I run with another mother for local parents who have lost someone."

Ann also volunteers at a local hospice, running a support group there as well. She regularly sends cards to grieving families, offering her support if they want it.

"I'll send a card with my phone number and email address. Some people respond and some people won't. Someone did that for me, a woman from Waterford. She lost her son to suicide. I didn't know her. She sent me a card and I reached out to her. It helped me."

Ann

Ann

Apart from her volunteer work, she commits much of her time to developing The Brian T. Dagle Memorial Foundation, Inc., a 501(c)(3) non-profit organization. Her background in marketing, fitness and even retail management help expand this new venture. She networks, coordinates and schedules events for the foundation's benefit. The day after we met, the Foundation was holding their first "dine out fundraiser" to support the organization's initial start-up costs. At the end of the month she'll hold a forum on suicide prevention and awareness. Later in the year she's planned fundraising 5K's and suicide prevention walks. Her ultimate aspiration is to find the foundation a real home.

"It is our goal to have a healing center."

Ann's face brightens as she describes the future center. "I want an old house, a Victorian with a lot of charm. In my mind I just want a nice piece of property where people can walk the grounds. And lots of sunlight."

There will be private office space for grief therapists and a comfortable meeting room for support groups. Visitors can choose from a host of holistic services like massage therapy, Reiki, reflexology and grief healing yoga.

"I would have support groups not just for parental loss, but for siblings who have lost brothers and sisters, for people who are recovering from cancer treatments, and maybe even getting into groups for people who have family members with addictions." She says she would also consider providing services to those who have lost a pet, "because that's a huge loss too!"

She also wants to "run retreats, have speakers, and have mediums come in. Just some really non-traditional things. Whatever's going to help people heal."

She has been to see several mediums herself and feels confident that she made contact with her son.

"She was pretty spot-on with a lot of things," she says of one meeting. During these sessions, Brian would sometimes talk about what his brothers were up to.

"One of them had just gotten a tattoo. The medium said, 'Who has the tattoo?'" The psychic then went on to describe it in detail. Other conversations were more intimate.

"Every time I saw her, she said, 'He was not in his right mind when he did this. It went too far.' Which I know. And he just said that he loves us all."

Ann says she doesn't need a medium to communicate with her son. "I tell him every day that I love him and I miss him, and I try to talk to him. I do think that he knows everything that's going on. He knows about what we're doing for the Foundation, and he's with his brothers all the time."

She thinks that maybe the Foundation wasn't only her idea. "Maybe it is Brian who's telling me to do this, because that's what he would have done. Help people."

In the first two months after Brian died, she started seeing hawks everywhere. "I saw probably five or six different hawk sightings. One came right to the backyard, flew low, and sat on a branch. Going out in my neighborhood on a street sign, a hawk was sitting there. I was walking with a friend on the Cape Cod Canal, one flew right by me. I haven't seen them since, but shortly after he died I saw so many hawk sightings. I was like, *Wow*. There might be something to this."

She adds, "I have a picture of Brian with a hawk on his arm from when he was 10 years old. He went to a county fair. People say a hawk is definitely a sign that they are here and they're acknowledging their presence with you."

Ann's advice to the grieving is to find whatever it is they need to do to get through the rough patches, even if that means doing nothing for a while.

"I tell them to do whatever they need to do. Don't listen to anybody else. Do whatever works for them. If they need to stay in bed all day, then do that. You need to just go with the grief. You can't fight it. You can't go around it. You have to be in it. I tell everybody who's going through it: it sucks, it's painful, but you just have to be in it. That's the only way to get through it.

"What I used to think was a long time is not a long time. I've learned it's not. There's no time limit. It could be three years, 13, 30 – there's no time limit, but the pain softens. I'm a big ocean person. I tell everybody, it's like a piece of sea glass. When the glass first goes in the water it's sharp, and rough, and raw. And then over time it softens."

She encourages those who are grieving to do as much self care as necessary. "It's all about them. Whatever they need to do to take care of themselves is what they have to do. If they can't go to a family event, then don't go. I really haven't been to any family events. I think I've been to one or two in three years. I can't go. Brian was one of twelve cousins. I can't go and see the other eleven knowing there's somebody missing. It hurts too much. So I don't."

Above all else, Ann advises, "The best thing is talking to others." What she's doing with her volunteer work and the foundation makes her feel better, too.

"Helping others helps me," she says.

When asked what she's learned from the past few years, she answers without hesitation. "I learned that I'm stronger than I thought I was."

She talks about the time her son Matthew talked about joining the military. Her first reaction was immediate fear.

"No, you can't," she whispers as she recounts the day. "If I ever lost you, I wouldn't survive."

"People say, 'I would never survive.' I used to say the same thing. You're stronger than you think you are."

As for her views on God, she mixes what she learned growing up Catholic with more spiritual concepts.

Why Go On: Connecticut Residents Bring Dark Days to Light

"I believe in Heaven. I'm hoping that he's there. Spirituality has really come more into play now. I'm looking for signs that there's more to this life than here on Earth and perhaps he is still with us. Life hands us stuff for a reason. We have choices."

Instead of giving up, Ann chose to transform her mind and her spirit. She's used her renewed sense of self to help pull others up from the depths of grief. Ann has shown that no matter what befalls you, hope remains as long as you are open to it. And now, for many, hope is Ann herself.

Jenifer

"I have the word 'hope' everywhere in my home. It's just my word."

When the going gets tough, the tough go biking.

I met with Jenifer at her home in Cheshire, Connecticut. We chatted on her back deck one warm summer day. Fenway, her adorable curly-haired dog, kept us company.

Jenifer's style is sporty chic. She's dressed in a t-shirt and striped shorts. Her brunette locks are cropped short. A silver necklace sparkles around her neck. From it hangs a pendant in the shape of the word "hope" written successively six or seven times in a circle. She's unexpectedly soft-spoken considering her ambitious personality, but when she speaks, she speaks rapidly.

Jenifer is a social, energetic person. As a kid she spent most of her time hanging out with friends and playing sports. As a young adult, she actively engaged in fitness activities, often going on long distance bike rides. For many years she and a friend did a cycling tour fundraiser for Multiple Sclerosis in Windsor, Connecticut.

"We started doing it year after year to raise money for MS. It was a 25, 50 or 100-mile bike tour. We started out doing the 50 and then we did the 100 one year."

Throughout her 20's, she occasionally experienced strange, transient sensations in her extremities.

"I started getting all of these weird things happening to me – tingling in my toes and my feet. I would ignore it half the time. Then it would go away and come back again. It was just little stuff that went on for ten years."

After Jenifer had just turned 30, a friend from an aerobics class set her up on a blind date with a guy named Don. "She introduced us and that was it. He called me not too long after that and we went on a date. Within ten months we were engaged."

Faith is strongly weaved throughout their family. In fact, two of Don's three sisters are nuns.

"My 'nun-in-laws' I call them," she says, chuckling.

Shortly before meeting Don, the curious tingling feelings intensified. One day she lost feeling in the entire right side of her body.

"I woke up one day, took a shower, went to dry off, and half of my body – like if you cut me in half – was totally numb and tingly."

Jenifer

She sought the help of a neurologist to find out what was going on. Finding a diagnosis wasn't easy or immediate. A litany of tests was performed. MRI's. Brain scans. Spinal taps. Neurological disorders were gradually ruled out one by one, including Lyme Disease, Lupus and Spinal Meningitis.

Testing went on for years without a firm diagnosis. At 33, she was pregnant with her first child. During her pregnancy and after ten years of symptoms, she finally found out what was wrong. She was diagnosed with Multiple Sclerosis.

Multiple Sclerosis (MS) is an immune disorder that attacks the body's myelin, a fatty substance that protects nerve fibers. The destruction of myelin can produce a variety of symptoms, including tingling, numbness, dizziness, fatigue, difficulty walking, vision problems, cognitive changes or pain.

It is estimated that approximately 400,000 people in the U.S. and 2.5 million people around the world are stricken with the disease. It is two to three times more likely to affect women than men. Connecticut is believed to have about 6,000 cases alone.

Many of those with MS do not exhibit any symptoms. "You could pass 50 people a day on the street that have MS and you wouldn't know it," she says. MS sufferers sometimes have a difficult time relaying their symptoms.

"I would get all of these weird things happening to me and it's so hard to explain. *My foot fell asleep and it's not going away*, or *Now it's traveling up my leg.* Or that heavy, heavy feeling like you feel like you have wet jeans on. People think you're out of your mind."

Her diagnosis of MS was a double-edged sword. On the one hand, she knew there was no cure. On the other hand, she was "relieved to finally find out what it was. But then again scared, because I'm pregnant and they're putting me on steroids and stuff. I'm saying, 'What's going to happen to my baby?'"

Fortunately, her daughter Cara was born perfectly healthy. Between caring for a new baby and dealing with her MS diagnosis, Jenifer needed to quit her job. But that did not mean her work was over.

Her primary motivation became raising money for MS. Ironically, this was something she already had experience in, having participated in all those bike tours for MS years earlier.

In 1999, one year after Cara was born, Jenifer got involved with the Connecticut Chapter of the National Multiple Sclerosis Society and participated in her first Walk MS. She and her family had since moved to

Cheshire, where one of Connecticut's twelve walk sites is located.

Her team (eponymously named "Team Jenifer") began as a humble quartet consisting of herself, Don, Cara, and a friend. The couple had a second child, Patrick, who also participates in the walk every year.

In subsequent years the team grew exponentially. She is fortunate to have found a husband whose enthusiasm for finding a cure nearly rivals her own. Don's involvement in Walk MS was a vital component of Team Jenifer's success.

"My husband is very dedicated to the fight. He started contacting people and sending out mass emails to friends and family to do this walk every year, and it just got bigger, and bigger, and bigger. We started buying Team Jenifer t-shirts and giving them out to anybody that wanted to walk with us. Then it got up to like, 100 people."

Jenifer's MS symptoms remained mild for many years, but these days her mobility is significantly affected. She has a pronounced limp and describes her right leg as "dead weight." Walking is a delicate process. Since she can't lift her right leg normally, she must tip to the left and swing her right leg forward. One false move and she'll plummet to the floor. Any number of tiny obstacles can trip her up: a rug, a crack in the concrete, and more.

"I have to think about every step I take on my right side," she says, "because if I don't, I'll fall."

Having one immobile leg turns lots of little things into big things – like tying her shoes, for instance. Many times she has to physically lift her leg up with her arms in order to move it.

Driving is a special challenge. Getting into the car is difficult with one immobile leg. Using the pedals poses another problem.

"I can't get from the gas to the brake quickly. So if a car came out in front of me, I wouldn't be able to move my foot over. So I drive with two feet. I'm sure as I progress I may have to get hand controls."

If she knows she'll need to walk around for an extended period of time, she uses a scooter. For the past four years she's been relegated to using a cane, a device she shunned for as long as she could.

"I don't like to conform to it, but sometimes I have to. I'm very stubborn when it comes to having to use assisted devices to get myself around when I never had to do that before."

Jenifer adheres to a strict daily regime of prescription drugs. This includes periodic intravenous infusion therapy in the hopes of slowing down the progression of her disease. She was forced to discontinue one drug she used for four years after testing positive for antibodies that indicate an increased risk (about 1 in 150 chance) of developing a fatal brain infection.

She discusses how difficult it is to be a healthy, independent person who is becoming increasingly disabled. The continuous struggle can be emotionally taxing.

"I try to be so positive, but there are times that I could bawl my head off. Especially if I fall in my house in front of my kids and I have scratches and black and blue marks on me. Or I'll be putting clothes away and I fall and my whole family comes running. It's not fun."

Apart from her impeded gait, she looks healthy and strong. She has a tanned, toned glow that exudes energy and vitality. There's a good reason for her muscular physique.

Jenifer is a fitness instructor.

In 2008, she was having a typical day at the gym when she started chatting with one of the trainers. The center had just introduced Spinning classes, which is essentially indoor cycling on a stationary bike. During the conversation, the trainer gave her some life-changing advice.

Knowing that Jenifer had been addicted to biking before she developed MS, the trainer encouraged her to give Spin class a try. "Go at your own pace," she advised.

"And I did," Jenifer says, letting go of a huge breath of air. "I tried it and I could not believe how I could function on this bike." Spinning changed everything. It gave her purpose, it gave her a challenge, and it gave her a place where MS didn't exist.

She was almost immediately obsessed. "I'd go. Every day, every day, every day, till I got addicted to it."

The bulk of the peddling work is done by her left leg, so her right leg is able to go along for the ride.

Seeing how well she was doing on the stationary bike, her trainer suggested pursuing a spinning certification to become a teacher.

Her initial response was, "I could never do that."

She soon changed her mind. Despite her nervousness, she took the course. "I was even nervous to walk into this gym where I had to go to get certified." She feared what people would think, seeing a woman with a noticeable limp trying to become a fitness instructor. But Jenifer never shies away from a challenge, so she pushed through the fear.

Her teacher gave her the same advice as her trainer: *Go at your own pace*. She completed the course and was awarded the certification.

She started teaching classes at her local gym – first in tandem with other teachers, and then on her own. She now teaches classes at two different gyms and makes it a point to spin every day. It's the one time of day where all of her limitations are removed. When she's spinning, she is unstoppable.

"Just the feeling that I get when I'm doing this makes me feel normal."

While spinning is easy, sometimes getting to class isn't. "One of the gyms I work at has about 15 steps to climb. I have to do them one at a time, holding onto the railing. I feel like an ass, and I feel like everyone's watching me, but once I get up there and in that room I'm totally fine."

New students unwittingly offer help as she shuffles to class, having no idea she is the instructor.

"Are you okay?" they will ask, watching as she makes her way to the bike at the front of the room. When class begins and they see that she's the teacher, her students' reaction is generally pretty much the same.

"Holy crap!" she says, with a big belly laugh.

Jenifer provides special inspiration to her students. Getting the motivation to work out is hard for a lot of people, but to see a woman pushing through a disability to not only complete a workout but also enjoy the liberation it brings, is an amazing sight.

"Even to me, to look down at my legs, to see myself on a bike and pushing that hard, it's mind boggling."

Jenifer has pushed hard for herself, her fellow sufferers of MS, and many other people she feels compelled to help. Many of these people live in her town of Cheshire.

The day we spoke, it was almost the seventh anniversary of a tragic event that happened less than 5 miles away.

In July of 2007, the lives of Jennifer Hawke-Petit and her two daughters Michaela and Hayley Petit were taken during a morning of burglary, violence, sexual assault, arson and murder. The family's patriarch, William Petit, was the sole survivor of the grisly event. While the rest of Connecticut refers to it as "the Cheshire home invasion," for the people who live there, it's "what happened."

"It was so devastating here," Jenifer says. For weeks afterwards the collective grief lingered on the faces of everyone in town.

Jennifer Hawke-Petit also had MS. She had attended an MS dinner, seated near Jenifer and Don, along with a host of others.

When she heard the news, Jenifer couldn't believe what happened to the Petit family.

"Every single person in this town was devastated by this and wanted to do something." She was one of those who followed through.

Two years before the Cheshire murders, her next-door neighbor's husband lost his fight to esophageal cancer. Jenifer and another neighbor found a way to honor his memory by selling luminaries throughout the neighborhood and donating the proceeds to the American Cancer Society.

But what type of thing could be done for a community shaken by such a horrifying tragedy? As Jenifer and Don brainstormed ideas, they thought of the luminaries. They decided to once again sell them and donate the proceeds to charity, while burning a candle in memory of the Petit women.

The idea rapidly escalated beyond their wildest expectations. "We just told a handful of people from Team Jenifer and then it all of a sudden exploded. We asked an attorney friend to help us become our own non-profit with a 501(c) 3 status."

They picked a day to light up the town and word spread like wildfire. "We laid in bed at night, going, 'Holy cow.' We couldn't put the brakes on it if we wanted to. People started calling us, saying, 'I want to help.'"

Bozzuto's, a local wholesale food distributor, offered storage space in their warehouse for thousands of luminaries. A graphic designer created a graphic for the luminary bags pro bono. A committee was formed to handle the needs of this budding non-profit business. A town in mourning came together in harmony and hope.

Jenifer, Don and their cadre of volunteers scrambled to organize street captains and frantically stuffed paper bags full of supplies for purchase. One day William Petit and his sister Hannah Petit-Chapman visited the warehouse as Jenifer and her team were sprinkling thousands of luminary bags with sand.

"We were nervous. I mean, I didn't really know him," she says.

Both expressed their gratitude for Jenifer's compassionate initiative to do something for their family. To show their appreciation, they volunteered too.

"They got down on their hands and knees and started digging shovelfuls of stand and putting it in these bags. Now they are part of our committee and I am friends with Hannah, Bill Petit and his wife – which I never, ever, expected to happen." (Petit remarried in 2012. His wife, Christine, gave birth to William Petit III in 2013.)

The luminaries were a tremendous success. On January 6, 2008, the entire town of Cheshire lit a candle in memory of the Petits.

"Every single solitary house, every single street – everybody bought these luminaries. I don't know how we did it. This whole town lit up."

Jenifer's team sold an impressive 130,000 luminaries, raising an equal $130,000 for charity. The first year's profits were donated to the Petit's MS Fund called Hayley's Hope & Michaela's Miracle Memorial Fund.

The luminaries became an annual town tradition. Over the years, Cheshire's Lights of Hope changed their mission statement from a message of remembrance to helping the community as a whole.

Each year, proceeds are given to organizations including: the American Cancer Society, Cheshire's Food Pantry, Cheshire Youth and Social Services, Cheshire's Lights of Hope Scholarship Fund, and the Petit Family Foundation. Lights of Hope raised $7,000 to benefit various charities in Newtown after the shooting at Sandy Hook Elementary School. They also set up 1,000 luminaries in Newtown on Christmas Eve.

In 2014, Cheshire endured two more tragic events involving two recent Cheshire High School graduates. "A 19-year-old girl was killed in a car accident. Four days later, a father shot his 19-year-old son then killed himself, leaving a wife and three young daughters. We decided to sell luminaries and use our HOPE sign, which we placed on the Church Green, to raise money to help these families. We asked residents to purchase one luminary for $5.00 and place it in front of their home on

New Year's Eve. We raised over $8,000."

Since its inception, including the two years before its official incorporation, Cheshire's Lights of Hope has raised over $675,000.

After the Lights of Hope event concludes each year, it's back to work on the Walk MS event in the spring. At close to 200 members, Team Jenifer is now one of the largest Walk MS teams in Connecticut, thanks to Jenifer's passion and marketing skills. Early spring brings another event, a brainchild of her husband Don.

A few years ago, Don had the idea to start a beer tasting fundraising event. The evening features an array of microbrews for sampling. Craft beers were exploding in popularity, and so did Don's idea.

Every year around St. Patrick's Day, Team Jenifer's beer tasting event offers samples from about 30 different distributors from around Connecticut.

Between Walk MS and ten years of beer tastings, Jenifer and Don have amassed an impressive $300,000 for the MS Society toward finding a cure. Adding this to what has been raised through Cheshire's Lights of Hope, she has grossed nearly a million dollars for charity.

Jenifer's efforts have won her much attention and accolades. In 2008, she and Don won the MS Community Champions Award. The following year, she was chosen to be the 2009 Travelers Walk MS Spokesperson for the Society's Connecticut Chapter.

"I'm not the type of person to sit in a corner and feel sorry for myself. I think the MS Society saw me as a positive person, so they asked me to be their poster person for the state of Connecticut years back. I went and had a photo shoot with [WTNH anchor] Darren Kramer. I was on all these posters and flyers, appeared in commercials, stuff like that."

While she is focused on finding a cure, she's comfortable in the limelight. "I was honored to do it and I'm not shy about it. I'll volunteer for anything." That said, she is modest upon any mention of her awards and accomplishments.

"Our goal isn't to be on TV or be in a commercial, or any of that kind of stuff. We're doing it because we want to do it. We want to raise the money to find a cure."

Despite her unending energy, day-to-day living is becoming

increasingly difficult. The MS is progressing on her right side, now limiting her use of her right arm and hand.

"Little things like putting earrings in or clipping a necklace – some things are so difficult. It's cutting me in half. It's hitting my core."

She's already learning to do more things with her left side. "I basically trained myself to text left-handed, eat left-handed. I can still write a little bit; my writing is kind of weak. It's hard for me sometimes to grasp the pen."

She tearfully acknowledges that in the future she may have to start using a wheelchair. "I know it's coming. I just don't know when."

Still, she manages to keep an upbeat attitude, and suggests others with MS do the same.

"Be positive and try to exercise, because that makes you feel good here," she says, motioning to her head, "and it makes you feel good here," now to her heart. "Whether it's walking, or running, or biking or swimming, find a type of exercise to make you feel good. I know people look at me and see me as an inspiration to them at a gym when they look at me hobbling in. Will I use my cane? No. I will crawl before I do that in the gym."

The word "hope" is Jenifer's mantra. Hope is carved in a wooden block that sits atop a dresser. It adorns the walls in typographic art.

"I have the word 'hope' everywhere in my home. It's just my word."

It even adorns her body.

A few years ago Jenifer had the Spinning® logo tattooed on her leg with the word "hope" behind it in big red letters. "I see it when I have my shorts on while I'm spinning, and it's a motivator to me."

She entered a contest by spinning.com, which led to being featured in an article on the site because "they were so moved and touched by what I wrote." After that, she was given free admission to a spinning conference in Miami, which she attended with three of her friends.

"It was amazing, amazing, amazing. People from all over the world were there."

A few days before she left, Don suffered a freak accident that rocked the family. One evening, he stumbled on a small set of stairs, landed on his hands and knees, and ruptured both of his quadriceps. This necessitated a major surgery, including thirty staples across each of his knees.

The accident put Don in immobilizing metal leg braces for eight weeks. "It was hell," she recounts. "He was like the tin man." Jenifer, used to having the help of her husband, was now a caretaker with mobility issues of her own. Fortunately, years earlier they renovated their home to make it handicapped accessible. Even still, Don's recovery was excruciating.

"In the beginning when he first came home, we were in tears because it was so hard. It was so hard to just get through your daily living stuff. He's been helping me all these years, and now it's flipped. It was crazy."

She recalls bringing him to the doctor. With Don suffering from a massive leg injury and she with a distinct limp, the couple was a sight to behold.

Jenifer quips, "We looked like, 'Who did it and ran?'"

Though the incident tested their mettle, it made Don better understand his wife's struggles. "He was now realizing how being in a handicapped world is. He saw a different side of it himself."

Jenifer acknowledges the importance of Don's support and how lucky she is to have him.

"A lot of couples are married or involved in a relationship and this happens. You're diagnosed and that person can't deal with it and they take off. He's not like that. That's another emotional part of it. He could've."

The family leans on God, too, for support. "Faith drives us in both of our families, so that helps a lot."

Jenifer's "nun-in-laws" are her chief campaigners of divine help. "If they can't come and walk for me, they will do a living rosary prayer for me, for the walk. So, it's pretty cool."

Her children Cara and Patrick are just as compassionate as their parents. Posted on her fridge is a newspaper article with a photo of Cara and a friend flanked by two nuns in full habit. Cara co-founded an 80-member club called "Sister to Sister". The club connects students from her school with the elderly nuns at Sacred Heart Manor in Hamden for a social visit. Both the students and the nuns enjoy the interaction and shared wisdom the experience brings.

"I've learned to be, and so has my family, very compassionate. My kids live this. They were born into this. We'll be walking somewhere and they'll be like 'Mom, here's a little thing here, be careful,' or 'There's a ramp here.' They're so intuitive, they're so aware, they're constantly opening doors for people and helping people. I just think that's happened to all of us because of this and we know what disability does to people, whether it's mental or physical."

Multiple Sclerosis has added a dimension of complexity to Jenifer's life, but that doesn't stop her from living as fully as she possibly can. "I'm not going to give up, and I'm going to keep pushing, and I'm going to keep spinning until I can't anymore."

Jenifer's message is clear. Keep going. Keep pushing. Be kind. Be a light in the darkness. Be thousands of lights in the darkness. Start walking. Walk alongside others and fight together. Have hope. And, if you want to, get on a bike and ride.

Tod

"Life isn't about finding yourself. It's about creating yourself."

Throughout his life, Tod has had an intimate relationship with the sea.

"I am on the water six weeks of the year somewhere in the world," he says. Tod met with me inside the art studio adjacent to his home in Mystic, Connecticut. Throughout the structure wafts the delightful scent of paint and wood shavings. Hanging from the stairwell are dozens of hats he has collected from cities around the world. His artwork peeks out from every corner in the form of painted landscapes, model ships and pencil sketches of spiritual beings.

Much like the sea, Tod is unpredictable and impossible to contain. In one breath he'll talk about Bill O'Reilly's new book and question the validity of climate change. In the next he'll discuss his experiences with peyote and share conspiracy theories. He's the consummate maverick, transforming from a pleasant ripple to a tidal wave without warning. He's often pretty intense, until he laughs. With even the smallest chuckle, his blue eyes crease and twinkle with uninhibited joy.

Above all else, one thing is certain: Tod is true to himself.

He was born in Youngstown, Ohio, but his family moved to Stonington, Connecticut when he was three. He was the eldest of five children, and the only boy.

Why Go On: Connecticut Residents Bring Dark Days to Light

He describes his parents as cold and unaffectionate. "I don't recall a lot of hugging or holding," he says.

The comforts of home were taken away from him when he was sent to boarding school in 5th grade. His teachers were abusive.

"In the early 1950s, schools had permission to discipline you or teach you as they felt necessary. There wasn't anything you could do. You lived with it and tried to avoid it."

Tod had a plan. He'd get himself kicked out, hoping the next school would be better. It didn't work. He encountered the same problems with each new school.

"You go to the next one, next one, next one, and ultimately you're going through about every boarding school in New England."

He also struggled with learning disabilities. "Whether I had dyslexia or whatever, learning to read and write was not easy." Tod is an extremely bright person and a creative, artistic learner. His style didn't fit into schools' one-size-fits-all approach to education.

In 8th grade, he found art. "My mother was an artist, so I picked it up from her. It was natural. I like doing things with my hands. It was a way to get away."

At age 16, he found a permanent way out of the vicious boarding school circle. Enter *The Albatross*.

In 1960, 34-year-old Captain Christopher Sheldon acquired a ship called *The Albatross* and founded the "Ocean Academy," a nautical prep school. Dubbed a "floating classroom," *The Albatross* had a long and intriguing history.

Built in Amsterdam in 1920 as a schooner, *The Albatross* was used by Dutch and German governments until the early 1950s when she was purchased by American filmmaker and novelist Ernest K. Gann. Re-rigged as a brigantine, she sailed the Pacific Ocean for a few years before becoming the set for Gann's 1958 movie entitled, *Twilight for the Gods,* starring Rock Hudson. Two years after that she was in the hands of Chris Sheldon.

When Tod found out about Captain Sheldon's new school, he foresaw great possibilities ahead.

"I'm thinking to myself – wait a second… putting on a bathing suit and t-shirt, sailing around the world – maybe school isn't such a bad thing." He already knew how to sail, so for the first time he'd be the star pupil.

Tod's parents gave him their reluctant permission to board *The Albatross*, but they warned him this was his final chance to straighten up.

On one of his first days at the nautical school, he remembers Captain Sheldon handing him a brochure with a passage that read:

"The sea is one of the great molders of character."

And so, in the fall of 1960, he embarked upon a journey along with a crew of four teachers (including Captain Sheldon and his wife, Alice), a cook, and thirteen other students. They sailed to exotic locations like Bermuda, Trinidad, the Panama Canal and the legendary Galapagos Islands.

Tod was finally thriving.

He even found a surrogate father in Chris Sheldon. Tod describes him as the first person he met with a "non-selfish, positive attitude."

The students, all boys, quickly developed a strong bond. The demanding work on the boat necessitated this. "We were a team. We learned how to sail the ship and work together." The boys' training included learning the names of dozens of ropes and climbing 85-foot tall masts. These exercises built confidence and gave them a sense of purpose.

One of the boys didn't last. Tod explains the student's exit in one word: "nonconformity." The remaining twelve boys lived, ate and breathed the sea.

The morning of May 2, 1961, began like any other day. By this time the crew had been at sea for eight months. Tod approached the helm and relieved fellow student Chris Coristine of his duties. Five minutes later the nightmare began.

Suddenly, a single bolt of lightning cracked against the sky and a violent storm emerged. The rare and dreaded phenomenon called a "white squall" struck the ocean.

Tod explains that a white squall (also known as a "microburst") is when a "column of cold air comes crashing down on the water. It's like throwing a big rock there. It goes down, a wave comes up." A solid wall of water barreled toward the ship. "Next thing you know – *Bang*! Over we go."

Organized chaos ensued. Captain Sheldon commanded him to

turn "hard to starboard," or away from the storm. Tod questioned the skipper's directive. He thought it better to turn *into* the wind to dispel water from the sails and, with a little luck, help blow the ship back into an upright position. He disobeyed the Captain's orders and veered toward the storm.

Sheldon grabbed the wheel, shouting, "Are you trying to kill everyone aboard?"

Neither Tod nor Sheldon's efforts righted the ship. *The Albatross'* open sails filled with water and dunked down into the deep abyss.

Tod pulled his friend Phil up and over a rail to safety. Another student, John Goodlett, rushed to release the lifeboats and became entangled in the rigging. Two other boys ran below deck, either to retrieve personal belongings or to save others. Another boy tried to unfetter the ship's sails. The latter four boys would not live to tell their tale.

Tod, his friend Chuck Gieg, and Captain Sheldon were the only survivors who had been on deck when the squall struck. Ten others managed to find their way up from below. This was no easy feat.

"Take a narrow, dark thing with no windows, turn it all upside down and fill it up with water and find your way out," he explains. A few boys were blown out through the ship's dumbwaiter from a buildup of air pressure. "Others came up through ladders and other things."

The ship's cook, George Ptacnik, and the captain's wife Alice were trapped in the chart house below deck. Tod and Chuck swam down in an attempt to break them out.

"We could feel them on the other side of the door responding to the door handle. We couldn't pull it open because the water pressure was so great."

The two boys eventually gave up, knowing they couldn't save Alice and George.

In less than 90 seconds, *The Albatross* was engulfed by the ocean. There had been no time to send out a distress signal. Tod, still below water, had lost direction, will, and air.

"At about 65, 70 feet underwater, I let go. Blacked out. Saw my life passing in front of me."

He says he saw a white light. "Everybody says, 'it's the light at the end of the tunnel.'"

He disagrees. "You don't see the light until you're born. It isn't the end of the tunnel, it's the beginning. It's the light at the beginning of a new life."

He miraculously re-emerged above water. "I look around and all I can see is debris, with the last of the mast sliding by me. I hollered out for Chuck, 'I'm here! I'm here!' One by one, people popped up."

John Goodlett's fatal efforts to free the lifeboats ultimately saved the surviving boys' lives. Now the only problem was how to empty and level out two 19-foot lifeboats flooded with water. A single life preserver helped keep all 13 survivors afloat while they figured it out.

"The lifeboats had watertight tanks in them to give them buoyancy and floatation. They broke loose from so far down that the pressure had collapsed these tanks. The only thing keeping them afloat was the fact that they were made out of wood." The tanks also contained valuable provisions, food, and maps – all of which were destroyed.

In an amazing display of camaraderie and solidarity, the survivors worked together in a time when panic could have easily overrun the crew.

"We came together. We knew we had to work together as a team. There was no screaming, no panic, no carrying on. We all knew we had to survive."

For the next eight hours, the boys emptied the lifeboats of water one handful at a time. Exhausted and traumatized, they waited and prayed for someone to find them in the middle of nowhere.

Sheldon waited two hours to see if any other survivors turned up. None did. Teacher Alice Sheldon, cook George Ptacnik, and students Chris Coristine, John Goodlett, Rick Marsellus and Robin Wetherill had perished.

The crew started rowing. Tod says they talked about "how insignificant we felt. How nobody in the world knew of our incident." They wondered if they would ever be found.

Though they were close enough to see the lights of Havana, Cuba was not a viable destination, as The Bay of Pigs invasion had occurred just three weeks prior. The boys watched ships veer away time and time again, thinking their tiny vessel harbored Cuban refugees.

By dawn, the young men were out of flares and nearly out of

hope. They spotted a giant freighter and rowed toward it like mad. Their exhilaration soon turned to fear.

"They came right up on us and pointed their guns at us," Tod explains. "You had to realize, here's a 300-foot ship and we're down here in this little rowboat." No one knew what was going on.

At first, the crew of the Dutch *Gran Rio* was overtly suspicious of the students' unbelievable story. During this time of high tension with Cuba, the Dutchmen were distrusting of these deeply tanned young men in the middle of the ocean. They dropped a rope down and ordered Sheldon to climb up. He complied.

The *Gran Rio* called the Coast Guard, who in turn called Darien, Connecticut, where Chris Sheldon's identity was verified. The crew of *The Albatross* was welcomed aboard and the boys were saved. The *Gran Rio's* captain later admitted, "We didn't want to get involved in an international incident. We were going to leave you on the high seas."

By the time the crew arrived in Tampa, the entire world knew of their tragedy at sea.

"There were hoards of reporters on the dock," Tod says.

He arrived onshore clutching their sole life preserver, which is now displayed in his studio's stairwell. After descending the gangplank, he expected a long and loving embrace from his parents. Instead, his father greeted him with the words, "You dumb sh–, you can't even do that right."

"I knew I had changed. He hadn't," he says with conviction.

He returned home with a profound burden on his shoulders. He knew his decision to steer into the storm was correct, but he couldn't shake a sense of responsibility for the death of six of his crewmates.

"That was a hell of a load to live with. There was no youth counseling or anything else, so I lived with it. It was all bundled up inside."

Not to mention the fact that his time on *The Albatross* had made him a changed man. He had seen things. Not only the heartbreak of a shipwreck, but loads of other things, too. Animals. Colors. Landscapes. Poverty. Artifacts. The World. He returned home to find he had nothing in common with his peers.

"I had gone out, circumnavigated the world, and come back to my friends in high school. Ninety-nine percent of 'em hadn't been across the street in the town they lived in."

When he returned to school for his final year, administrators didn't want to credit his time at sea, telling him, "You're going back to the 10th grade. You haven't been in school for a couple of years."

Seventeen-year-old Tod was not going to tolerate this. He responded, "I don't think so. Have you been to the Galapagos? Have you studied Darwin's Theory of Evolution? Can do you do celestial navigation?" He convinced the school to put him where he belonged: 12th grade.

After finishing high school, he graduated from the Portland School of Fine and Applied Art in Maine, now known as the Maine College of Art. After that he enlisted in the military instead of waiting to be drafted into the Vietnam War, giving him the freedom to choose which branch he wanted to join. He looked for any way to weave art and creativity into his service.

"That becomes map making. Cartographic drafting." He was trained in the relatively new Decca Navigator System that was being put in place in Vietnam at the time.

"The biggest use for the Decca was to put it into medical rescue helicopters. It's like an early GPS. If they were out on patrol and they got caught, they could radio in the signals. We could send a helicopter in without someone setting a flare up and telling everybody in the world where you were. Survival rate of personnel went up. Survival rate of equipment went up."

Soon, Tod and his colleagues noticed something was wrong.

"All of the government-issued charts were 1,000 feet off." His background in celestial navigation led to this discovery. "We put our two systems together to prove that the government charts were wrong. So we set about remapping Vietnam."

His work earned him a Bronze Star.

After serving three years in the military, he held a string of unusual jobs. First, he wielded a top-secret security clearance for a company that did "all the briefing information for the pentagon." Later, he worked on "simulations and animations for the Apollo moon landing."

He moved back to Maine, then to Florida, and back to Connecticut again. He married and had a daughter, before getting divorced and remarried. As the years passed, he still couldn't forget his fallen crew members. The spirits who departed May 2, 1961, haunted him.

During the late 1980s, about 25 years after *The Albatross* sank, the deceased began communicating with him through art. He showed me a divinely-inspired white pencil sketch against a cerulean background.

"These came as automatic drawings. I would sit here and I'd start to do a painting and all of a sudden something would take over. Christ would appear, and this whole energy of life would appear. I had no control over it. I had no answers. I went to psychics. I went all over the place to try to find out, *Who are you?* I got no answers."

Tod gathered his sketches and headed south. "I went to an art institute in San Miguel De Allende, in Mexico, knowing there was a guru down there that would take me into a peyote experience."

He found the shaman and showed him his drawings. He told him about what happened on *The Albatross*.

The shaman told him, "These are the energy spirits of all the boys that drowned."

He brought Tod down into a peyote cave two hundred feet deep

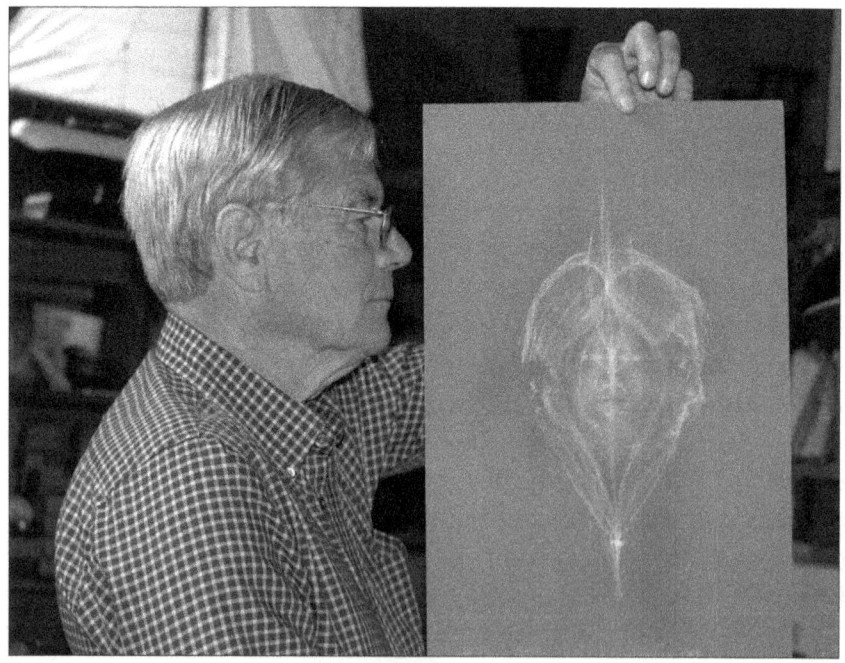

Tod

in the earth for a spiritual cleansing. First he aligned Tod's chakras using a tuning fork.

"He said each note, each energy center, is related to one of the seven major colors of the rainbow. Each of those is related to one of the major notes of the music scale."

He rang the fork at each of his chakras, bringing vivid color to the dark, desolate cave.

"*Bong...*" Tod hums, reproducing the sound of the fork, "like that, and you see red in the whole room. And this is a totally black room."

Next, came the peyote. "We eat this wretched stuff. Next thing I know – oh boy. Talk about being on the moon? We're on Pluto! Wow."

The shaman contacted each soul who died on *The Albatross*. "He said one by one each one of the crew that died came to him and said, 'It's okay. We're okay.'"

The drawings that inspired this journey are mesmerizing. Soft white lines form a three-faced being of sorts. Facing left is a young boy, facing right is a mature man, and facing straight forward is a hazy white spirit.

"I drew this in '87. Here I am, a child," he says, pointing at the left side of the picture. "Here I am standing here today," he says, pointing to the right. "You'll see my exact profile as it is today, in that painting," he explains, shifting to show his silhouette in comparison.

"It's like Dorian Gray's portrait," he says.

Ten years later his profile would make an appearance on the big screen.

In 1962, Tod's friend and shipmate Chuck Gieg wrote a book called *The Last Voyage of the Albatross*. About thirty years later, a screenwriter adapted the book into a feature film called *White Squall*. Chuck and Tod were consultants for the movie.

The 1996 film directed by Ridley Scott starred Jeff Bridges as Captain Sheldon, Scott Wolf as Chuck and Balthazar Getty as Tod. None of the other survivors allowed their real names to be used or had any involvement in the film.

White Squall provided an overtly fictionalized version of the voyage. Tod doesn't seem to mind the wide-reaching liberties of the film, except for one: the scene where the ship rights itself before tipping back over for dramatic effect.

"In the sinking scene, a steel ship would not roll over and come back to the surface. It's like throwing a hunk of lead over the side. It ain't gonna float back up. That was a major flaw."

In the movie, the ship takes ten heart-wrenching minutes to go down as opposed to its true ninety-second descent. Watching the scene is not easy for him, particularly the depiction of his failed attempts to save the skipper's wife.

One of the movie's biggest fabrications was, in fact, written specifically for Tod. After the survivors arrived in Florida, everyone went their own way and no one was questioned about what happened. In the movie, something else transpired.

"I talked to Ridley about being blamed for it and everything. So he says, 'Okay – we'll make a whole courtroom scene. I'll put you on trial and I'll let you stand up and defend yourself.'"

Scott crafted a tribunal scene to determine the cause of the wreck. "We put that in the movie in order to get the monkey off my back." In real life there was no investigation because the foreign-registered *Albatross* sank in international waters – releasing the U.S. Coast Guard of any jurisdiction. The *White Squall* scene was the only way in which Tod could be publicly exonerated of any responsibility.

The pivotal moment comes when young Tod (Balthazar Getty) is seated at the stand and asked about which way he turned the wheel – and why. He explains that he turned into the wind to "spill air from our sails." He's then asked why he didn't follow the Captain's order. "Because… I panicked," he replies.

This is when the "real" Tod makes his film debut. Cast as his own father, he stands up and cries out in the middle of the proceedings.

"You *know* that's not true, Tod!"

The moment is powerful, both on screen and in reality. As they filmed, the scene elicited an emotional reaction from the entire cast, from the extras to the stars.

"Jeff Bridges and I were in tears, crying. It was really an emotional day." Extras came up to him and apologized, fearing their sobs may have ruined the take.

At last, Tod was finally absolved of any wrongdoing. In addition, facts became evident over the years that *The Albatross* was not a safe vessel to begin with.

Modifications made by Ernest Gann for *Twilight of the Gods* made the ship top-heavy – eliminating any possibility of righting herself after the squall. His addition of heavy steel spurs, a square rig and a lighter engine greatly altered the balance point of the boat.

"We *never* would have come back. Period. There was no alternative to it once this event took place. When we took the knockdown, the ballast shifted and never had a righting moment." Once the ballast shifted, the sails filled with water.

"That was the greatest factor in the sinking. With a keelboat, you could take a knockdown and it would come back up. Not in this case. Had the ballast been fixed, the ship might have survived."

He adds, "It made no difference which way the helm was turned. We were not moving, so the boat did not change course." One small comfort is that this type of disaster will never happen again. In the mid 1980s, the *Marques* and *Pride of Baltimore* both tragically sank due to ballast shifts "and resulted in the U.S. Coast Guard making a rule that all round bilge sailing ships had to have a fixed ballast," he explains.

Over fifty years have passed since the disaster at sea. Tod still thinks about the experience frequently "to remind myself of how valuable life is, how fragile it is, and to say thank you for the experience, because it gave me that opportunity to see beyond, so to speak. To not just take things 'for here.'"

Through the years he has learned that your circumstances aren't what's important; it's your choices.

"Life isn't about finding yourself, it's about creating yourself," he says, borrowing a line from George Bernard Shaw. "You become that person. You find out who you want to be and make that happen. Then you're happy with yourself."

He makes an analogy that people who are unhappy are like someone who steps in the same pile of dog poop every day. Instead of stepping in it, he says, "Walk around it. If you don't like the environment you're in, don't step in it. Step around it! Or, pick it up and remove it. You have a choice. You've really got to say, 'I believe in myself.' It's having some self esteem and respect. You've got to put it behind you and move forward."

He tells me about a rather amazing experience he had on a cruise ship in the Mediterranean Sea. While socializing with some friends, a talkative man walked up and started chatting away.

At one point Tod tried to share his story about *The Albatross*, but each time he started to talk, the man shut him down. At some point, he made it clearer why.

"My very best friend growing up in Montreal was on some kind of a school ship or something. I think it sank," he said.

"Oh, you mean Chris Coristine?" said Tod, knowing his Chris was from Canada. Chris was the young man he relieved from duty that fateful morning – who died five minutes later.

"Stuff like that makes you…" he says, trailing off to make a motion depicting his hair standing on end. "The guy just went sheet white," Tod says.

He gave the man a heartfelt solution for both of them. "Why don't you bring him to me from the day he left, when you grew up with him, and I will bring him back from the day that he died, to you, and you can take him home and have closure?" The man agreed.

Today, Tod lives a quiet, content life with his elegant wife Lisa, to whom he's been married for over 25 years. He continues to follow his passion for art, taking great delight in sharing it with others.

At one point I remarked that one of his paintings of the shoreline was my favorite. I adored the smooth, deep blue of the ocean. He sat down at his desk and before I knew it, he was in the midst of recreating a miniaturized version of that very same sea scene.

"You said you liked that one, so I did it for you."

To watch him work is a pleasure. He transforms into a playful, cheerful soul – whistling, content, and charmingly childlike. Any bit of tension noticeably dissolves and he seems every bit at home.

"I don't have to be Rembrandt. I don't have to be anything else. I just have to feel that I've accomplished something positive. It's an ongoing process every day. At the end of the day, I want to accomplish something. I want to feel that I've done something. That's my value of being here. That's why we're here. It doesn't make any difference how big or how significant it is, as long as I have accomplished something, I feel like I have self worth. Because I don't believe we were put on this earth to do nothing. From all the negative things that have happened, I try to find the positive," he says. "I take it one day at a time, do the best I can for each day and be thankful that I have it."

Tod is a whirlwind of ideas, opinions and fascinating stories. He's endured change, isolation and grief. One morning in 1961, he chose to steer toward a storm and it changed his life. Never to back down from a challenge, he's surely faced a few more squalls since. But now, Tod knows he can stand by what he believes and know that no matter what, he is worthy, loved and free.

Corrine

"You get courage by facing fear. You cannot get it unless you face it. Do not be afraid to face it."

Corrine's crystal blue eyes sparkle like the seawater that splashes a few hundred feet from her doorstep. She's warm, caring, acutely perceptive and quick to offer frank opinions about life. With Corrine you can expect to hear positive, motivational words and feel a true sense of hope for the future.

Without hesitation, she greets me with a tight embrace. Some of the first words out of her mouth reflect her deep love for her two daughters, cooing, "They are the coolest people." Every mother is grateful for the health, happiness, and well-being of their children, but for Corrine it goes a bit deeper.

She sits on the couch, clad in shorts and bare feet. She nimbly bends one knee into her chest like a woman half her age. Her apartment is bedecked in a neutral, beachy vibe, with comfy wicker furniture and a Christmas cactus blooming in a sunny spot in the kitchen. A plaque on an end table reads, "Life is fragile. Handle with prayer."

On the wall hangs a picture of an 18-year-old Corrine standing in the woods. Her hippie hairstyle is long and wavy, her expression quiet and inquisitive. Next to it is a photo of her adult daughters Lee and Robin, who look happy, smart, kind, and greatly resemble their mother.

Her mother was a stay-at-home mom and her father was a police officer before he became an insurance investigator. She says she doesn't remember a lot about her early childhood except for a few key events. Her most vivid memory occurred when she was 10 years old.

A major fire at her home destroyed all of her possessions. The home had to be completely gutted, resulting in a three-month stay at a nearby motel. The event devastated her. The old saying "you can never go home again" rings true here, as her family life would not return to the way it was before the fire.

Her newly renovated home felt like an "empty, cold shell" that would soon become far colder. Unbeknownst to Corrine, her father's infidelities left an indelible stain on his marriage – and her mother wanted him gone.

"I remember my father and mother screaming at each other. The next thing I knew, my father never came back. That was traumatic."

After that her father occasionally came to visit, but he was unreliable at best.

"My father would call and either be two hours late, not show up, or bring us to a fife and drum muster. I will never forget that feeling of waiting outside and him not coming and feeling so abandoned. I think that carried through my whole life."

After her parents split up, she gravitated toward boys, alcohol and drugs.

"I was probably about 11 or 12 the first time I drank. I think I only drank one or two beers and I was really sick. God knows why I didn't learn, but I didn't."

She used drugs recreationally, but they weren't her vice of choice. "We would sit in the auditorium in the morning at 13 years old and figure out who was going to get what. At that time you had THC, speed, those kinds of things. I was afraid of drugs. I did some, mostly smoking pot. I didn't even like smoking pot, I just did it."

She wistfully describes meeting Bruce, her first husband. "I met him and he was just so cool," she says. Bruce was a mellow, long-haired and bearded musician who spent his spare time jamming out to The Allman Brothers Band.

Corrine was just 15 when she became pregnant with Bruce's child. Afraid to tell anyone, she kept the pregnancy a secret. For over eight months she told no one but Bruce. Despite it becoming incredibly obvious, her friends didn't say a word. Corrine felt afraid and helpless.

"You can understand these issues of being alone. A lot of people later told me they knew, but I just isolated. That's what I do. At 8½ months I told my father because it felt safer than telling my mother."

His response: *You're getting married.*

"We got married two weeks later and my daughter was born five days later." She gave birth to a happy, healthy baby girl who they named Robin.

Despite being thrust into young motherhood, she describes her late teens as "a really good time in my life. We moved to another place right on the water and it was the best time. We had this beautiful little redheaded girl. My friend Marie almost lived with us and our friends would come over for parties."

This is when she started drinking. Back then the routine was harmless and fun, and she could drink responsibly.

The early stages of her alcoholism were faint but insidious. "Marie would come over and we'd buy big jugs of wine. It was very *adult* to have a glass of wine. We would drink glasses of wine all night long. We took care of my daughter and would just sit and play Pinochle. We weren't out partying; there weren't any drugs. It was just sitting at the house, drinking wine, playing Pinochle. So it seemed fine."

Soon after Robin was born, Corrine wanted another baby. "It was a very easy decision. I walked by somebody holding a pink bundle and I was like, *I want one.*"

At age 18 she gave birth to her second daughter, Lee.

Reveling in the good life didn't last forever. She realized she "never had a childhood. I started feeling like I missed something. I worked at night as a bartender and alcohol became more prominent in my life. Somehow I started moving away from my husband and we ended up getting a divorce."

After she and her husband split up, Corrine moved out. They agreed that the kids would stay with Bruce, but she came to the house every day to care for the girls. She worked at a restaurant in New Haven, where working after hours meant late nights spent drinking and unwinding. Evening revelry trickled into early mornings, after which she would go to Bruce's to make the girls breakfast, get them ready for school, and return before they came home.

"It was almost like I was there, but I didn't sleep there. It must have been confusing for them."

It was a confusing time for Corrine, too. She was a vulnerable young woman looking for love. One night she met a new man named Henry.

"He's a musician, very charismatic, and I was just a lost soul. Truly, just a lost soul."

Soon, the two were married. The couple lived in his parents' upstairs apartment. Henry was a musician waiting to be discovered, with no interest in holding a day job. Despite dropping out of high school, Corrine held good-paying management positions. She footed all of the bills, including paying rent to Henry's parents, whom she also helped care for. She set out their pills and ensured they made it to their doctors' appointments.

Henry's bitterness increased over time, resentful of a world that didn't appreciate his talent. Still, Corrine held out hope that he would find and keep a good job.

"So I'm working and I'm taking care of all this stuff, and he's sitting back and playing his guitar. And I'm drinking more. Like, a lot more."

Henry had been hiding another unpleasant trait: he was physically abusive.

"This story is as classic as it could be, because it's vicious. You think that love will be enough, but it's not. They hit you. You don't tell anybody – or I didn't tell anybody – and they say they're sorry. This kind of abuse with him was like twice a year. There was a long time to fall back into that lulled sense of safety."

Henry effectively silenced Corrine from speaking out. Any time she criticized him, he'd bark back, "You're a drunk."

"He used it every opportunity he had," she says. "And he was right."

Soon, her life would be consumed by a new problem. When her daughters Lee and Robin were 18 and 21, tragedy struck.

After Robin returned to college after a holiday break, her doctor left a message with Lee asking Robin to call the office as soon as possible about an urgent matter.

"Right then, I knew."

Corrine

Corrine immediately called the doctor. Since Robin was an adult, they refused to give her any information.

The feeling of helplessness was excruciating. "What do you mean you can't tell me? I'm her mother."

All the doctor could say was, "I do believe you should get here as soon as possible tomorrow."

The next day, she took Robin to the doctor. Corrine was not allowed in the office.

"I will never forget this. I sat outside and I could hear my daughter crying. That was my *baby*," she says, with heaviness. "That was the most heart wrenching time."

When she was let into the office, she remembers the doctor looking at Robin's hair.

"She has long, auburn, strawberry blond hair and it was down to here," she says, gesturing below her chest. "The doctor looked at her hair first, because he knew it was going to fall out."

Robin was diagnosed with a rare form of cancer, with less than a dozen cases known in the United States. The cancer was so rare that her doctors had to research extensively to formulate a treatment plan, as they had no standard protocol for her particular case.

Their resulting plan was a dangerous, but potentially life-saving strategy. They developed an experimental and aggressive course of treatment called a "rescue." They would deluge Robin's body with as much chemotherapy as it could stand without killing her, essentially shutting down her immune system until it could be healthfully restarted.

Doctors told Corrine, "We need to do this fast and furious. We have one chance." If it didn't work, she wouldn't make it. Robin was given a 15% chance of survival. She broke out in a cold sweat and hives when she heard the news.

Robin was assigned a roomy suite at Yale New Haven Hospital. Fortunately, Corrine and her ex-husband Bruce maintained a great friendship. The two worked together to give Robin the support she needed.

"We went in and we brought everything: music, books, and we're going to keep her as comfortable as we can – no idea what we're in for." She promised Robin she would never be alone during her recovery. Despite drinking daily, she kept her promise and ensured

Robin was never by herself in the hospital.

During Robin's nine months of treatments, she became grievously ill. "She was really sick. Lost her hair. Because it was so aggressive, she couldn't have flowers or plants. I would have to have masks and gloves on. She was really put in a bubble. It was a grueling, grueling, grueling thing."

It was around this time that Corrine made her first connection to God. "I remember going down to a chapel one of the first times I was in that hospital."

She knelt down and prayed, saying, "God, I know that if you take her, she will be fine with you. Just show me how to do it."

She recounts the moment with tears streaming down her face. "That was the moment I knew that God will see me through everything, and still to this day that is with me."

Throughout Robin's entire ordeal, Corrine went to work, slept at the hospital, and lived with an increasingly abusive husband.

Not only was Henry violent, but he owned guns. He'd wave his weapon and rant, "I'm gonna take this gun and I'm gonna start with this one, this one, this one," she recalls, pointing at invisible people in the distance, "and then I'm gonna come back for you. He would say that to me all the time. So I would hide the gun. It was just horrible stuff. I was drinking the whole time. I remember I would go home and drink before I went to the hospital."

After Robin completed her treatments, it would be a year-long wait to verify if she was in remission. After that year, Corrine and her family sat in the lobby of her doctor's office, waiting to learn if Robin would live or die.

"We're sitting there so scared. We see the doctor walking back and forth."

She watched the doctor pass by several times until he noticed Robin sitting there. "All of a sudden he caught sight of her, and he went like this." Corrine smiles and gives a double thumbs up. "I will never forget that moment. It was just the coolest thing. That was 17 ½ years ago and she's been cancer-free since then."

Robin's anguish was over, but Corrine's was getting worse. Watching Robin deteriorate had drained her. Henry's cruelty and neglect whittled away whatever self-esteem she had left. All of that built-up tension reared its ugly head.

"Either coping with my daughter's cancer or the domestic violence alone would be enough to beat somebody down. I had 'em both going on, and functioning the whole way."

But now, everything in her life was crumbling. It started with the couple being kicked out of Henry's parents' home by another relative.

"We had nowhere to go. I was exhausted. I had no idea I could go to AA. I had no idea I could stop somebody from hitting me. Henry got angrier and angrier. He was always hitting me and always yelling at me, and it was just horrible.

"All those years I never called the police, never threatened to, never said I was going to leave – none of it. Because you just don't know. Domestic violence is like alcoholism. It creeps up on you. They're nice, and it's fun, and then little by little, all of a sudden you're in this horrible hell."

She bought a new house with funds from her 401K. "At that point I was so scared of everything and I was drinking all the time. I had no control any more. I had no fight in me. I just kept moving like a hamster on a wheel."

Her work life was next to be affected. "I lost my job because they sold my department. I could have gotten transferred if I wasn't drinking the way I was. I got another job, but I was not capable of doing it. I smashed up my car and lost that job."

As tensions in her life escalated, she could no longer handle Henry's abusive behavior. She sought help from an elderly neighborhood couple. She told them she needed to call the police on her husband, but she couldn't go through with it and returned home.

Henry found out that she almost called the police on him and became enraged. He struck her legs with a baseball bat. Then he threw a telephone at her.

"You said you were gonna call the police? I dare you," he said.

So she did. After 20 years of abuse, Corrine finally stood up for herself.

"The police came in. They took him away. I went to court the next day. A victim's advocate told me what to do and I did everything they told me. They put a restraining order on him and he was gone."

Unfortunately, her life was still being held hostage by alcohol.

For the next two years, she would drink every day until she passed out.

"The first year I was eating. The second I was not." Her relationship with her daughters was non-existent. She rarely interacted with anyone.

"My friends would bring me food. They would sit with me. After a while they would just leave it outside. I couldn't eat because my body was being poisoned. I got to the point that I couldn't walk – well I could walk to get alcohol – but I had no leg muscle. I would just sit in my house and drink. I literally did nothing else. Drink, pass out, come to, drink, pass out, come to – and the circle continued."

One day, someone knocked on her door. She didn't answer, afraid it was Henry coming back to hurt her.

"Even if I didn't think it was my ex, I could barely walk to the door and would never let anyone see me like that."

A woman named Denise from the U.S. Census Bureau left a tag on her door handle with her contact information. She ignored it. Denise visited a second time and left another tag. Then a third. Corrine finally called to explain that she was simply too sick for visitors.

Denise somehow convinced Corrine to allow her to visit. The two spoke for a while and over time became friends. She had no idea how significant this new friendship would be.

Shortly thereafter, Corrine was rustled from unconsciousness one evening by a troop of emergency personnel.

"I heard banging on the windows. Marie could not reach me for 24 hours and she called the police. That's why I'm alive today."

She was admitted to the hospital. "They took me in and I was in shutdown. I ended up on a liver transplant list. I weighed 90 pounds. I was malnourished and emaciated. I had no muscles, liver, or kidney; everything was going down."

One of the 11 doctors assigned to her case told her, "If you had laid there for three more days, you would be dead."

She was released after a 15-day hospital stay. The first thing she did was look for a bottle.

"I called a cab to go to a package store, got a gallon of wine, drank half of it, and called the ambulance again. That was the last time I drank. That was 9½ years ago and I haven't wanted a drink since."

Soon thereafter, she received an unusual offer of help.

Corrine

Denise from the Census Bureau invited Corrine to move in with her and her husband Ed to recuperate for the next few months. She accepted the offer. The day she moved in, Denise pointed to bedroom and said, "You just have to lie on that bed till you get better."

"They fed me, they brought me to the doctors, and I laid on that bed and I learned to get better. Isn't that a miracle? She was just trying to take a census."

She started going to AA, but she can't remember much about her first few meetings.

"These women would come to the house every day. They would pick me up, they would walk me to the car, and they would bring me to a meeting. I didn't even know where I was. I would sit down, they'd bring me back out to the car, they would bring me back to my house, and they came back the next day. They kept doing that until I could get it."

She has immeasurable gratitude toward those who helped her reclaim her life.

"I love those people in a way that no other can touch. God sent them to me. No doubt about it. To show me the way and give me a safe place to fall while I healed, emotionally and physically. I am grateful beyond words.

"There's a saying in AA: 'God will do for you what you can't do for yourself.' I didn't know to go there, I didn't ask to go there, I didn't look to go there. These women came and brought me there. I started going to meetings and all I knew was that people loved me."

For the first time, Corrine loved life. Each morning, she counted her blessings. "Nobody's hitting me, I'm not drinking, and I'm not sick – I'm so happy. I still to this day do not forget where I came from."

Her appreciate for AA is almost palpable. "I walk into a meeting and I'm with people who know me. I could walk into a meeting in New York City and never have met those people and they know me – because we know each other.

"The thing that comes from AA is they teach you how to live differently. Some people drink because they're mad. There are reasons – they call them character defects. Mine is fear. I drank because I was afraid. But look at what I've been through. Why should I be afraid? I've been through Hell and I'm still alive. I learn to call somebody or go to a meeting when fear kicks in.

"My sobriety has been amazing. I have no doubt I'll be fine. I do what they tell me – just like when I went to the court that day and did what the victim's advocate told me to do. You know why? Because what I do doesn't work."

Corrine's brush with death nearly ten years ago still teaches her today. "My liver rejuvenated itself. Not to the point of no disease, but it got better. It got better only because I never drank again. My doctor tells me that through a doctor's care and the miracle of the body itself we can heal, but his frustration in this type of disease is that almost all of the time the patient will drink again and then the liver doesn't stand a chance. He tells me how difficult it can be to work against the part of the disease that he cannot help — the alcoholism part. I am grateful beyond words to my doctor for sharing this with me. It keeps me green and grateful."

She knows now that her tendency to isolate is something to keep in check. "I can't be alone when I'm in trouble. There's not a minute I have to be alone. I have God, the fellowship of AA, and my kids are back in my life. I have self-love. I know today that I'm good enough."

Her feelings of self-love come after years of self-imposed silence. "When I tell my story I say at the end of it, 'I was 8½ months pregnant before I told anybody. I got hit for 20 years and I never told anybody. In this program I learned I have a voice. It's a beautiful voice, it's mine, and I honor it. I honor every feeling I have. I don't have to hide anything and that's a miracle for somebody who went through what I went through."

Corrine considers her road to sobriety a relatively easy one. "I'm one of the lucky ones. Some people had to fight to get sober. God gave it to me. He took me down hard and it was a vicious time, but he gave me the gift. I didn't seek it, and I cherish it."

She reminds fellow alcoholics to keep active in their recovery program no matter how much time they have in. "Having more time in sobriety does not make us any less apt to have a drink. If we have one day or we have 40 years, it makes no difference. The possibility of you having a drink is the same. The only difference is how you work the program."

She refers to spirituality as one of her favorite topics. "I know that everything starts and ends with me and God. Anything in between is none of my business." She points to her chest to indicate the place she finds her Higher Power. "It's here. It's in my heart. I am *so* grateful for that. It's not a church, and it's not a structured religion. It's me and God and the feeling. I could sit when I'm in bad place and just say, 'God put your arms around me,' and I know it's okay." A calm, peaceful feeling envelops the room as she speaks.

"It doesn't matter what happens with my life as long as I stay out of the way and let it be God's will. I really believe that. Sometimes I'll start to question God, and I stop. I guess the best way to put it is, *Look at my life.* How could I have any doubt?"

She urges victims of domestic abuse to know they have the power to change their situation.

"You don't have to be hit. You don't have to stay there for another minute. Do not be afraid. Period. There is a life waiting for you that will be amazing and safe, where nobody hurts you and nobody makes you feel bad about yourself. Go there. Today. Now. Look up the domestic violence hotline. Don't be afraid of what the guy's going to do to you, because that's what holds most people back. That or thinking the abuser is going to change. They're never changing. "

For many years Corrine never thought she'd have the courage to change her life, but now she knows differently.

"The thing that has made my quality of life so much better is that if I am afraid, I walk to the other side. That is courage. You get courage by facing fear. You cannot get it unless you face it. Do not be afraid to face it. My whole life I was paralyzed with fear. I don't have to be afraid anymore because I've walked through it and I've seen what happens. And look at me today. I'm a miracle, many times over."

Now she is focused on helping other people.

"The most important thing to me in life is that I help other women and men be aware that they don't have to stay where they are, because nobody ever told me. I hid it so well that nobody ever felt they had to. No matter where you are, there's a way out. My goal in life would be to help people find a way out."

After years of looking for love, she finally found it in the most important person: herself. By finding her voice and allowing it to be heard, she was able to appreciate the love that had been there all along, just waiting for her to find it.

Chris

"First and foremost, you do have worth and you are loved."

I met with Chris at the public library in Woodbury, Connecticut. He's close to six feet tall with a solid build, dark hair, brown eyes, and a sonorous voice. Despite having a strong presence, his demeanor is cheerful and relaxed. He's the kind of guy who can be assertive without being aggressive. Today, he's brought with him a bulky backpack, as if he's headed off for an adventure.

Chris grew up in Wantagh, Long Island, a suburban hamlet bordering Levittown, New York. He was the only child born to his Italian father and French mother.

He speaks adoringly of his father, a Korean War vet. "My dad was a good dad. I'm really lucky to have him." His father used to carve toys out of wood for him, a memory he holds dear. Another important memory occurred when he was three or four years old. While the family was vacationing in Bermuda, Chris dove headfirst into a swimming pool.

"I never had been in the water before, but me being adventurous... I'm going in. It was the deep end. I got under and I'm like, 'Whuh-oh...'" he says, laughing. "I look up and I just see this splash, and my father grabs me. Most people are going to say, well big deal, most dads are going to do that. But my dad didn't know how to swim. He was frightened of water. He figured out how to swim. He just used instinct. He got up to the side, handed me to my mother and lifted himself out."

His relationship with his mother was considerably different.

"She was physically abusive. She used to hold me up and use me as a punching bag. She would literally wind up."

His father bore his share of abuse as well.

"She hit him with a pan once. I just remember hearing him screaming in the kitchen and I hear *twang!* And my father's walking out, holding his head. That's how my mother was when she wasn't getting her way."

This confrontation had a profound effect on Chris. "That incident molded my view on how to treat women. I never saw my father raise his hand in anger to my mother. He taught me the value of women and how they should be treated, no matter how angry you may get."

Chris and his mother constantly butted heads. "I was a pain in the ass. I was a really rebellious person. I was always breaking her rules, because her rules didn't fit me. They were too controlling."

When he was nine years old the family dynamic changed.

"Chris, we need to talk to you," his mother told him. "Daddy and I are going to get divorced."

"I remember my whole world was just like..." He makes a whistling sound to represent his descent into sadness. His parents gave him the choice of whom he wanted to live with.

"I looked at them and gave the only answer I could give, which was, 'Whoever stays in this house.' My whole world was being turned upside down." His parents' divorce was enough to handle; he didn't want to move, too.

He inadvertently chose to live with his mother.

"Deep inside, I was like, *Ugh. You're kidding.*"

After the separation, his relationship with his father changed.

"I kind of pushed away from him. Not because I didn't want to see him, but because the whole thing was so awkward for me. He had this little apartment, which I hated. I hated the fact that he had to be in that apartment."

Shortly thereafter, his father was diagnosed with lung cancer, which ultimately spread to his bones. Oddly enough, though he smoked two packs of cigarettes a day, doctors claimed his lungs were "clean as a runner's."

Chris

He believes his father's cancer may be connected to the use of Agent Orange in Korea. After the war, his father worked for Trans World Airlines and was surrounded by jet fumes for many years. "That could have done it, too," he says.

His father was shuttled back and forth between the care of Chris' mother and grandmother. At that time, New York State required a one-year waiting period for divorcees, so even though his parents had split up, technically they were still married. Chris' grandmother eventually kicked him out, saying it was his wife's responsibility to care for the sick man.

His father underwent radiation treatment, but he refused chemotherapy due to a debilitating fear of vomiting. This choice led to his rapid deterioration. In his final days, the 5'10", 170 pound man had grown sickeningly gaunt.

"Seeing him wither away was the hardest thing. The last time I saw him in the hospital he was 90 pounds. My *father*..." Chris says, gasping quietly. "That's my hero. That's the man that saved me."

His father passed away at age 50 on Halloween in 1985. Chris was only eleven years old. He received a military burial and was laid to rest at Calverton National Cemetery.

"We're in the limo to bury him and my mother was crying. I couldn't understand why. I'm like, you abused the one thing that loved you, and now you're upset he's gone? Now I obviously understand the convoluted nature of relationships. She knew what she lost, and in that moment she probably realized everything that she had done wrong."

Unbeknownst to Chris, she was hiding her own health issues.

One day he and his mother were sitting on the couch watching TV. Out of the blue she dropped a bombshell.

"I have cancer," she told him.

"That's when she pulled her wig off. She was bald." He had no idea she had been wearing a wig. "I went back to watching TV and everything drained out of me. I was like, I don't know what to think right now, but my mother looks like the walking dead."

A week before Chris' father died, his mother had been diagnosed with terminal breast cancer. Doctors said she had four months to live and advised her to start making arrangements.

His mother dismissed the prognosis. "No. I'm not dying," she said. "I have my son to raise." She would go on to live another four years.

"If there's one gift that my mother left me, it's the power of the mind, because it wasn't even a wish. She made a *decision*. She decided it so clearly that it *happened*."

She fought as hard as she could to stay alive for Chris. The cancer went into remission for about two years before it returned.

"When the cancer came back, I think at that point she was spent." This time, his mother knew it was terminal. She needed to find someone to raise her teenage son.

Finding a guardian wasn't easy. His Italian side disapproved of his French blood. They considered his father's marriage to a French woman a travesty and would not accept him as one of their own.

He had an uncle on his mother's side, but there were family conflicts there, too. He did not have one family member who could take him in.

His mother had an old friend named Burt. The two had gone on one date long before she met Chris' father, but now they were just friends. Burt was a brilliant scholar and attorney, with degrees in Metallurgy and Civil Engineering from MIT.

His mother had no money left to pay a lawyer to prepare her will, so she asked Burt if he could help. He happily agreed. She also asked him to take control of the modest trust she set up for Chris' care and education. But who would become his guardian?

"Put my name down," Burt graciously offered.

Unfortunately, Chris never cared for Burt. He didn't know exactly why, but the more they spent together, the more he disliked him.

Burt accompanied Chris and his mom on a trip to France to meet some of his French relatives. It didn't go well. "I hated him. There was something I did not trust about him."

During one of his mother's final days, she talked to Chris from her hospital bed about his future. She asked him if he liked Burt.

"Oh yeah, yeah. I totally like him," he lied, not wanting to put any undue stress on his mother.

His mother said she was afraid Burt might let him experiment with illegal substances.

"I want you to stay away from drugs," she said.

Chris

"I won't do drugs," he assured her, lying again.

"Because I'm going to die," his mother said.

Chris says, "Then she told me that she loved me, that she was proud of me, and she hugged me."

His world was caving in on him. "Now I'm losing everything. I mean, now everything is like, legit f—ing gone, now, and nothing's ever coming back. That's when I knew it was over."

He left her room and went to a waiting area where a family friend and a doctor were also sitting. He felt overwhelmed and disconsolate.

"I'm 14 years old," he told them, his way of expressing the fact that he was just too young to handle this.

The family friend said to the doctor, "He and his mother were really close."

"That's when I realized the disconnect," Chris says. "My mother had no idea what was going on and she obviously thought everything was cool. And it wasn't." The realization made him feel even more alone.

A few days later, his guidance counselor pulled him out of math class. He assumed he was in trouble for a fistfight he got into the day before. He pleaded with the counselor not to tell his mother about the fight.

"Chris, just come with me to the office," she said.

"Mom died, didn't she?"

"I need you to come with me to the office."

"Mom died, didn't she?"

"I really need you to come with me to the office," repeated the counselor.

Chris chokes up. "That was a long f—ing walk."

His mother died in January 1989 at age 45. Chris was 14. Christmas presents sat unopened under the tree. His family was gone.

His mother was buried in Calverton National Cemetery next to her husband. Burt sat next to Chris in the car ride to the funeral.

"That was like a drive to the gallows. We turn in and I remember thinking, please let this not be real. I'm so sorry for being a bad son."

A soldier opened up his car door and said, "Mr. L——, I need you to sign this."

Chris thought the solider was referring to his father. "I'm sorry, he's dead," he replied.

He noticed the soldier's bottom lip quiver.

Burt nudged him and said, "That's you now."

Within a week, he had moved to Darien, Connecticut with Burt and his girlfriend Karen.

He says, "Burt drank every day. Heineken's and vodka during the day and then at the end of the night, White Lightning." White Lightning is a type of cider known for its low price and high alcohol content.

"From the get-go it was bad. My mother coddled me and now I've got a guy who expects me to be completely on my own. I really didn't know how to do it because no one taught me."

His first day at Darien High School was a bit of culture shock. He was used to working-class, tough-talking, no-nonsense Long Island in contrast to Darien, which he describes as "all polo shirts, rich people." It wasn't long before his classmates were asking the new guy to say, "Lawng Oyland" again and again.

"I'm dead broke. I roll in with my thick coke bottle glasses, a mullet, and Z Cavariccis. I look *way* different than everybody. I look around and I'm like... Ugh. It's gonna be a long four years."

The first three students he started talking to on his first day ended up becoming his lifelong friends. His ears perked up when he heard one of the guys, another young man named Chris, curse after getting a failing grade.

Me and you are gonna be friends, he thought.

He and his three new friends bonded immediately. They spent the day skipping classes, talking Metallica and telling offensive jokes. Chris showed the boys a thing or two about how they irritated teachers back in Long Island. The day ended with him being sent to the principal's office, which he blew off.

Back at home he was having far less fun. Burt promised him an allowance of $20 per week in exchange for doing basic chores like vacuuming, cleaning the bathroom and mowing the lawn. That was okay with Chris, who joked, "I'll lick the floor clean for $20 a week, you know?"

It seemed a fair deal until time went on.

"The toilet paper had to be a certain way, the shower doors had to be perfectly in the middle, the towels had to be perfect. All the cans had to face forward. When I vacuumed, it was never good enough. If there was one spot that I missed I'd have to redo everything. Guess who didn't take well to that?"

He never saw a dime of his allowance. "Every time I did something he didn't like, I owed him $5." The charges added up to the point where Burt claimed Chris owed him money.

Their relationship was horrible at best. Burt said he was a "screw-up" who would never amount to anything. He routinely threatened to break his jaw. Chris would tell Burt he hated his guts, to which he would respond, "Well, I hate yours."

He wasn't allowed to watch TV or stay out past 9 o'clock. When Burt went out to the bar, he locked Chris out of the house, which required him to wait on the stoop till he returned. He couldn't participate in after-school sports unless he came home, did his chores, then rode his bike back to school on an uphill, four-mile trek.

Chris had inherited his mother's car, but predictably Burt didn't think he was responsible enough to drive. Burt's girlfriend Karen drove it instead.

"Guess who decided to take his car for a joyride one day?"

While he and a friend took the car out for a spin, Chris made an illegal left hand turn and drove in through the exit of the Darien train station.

"We got busted by a cop on foot," he says.

He pleaded with the officer for mercy. He burst open the car door, dropped to his knees, grabbed the officer by the pant leg and begged to be let go.

"Please don't tell my guardian. He's going to kill me! Please, you don't understand!"

His efforts failed. Chris and his friend were shipped off to the Darien Police Station.

Inside the precinct, he told officers how horribly Burt treated him. "You guys are going to get a call tonight for domestic violence – if I live to grab the phone."

"I told them everything this guy did to me, how he drinks all the time."

Officers gave him a card to call in case of trouble. Karen came to pick him up since Burt hadn't returned home from work yet.

Once home, Karen sent Chris to his room. He contemplated running away.

"I start packing a bag," he says. He heard Burt come home and started shaking. He was halfway out the window when Karen opened the door to his room.

She quietly warned him, "You can't come home if you do that."

Having no place to run, he climbed back inside and faced his fate.

Burt's punishment was rough, but not draconian. He couldn't listen to the radio. Friends could not call or visit. He was not allowed off the property except to go to school. Lastly, Chris would have to move out when he turned 18.

In response, Chris ignored every one of these rules and stopped doing his chores. He told Burt, "I'm punished till I'm 18 and then you're kicking me out? I've got nothing left to lose."

Burt realized he was right and made a complete turnaround. He told Chris he could do anything he wanted as long as he was home by midnight every night. This newfound freedom encouraged him to start doing his chores again. But one thing hadn't changed – the bubbling rage between them.

One day Burt was looking for a fight. Out of nowhere he said, "Your parents were a–holes."

"You wouldn't be saying that if my father was alive," Chris responded.

Burt called his father a derogatory word, prompting Chris to grumble, "My father would f— you up if he heard that."

Burt heard "f— you" and flew into a vicious rage.

"He gets up from the table and comes bounding around before Karen can stop him," Chris explains. "I start backing up. He grabs me by the neck, puts me up against the wall and lifts me off the ground so I could barely breathe."

"You always threatened to break my jaw, maybe you'll break my neck," Chris hissed.

"Maybe I will," Burt replied.

Karen managed to tackle Burt and pull him off of Chris, who ran into the kitchen.

"I ran, I grab the phone, I grab the biggest butcher knife off the wall. I take the others, throw them in the trash can, put it behind me, and I turn around as he's starting to come near me. He sees the knife and I say, 'If you come near me, I swear to God I will f—ing kill you.' That was the first time I saw him stop dead in his tracks. I call 911."

When the police arrived, they ordered Chris to go outside. Another officer examined him and immediately noticed his bruised neck.

"He puts his light on my throat and he goes, 'Holy sh–.'"

After that, Burt and Chris were through. Chris moved in with his best friend from school and started the emancipation process. His new guardians treated him with kindness and raised him like their own son. He became so close with his new family that he considers them his stepparents.

Chris' life had stabilized, but he was not yet healed of his despair. That would come years later.

In his late teens, he was extremely vulnerable and suicidal. After living with his stepparents for about a year, he moved in with two young women named Debbie and Scarlett. His first taste of independence could have gone dangerously awry. Debbie and Scarlett gave Chris vital support.

"They helped save my life and they helped show me worth when I was living on my own." He believes that people like Debbie, Scarlett, his stepparents, and all the friends that have touched his life were deliberately put in his life to help save it.

He was finally free from abuse, but his self-esteem had been shattered. After graduating from high school, he tried college but dropped out. He worked as a bartender, drinking to excess on a daily basis. He lived in a dilapidated apartment without electricity. He was "pissed off and suicidal."

"I wanted to die. I was so pissed at religion. Who are they to tell me I can't take my own life?" he thought. "It's my life, I should be able to do what I want with it. It's not a sin. I don't want to be here. What have they given me? They've taken everything from me. Everyone else has love and I always felt like a stray dog."

He concocted a strange plan to commit suicide in a forgivable manner.

"If I die saving someone's life, God has to let me into Heaven. That's the reason I became a fireman."

He signed up for classes to become a firefighter. He had no idea how grueling the work would be, but he continued his long-term plan to kill himself.

Then, something changed. It happened during the fire attack portion of his Firefighter I live burn test. A fire attack realistically simulates the conditions a firefighter will encounter in the field.

"It's my turn to do the fire attack. I'm on the knob. We go in. It's all smoky. We go toward the heat and we're at the door. I feel the door and it's glowing at the top. The instructor opened up the door and it's just like: *Boom*. I just sat there and stared at it and it was like the first..." Chris pauses heavily to breathe. "It was the first epiphany I ever had, because my life flashed in front of me. And it wasn't the past.

"It was the future."

His epiphany was interrupted by a quick slap on the helmet from his instructor, who shouted, "Put it out!"

After the test, he was overwhelmed with joy. "That thing I looked at to take my life just saved it." He lets out an exhausted sigh of relief. "That day is just so important. I was just so thankful. Everything changed. I had purpose. It was everything. *Everything*."

Today Chris is a paid firefighter for the City of Stamford.

"I've never thought about suicide since. Every now and again that dark side pops up, but it's never serious, because I would redo every moment of my life. I have the best friends. I've been above the Arctic Circle. I've been to France. I've been across this country twice. I've driven up Route 66. I've saved a life. First and foremost, that is like, the biggest blessing. I've heard a human being's last words. It's an honor to assist someone to the other side."

When he starts talking about life, lessons and happiness, his demeanor lifts. He's lighter and more positive. His true self shines through.

"I'm probably the luckiest person on this planet. I'm not even lying. I mean it. Things could have gone so much worse than they did and every time somebody stepped in and helped me along the way." His gratitude toward his stepparents, whom he now calls "mom" and "dad," and friends like Debbie and Scarlett, show that kindness toward others can undeniably save a life.

The help he's received throughout his life inspires him to do the same for others. "Every day that I'm given a chance with the fire department, or with anything, to help anybody – I always try to give back and try to be a good example."

By 2010 he had quit drinking and chewing tobacco and became a vegetarian. He was feeling healthy, had a purpose in life and had made peace with his past. Then, in January of 2013, Chris felt an itch to spread his wings.

One day, he was home sick and watching YouTube videos of guys jumping off cliffs. He felt a pang of inspiration.

"I'm gonna do that," he thought. "Right then the decision was made."

He enrolled in jump school. He skipped the preliminary tandem jump that the majority of skydivers try first. This meant that during his first jump, he would not be securely harnessed to an instructor. Instead, two instructors would be at his side, using only their hands to hold onto him. His first experience made him wonder if he bit off more than he could chew.

"I almost didn't come back from it because of fear. I missed pulling my chute. I ended up grabbing my instructor's altimeter. He had to pull my chute, which meant I failed the jump."

Back on the ground, he felt deflated. He walked off by himself to think. He lay supine on a table, looking up at the clouds – and saw something.

"I swear to God this is true. A cloud made a figure of a wingsuit. As the cloud disappeared, there was a heart."

Even after this vision, he was still not sure he could jump again. He told one of the instructors, "If the regret on the way home is worse than the fear up there, I'll come back."

Regret was his friend that day. On the way home, he felt like a complete failure. He decided to give it another shot and has never looked back since.

Today he's done 150 skydives and passed his Accelerated Freefall Course, earning him the right to call himself a true skydiver. He says that once he conquered his fear, he found a whole new world above the clouds.

Why Go On: Connecticut Residents Bring Dark Days to Light

"You don't understand what's out there," he says.

Chris is no stranger to turbulence, so perhaps that's how he can handle the physical and mental stress of firefighting and jumping out of planes.

"Your biggest lessons are learned through chaos. People are trying so hard to make this world like heaven on earth. That's not what earth is for. You're here to make mistakes. You need the dark to see the light."

He lives with no regrets. The only thing he wishes he knew in his younger years is that he has value, and he hopes others are aware of their own value, too.

"First and foremost, you do have worth and you are loved." He repeats the phrase "you have worth" several times to stress its importance.

He references a quote by Ralph Waldo Emerson. "The love that you withhold is the pain you carry, lifetime after lifetime."

He also encourages people to make peace with their mistakes. "Don't hold it in and don't feel ashamed by it. Understand that was your

Chris

life's purpose and it makes you who you are. That's what you needed to learn."

Around his neck hangs a bone-colored turtle pendant. It pays homage to his friend Sean, a fellow firefighter who committed suicide about four years ago.

Of the turtle's symbolism, he says, "It has many meanings, but it symbolizes a navigator that always finds its way home. It's also a protector. It always reminds me of Sean. When I started jumping, I was really frightened and would ask him to stay with me in the sky. It was my place where he and I were together."

He believes the purpose of life is, "Soul evolution. Hands down." His perspective on his relationship with his parents illustrates just how evolved he is.

"I'm thankful for the situation that they agreed to put themselves in to help me. Their way out of this earth was a very painful way out, but it was something I had to learn and they took that on for me.

"I don't compare myself to anyone else. I don't think I'm better, I don't think I'm worse. I'm another human being here. If you really want to treat a person correctly, look at that person and say that person's my brother or sister and I unconditionally love them."

His philosophy of accepting the yin and yang of life helps him live in harmony. "Sometimes bad things happen. And yeah, we want to do everything we can to get rid of them. But this place isn't only yours, it's yours to share. All the bad things that happened to me, everything from my guardian trying to kill me to my mother abusing me, it all happened because I had things to learn. As soon as you realize that, you can release things. That's the important part.

"There's going to be bad people, because some people still need to learn. Even the really spiritual ones that want to make this the best place it could be and treat everyone with love have to be reminded sometimes that this is earth and it's not just there for your reality. There are six billion realities happening on this planet. Which reality you choose to vibrate with is all your choice.

"I can say with 100% certainty, that I have no death wish. But I understand the blessing if it was offered to me. So many people live inside their quiet little boxes and keep everything the status quo. I look back and my life has been one freaking tornado, some of which I've created. I've learned a gazillion lessons and I've had a great time. At the end of the run, I'm going to look back and feel like the only regret I've had is maybe back in college or high school I should've asked that girl out," he says, laughing.

"That's the only one. Other than that, there isn't any. Life's good. Life's really good and I'm blessed."

Stephanie

*"Life is short and it shouldn't be wasted.
The material things aren't important. It's the people in your life."*

I met with Stephanie and her mother Rose at the Southington Public Library. Stephanie looks "put together," wearing fitted jeans and a sheer top swirling with purple and yellow floral patterns, accented by a green camisole beneath. Her shoulder length straight brown hair curves slightly inward, framing her face. Beneath her dark-rimmed glasses, her soft brown eyes reveal a sensitive soul. Beyond her flawless appearance, though, is a young woman who has weathered storms.

Stephanie was, in a sense, named by her older brother Paul. "He had an imaginary friend named Stephanie so that's the name my parents went with," she says.

In a soft-spoken voice she says she was a "pretty quiet" child. Since she was young, fashion has been one of her main interests.

"When I was younger I had this sketchbook and I would sketch clothes. I would date it and sign it like it was some big deal or something," she jokes. "I guess I had some sort of style because everybody was always like, 'Oh I love your outfit.'" She was only three votes away from one of high school's highest honors: Best Dressed.

Her parents divorced when she was nine and her brother was twelve. The divorce created a rift between Stephanie and her father and she ultimately stopped speaking to him. Paul, or "Paulie," as his family affectionately calls him, encouraged his sister to work on her relationship with her father, even if that meant sometimes tricking her into it.

"Paulie would give me the phone when my father called, but he would tell me it was someone else. I think he wanted to continue the relationship because he wanted to keep the sense of family. I don't think he wanted to choose sides. It was in Paulie's personality to keep the peace," she says.

As for happier childhood memories, she shares the story of the vacation to Italy she took with her mother, grandmother and brother.

"It was in the summer of 2001. At that time I was 12 and Paulie was 15. We spent a month there and it was unbelievable. Our Nonni [Italian for grandmother] is from Italy and we stayed with her cousins." She adds that Paul was "proud to be Italian."

She imparts her favorite part of the trip. "Every day the whole country shuts down for a siesta from around 1 to 5 to be with family for lunch and to relax. One day after we had lunch with the family, we went to explore while everyone took their nap. Paulie and I took a bus into the city. To experience it with him was incredible. We were two young Americans in another country who didn't know the language, trying to figure it out and we managed."

A couple of years later, her life took a dangerous turn during the summer before her sophomore year of high school. It began with seizures.

"I had two seizures and I was taken to the hospital. They kept sending me home, saying nothing was wrong."

One morning while getting ready for school, she had a third seizure. She was taken to the Connecticut Children's Medical Center in Hartford for more specialized care. It was September 5, 2003, a day that was nearly her last.

"My blood pressure dropped into the 30's. I almost died that day. They put me in a medically induced coma to figure out what was going on. They had to talk to the Children's Hospital in Cincinnati."

She remembers nothing during the time of her coma. "The last thing I remember was going to the Children's Hospital and then waking up and being in the hospital. I was told I was in a medically induced coma, but I didn't know a week had gone by."

Stephanie

After she was released from the coma she had a lumbar puncture, or spinal tap, to remove fluid from her spine.

"Spinal taps – those hurt. I was awake for that. They try to numb you, but you still can feel it."

She became so ill members of the clergy came to her hospital room.

Her mother Rose adds her thoughts about these visits. "When she was sick, a priest kept coming in. So it's like, *Oh my God*," she says in her sweet, melodic voice.

Stephanie was eventually diagnosed with Hemophagocytic lymphohistiocytosis, or HLH. HLH is a rare disease that puts the immune system into overdrive, causing the body to begin attacking itself. HLH primarily affects infants and toddlers, but onset can occur in young adults and older patients. Mortality rates in children can be as high as 50%, but lessen as the age of onset increases. The disease is estimated to affect about 1.2 million people worldwide and is present in approximately 1 in 50,000 births.

She was only the third person in Connecticut known to be stricken with the disease. There are two branches of HLH, one called "primary," the other "secondary." Primary HLH is contracted genetically, while secondary HLH can be activated through viruses, infections, autoimmune diseases or cancers. Stephanie's was brought about by a simple case of mononucleosis she didn't even know she had.

There were a few bright spots during her two-week stay in the hospital. "It was great because all my friends came to the hospital and the nurses made it fun."

One day, the UConn Huskies visited. "Geno Auriemma and the girls' basketball team came. It was fun."

Most importantly, her devoted brother Paul was a permanent fixture in her room. "He took time off of work and he stayed there every day."

She returned home after two weeks in the hospital before beginning two months of chemotherapy treatments. The effects of chemo can be overwhelming, but Stephanie used it as a way to let her fashion savvy shine.

"I lost all my hair. It was tough, but I had different colored wigs. I had long blonde hair one day and short red hair the next day. So, it was not the situation you want to be in, but you make the best of it."

A year after being admitted to the hospital, Stephanie was given a clean bill of health.

Stephanie says she's always been the type of person who recognizes the fragility of life. "You really have to think – *anything* can happen. I mean, I could've just had mono, and this is what I had instead. Life is short, you know?"

After recuperating from HLH, her life regained normalcy. She attended Eastern Connecticut State University in Willimantic, majoring in Fashion Design and Merchandising, before returning to Southington to attend school closer to home.

Looking across the table at Stephanie and her mother, it's obvious they are important people in each other's lives. But it was Paul she was closest to.

Stephanie pulls out a photo of Paul and her. He is a little taller than his petite sister, has curly brown hair, a slightly mischievous look in his eye and a fantastic smile.

"We were like, best friends. He was my protector. I think he was brought up to be that way," she says, looking at her mother. "He would call me 'twin.' We were really close."

She says, laughing, "He was *always* around. Even when I didn't want him around, he was always around. He would hover. He was always there – even if I didn't know he was there, he was there."

Paul would always make the "I've got my eyes on you" gesture, pointing at both of his eyes before turning them around to point at his sister. All of her potential boyfriends had to live up to Paul's high ideals.

"That was not good. It's like he did a background check on everybody, I swear. It's like he knew things that I didn't know."

If he was overprotective, it was because he cared so much. "He was such a loving, giving person. If anybody needed anything, he would find a way to give it to you. If I needed anything he would give it to me. Even if I *didn't* need anything, he would give it to me."

As a kid, Paul had a variety of interests. He played the saxophone, was a Cub Scout, a Boy Scout and loved football. He attended Wilcox Technical High School and graduated with a concentration in HVAC. After high school he received a degree in Culinary Arts from the Connecticut Culinary Institute. He landed a job as a chef for the State Training Police Academy in Meriden, but he left to pursue his dream of opening his own restaurant.

Paul came down with what seemed like a really bad chest cold that slowly worsened over the course of a week. Stephanie says, "He was coughing and lying on the couch. He was saying his chest hurt, but he didn't want to go to the doctor because he just left his job and he didn't have insurance."

He asked his sister to go to the doctor and pretend to have his symptoms so she could get him a prescription.

She declined. "I told him I couldn't do that because they wouldn't see anything wrong with me. I've always felt bad about that."

Despite pleas from his family, Paul refused to seek help for fear of raking in medical debt.

Rose says, "I told him – just go. Don't worry. It will get paid. He didn't want to put that burden on us."

Stephanie says, "He didn't want to go to the doctor but we kept telling him, 'You have to go. You could have bronchitis.' He just didn't want to go."

Paul finally relented and went with his mother to a walk-in clinic. It was September 5, 2008 – exactly five years to the day after Stephanie almost died from HLH.

After the clinic did x-rays on Paul's chest, they sent him immediately to the hospital via ambulance.

Stephanie was working at a restaurant at the time. When she finished work around 11:00 p.m., her phone rang. It was her mother.

"Your brother's in the hospital. You should come."

Doctors said Paul had severe pneumonia.

Rose says, "His lungs were so congested. That's what was making his chest hurt. When we got to the hospital, they were trying to give him a needle."

Paul's family was escorted out of the room before they attempted a needle procedure to lessen the congestion in his lungs.

By the time Stephanie showed up at the hospital, medical staff was working on Paul in private.

"I came, but I couldn't go see him. They wouldn't let us in the room." Less than an hour after she arrived, the unthinkable happened.

While doctors were treating Paul, he suffered from myocarditis, an inflammation of the heart muscle, which can be fatal. Myocarditis is the third most common cause of sudden death in otherwise healthy, young individuals. Paul did not survive. Before she was able to see her brother one last time, he passed away at the age of 22.

When asked how the family reacted to Paul's death, Rose whispers, "Oh God," as Stephanie murmurs, "Not that well."

A wave of disbelief poured over the entire family.

"After, like *right* after, it's kind of – you're crying, but it's just like shock. So it's like you're crying, but you're not crying, because you just don't believe it. That night I called my cousins, who were like our brothers and sisters. I just… I didn't know how to say it. I called one of my cousins and she's like, 'You're joking. Not your brother.' Nobody could believe us. And I didn't even get to see him, so that made it worse.

"I would say the next month we were all zombies, just going through the motions but not really knowing what was going on. I didn't sleep, didn't eat, and couldn't concentrate. Nothing made sense."

Nearly six years later, emotions are still raw. Stephanie and Rose fight back tears when they talk about Paulie.

"I try not to get emotional around her. Because if I get emotional I know it's going to upset her," Stephanie says of her mother, to which she softly responds, "It's okay."

When asked if she feels Paul's presence is still with her, Stephanie replies without hesitation, "Yes." One way she senses Paul is through visits from moths. Many countries all across the world have folklore believing moths to be hosts for the recently deceased. While she and her mother were picking out flowers for his funeral, a moth flew over to Rose.

"There was one that landed in her hand and wouldn't go away. It just stayed with her. I see them all around everywhere, too."

In another instance, someone she knows visited a psychic who said that the spirit of someone who had recently passed was coming through and explained that they would be placing dimes around as a sign of their presence.

"After that I saw dimes *everywhere*," Stephanie says.

When it came time to say goodbye, her family was not alone. Turnout for Paul's funeral was immense. Three police officers were needed to control the traffic generated by his services, many traveling in from out of state.

"1,200 people had come through," Rose says.

Paul's warm heart and affable nature touched the lives of everyone he knew. His absence is still clearly felt. Even today, Stephanie says, "I just want to pick up the phone and call him."

Fortunately, she found someone special to help her through this loss. A year before Paul passed away, she started dating a man named Dan, whom she would eventually marry.

"He was there for me 110%. If he wasn't there, I don't know how I would've been able to get up in the morning."

Despite her boss offering extra time off, she went back to work two weeks after Paul's death to keep her mind occupied. She tried going to counseling and reading books, but admits neither gave her lasting relief. Her Catholic faith provided some comfort, but not enough.

What helped her most was the support of friends and family.

"People gathered at my mom's house. They brought us food and shared stories. It was nice to know we weren't the only ones grieving and that he was loved by so many people."

She says reaching out for help is imperative, and it's important to find someone to talk to.

"You need support. You can't try to do it yourself. I guess I should take that advice myself," she jokes. "It's hard to keep it all in – because I want to talk about it, but I don't want to get people upset." She adds, "I find it hard to open up to people I don't know."

She says it took her at least a few months after Paul's passing to regain any feeling of normality.

It's still difficult for her to reconcile why this happened and she continues to have tough moments. "Some days I have to just sit and think, let it out and have nobody bother me."

Unfortunately, just after she began emerging out of the shock and haze of grief, Stephanie's health took a step backwards. During a routine MRI in December of 2008, she had her first seizure in five years. The seizures had stopped since her HLH was treated, but they mysteriously returned and recurred about once every month. Her doctors could not pinpoint the source, but seizures can be triggered by stress. She believes the trauma of losing her brother could be the cause. Her seizures continued for the next four years.

Why Go On: Connecticut Residents Bring Dark Days to Light

Four days prior to the day we met, she celebrated her two-year anniversary without a single seizure, but the potential threat of reoccurrence prohibits her from driving. Unlike others who may see an aura or have other indications that a seizure is coming, she has no warning – only first becoming aware of a seizure after it's over.

Stephanie

"I'll wake up out of it and I'll know that it happened. Sometimes I'll bite my tongue and my mouth starts bleeding. One time I hit my head against the refrigerator and I had to get staples in my head."

Managing a family loss and a significant health issue, Stephanie carried on. She stayed in school, kept working and continued being a loving daughter and girlfriend. She is thankful for her decision to change colleges years ago, as it allowed her to see Paul during what would be his final days.

"I would've felt even guiltier if I wasn't living at home when it happened."

In 2009, she graduated college. She was proud of her accomplishments, but upset her brother wasn't there beside her.

"When I graduated I felt really upset that he wasn't able to see that," she says.

In 2012, she and Dan started a marketing company that creates websites for regional businesses. They also help these companies develop the Internet presence they need to be successful.

Stephanie

"We do a lot of restaurants. We branched out and did websites for lawyers, a horse stable and architects. So we're branching out into other areas."

She has a few personal and professional goals she's excited to achieve. Professionally, she says, "I'd like to grow my company and I would like to get back into fashion."

At the time that we met, she and Dan were not yet married. While sitting together at the library, the topic of her upcoming nuptials creates noticeable excitement. The energy at the table changes completely to one of positivity and hope as she discusses getting married and having children.

"The wedding planning is already in process," she says, adding that she's looking forward to "starting a family within the next five years."

A symbolic part of her wedding ceremony will honor Paul's memory.

"I will be getting a bouquet charm with his picture on it so I can carry him with me," she says.

In a lovely moment of maternal love, Rose expresses how proud she is of who her daughter has become.

"I think the world of her," she says, her eyes beaming with love. "I'm just happy that she's happy. You know, getting married, her business, and stuff like that. I love her boyfriend. I just love him. He takes good care of her and I'm so thankful for that."

She and her mother commemorate September 5th, the anniversary of Stephanie's brush with death and Paul's passing, together – though the activities vary from year to year.

"One year I had my family over for a brunch at my house so we were all together. Usually, I'll take the day off to spend with her and we'll do something together. Instead of making it a sad day, we'll do something positive."

Stephanie shows me her tattoo memorializing her brother. Wrapped around her ankle are a set of rosary beads, which drape down to the top of her foot. At the end is a cross, and beside it, the name "Paulie."

Visitors to Southington can find two memorials dedicated to Paul. Rose's parents purchased a lamppost and had it installed directly across from the Sons of Italy club on Center Street in Southington – of which Paul was a proud member.

"So the light's always shining," Rose says.

Paul's father, a welder, created a stunning memorial of his own. The monument is a metal cross, at least eight feet in height, embellished with symbols imbued with meaning.

"It's really pretty," Stephanie says. "There are symbols on it that mean something for each of us. The roses are for her," she says, pointing to her mom. "There's a big heart for Paulie and little hearts on the side for me. Then at the top there's this empty circle for the emptiness that my dad feels."

Stephanie and Rose graciously offer to drive down to the memorial since it's only a couple of miles from the Southington Public Library. I follow behind in my own car, keeping an eye on Rose's personalized license plate that pays homage to her son. The cross is located on property that Paul formerly owned but has since been transferred to other members of the family.

She leads me down a small road and into a remote parking area slightly offset from the Southington Rail Trail, a broad and flat paved route perfect for walkers, runners and bikers. It happened to be a sparkling day. The sun was shining bright and it was warm, but not too hot. For a moment it seemed a cruel juxtaposition to see a young man's memorial silhouetted against such a gorgeous blue sky. But as we walked closer, I recalled Paul's warm, loving nature and concluded that the ambience could not be more fitting.

"That's Paul's car right there," Stephanie says, pointing to a vehicle on the property behind the memorial, which gives the vague impression he never left.

The memorial's height alone makes a dramatic impression. The cross' black design is adorned with a multitude of roses and heart-shaped swirls. Mounted in a base of concrete, the memorial is encircled by a ring of rocks and a bed of hostas. A framed photo and biography about Paulie leans at the bottom, unscathed by six years of sun and harsh weather.

The three of us linger for a little while. Rose expresses her difficulty understanding why God would take her son away. I think about Paulie and the love he has for his sister. Some believe that those who have passed on remain alongside their loved ones, guiding and watching

Stephanie

over them. If that is true, one can be fairly certain that he was right there with us, keeping a watchful eye on his beloved twin.

Stephanie uses happy memories of her brother to help keep him close. Their trip to Italy is one she thinks of often. "To have this once-in-a-lifetime experience with my brother is indescribable. I'm so glad I have these memories of him and that he was able to experience it."

When Paulie was alive, his relentless attachment to his sister may have caused friction, but now it's one of the things that she misses the most. "As much as I hated that he was always there, I kind of miss that too," she says.

She knows that if he is still watching over her now, his unwavering love for her remains. "I could do no wrong in his eyes. I know he would just be so happy with anything I'm doing. With my company that I have, he would just be so happy and he would want to be a help in any way possible. I know he would be proud of me no matter what."

Despite everything she has been through, she knows that each and every moment helped create who she is, living a life she loves. Apart from the loss of her brother, there's nothing she would go back and change if she could.

"Even with all the health issues, challenges, and heartbreak, I wouldn't change anything because it wouldn't lead me to where I am now."

Though the struggle has been hard, it's helped her prioritize what matters most in life.

"I know for sure that you have to cherish every day. Life is short and it shouldn't be wasted. You should tell the people you love that you love them and never leave on bad terms. You never know when the last time you'll talk to them will be. I know that sounds depressing, but to be sick at 14 and lose my brother five years later, it puts things into perspective. The material things aren't important. It's the people in your life."

While Paul's death created an empty space within the family, his legacy illustrates the importance of living with love and compassion. He may have been taken from the world too soon, but his kind and caring existence will live on eternally. Paul's dedication to his friends and family reminds us of the lasting effects of kindness. While our spirits may move on to another plane, the results of our good deeds will continue to warm the hearts of those we loved for many years into the future.

Angelique

"It's all about the choices you make."

Her name is Angelique, but her friends call her Angel. She lives in a quaint, family-friendly development in Groton with her husband and two sons, Ryan and Aaron, ages 11 and 12. Ashley, her 24-year-old daughter from a previous relationship, lives in her own apartment but visits regularly – including the day I came to visit.

"She's a very humble person," Ashley says of her mom. It's not the typical way a child would describe her mother, but it's accurate.

Angel's family is close-knit, loving, and full of humor. Though she's had the lion's share of problems, she has worked hard to triumph over loss. Sometimes that triumph was not without sacrifice.

She and I sit down at the dining room table to talk. Her sons scurry off to parts unknown. She carries a pack of smokes to the table with her, but she never lights one.

She tells her story with the occasional hushed tone in all the right places, but is open and honest with her children about where she's been and what she's gone through. She's blunt in a most refreshing way. She's outspoken, but tolerant. She's serious when necessary, but humorous at every opportunity.

Angel was born and raised in the projects of Chicago, Illinois. She almost didn't survive her first year.

"I was born sick," she says. "I was born with pneumonia and a hole in my heart."

Doctors told her mother that she wouldn't live more than a year, "So she named me Angelique, which means 'little angel.'"

She recovered from the pneumonia, and the hole in her heart miraculously closed on its own – an early testament to her strength.

The resilience that sustained her as a baby are still evident in her confident presence today. She's tall and leggy, with a warm, radiant smile. Today she's dressed in a dark blue t-shirt and shorts. Her wavy hair is pulled back in a no-fuss ponytail. Her blue-painted fingernails hint at a creative side, evidenced by her interests in choral and culinary arts.

She describes herself as a "tomboy" as a child. She has two older brothers and an older sister, and lost a younger brother to SIDS when he was two years old. She comes from a unique mixed heritage; her mother was Czechoslovakian and German, and her father was African American and American Indian – specifically, Cherokee, Seminole, and Blackfoot.

She jokes about her light brown skin. "I came out this color. I came out the lightest one," she says, comparing herself to her siblings.

"My father was one of those guys that wanted to be around when he wanted to be around," she says. "My mom was a welfare mother and basically raised the four kids by herself."

Her mother married the father of her two eldest children right out of high school. Though they split up and she went on to have children by other men, the couple never officially divorced. They remained estranged until her death in 1993.

Her parents both struggled with substance abuse. Drugs and alcohol spoiled not only her parents' lives but also many others in her life. Angel made the conscious decision to stay away from all addictive substances, because she wanted something better for her life.

"I come from two parents that were drug addicts and alcoholics. I watched what everybody did while they were either drunk or high off of something. I had an ex-boyfriend that shot his best friend in the face and went to prison because he was high.

"I think I tried pot twice. Didn't like it; made me sick, both times. Only thing it *did* do that was good, it made me ace an algebra test when I was in high school. I'm like, 'What?'" she jokes.

She never went further to try any other kind of drugs. "The only bad habit I have is smoking cigarettes," she says.

Angelique

Life in the projects was hard. Danger, temptation and crime lurked around every corner.

"You are always looking over your shoulder. Being in a high poverty area, you've got all that trouble that comes along with it." Gangs were a huge part of that. While it was mostly men joining neighborhood gangs, women, too, had the opportunity to either join a gang or date someone in one.

"In the projects you either ran with these people or you didn't. Luckily for me I never had that issue."

Her mother worked hard to keep her kids on the straight and narrow, despite her own involvement in drugs, alcohol and other iniquities.

"By the time it got down to me – because I was the youngest – my mother had a really, *really* tight leash on me." She was expected to be home every night before the streetlights flicked on. "My mother tried her best to keep me out of it. At that age I didn't understand what she was doing, of course. Now I understand why she did what she did."

Angel started working in her early teens.

"I was going to school, going to work. Going to school, going to work." She started out with summer jobs. "I worked for the park district cleaning, sweeping, grounds keeping, stuff like that." Later she worked at Bears and Bulls games as an usher for security giant Andy Frain Services.

Working kept her occupied and out of trouble. So did school. Her mother sent her to a regional magnet high school instead of a public high school. She applied to several schools and was accepted to all of them. She ultimately chose Curie Metropolitan High School and attended as a drama major.

"Back then I was into drama and singing. I did *West Side Story* and other shows, but my main thing was chorus. I used to do advanced city chorus for the city to try to keep me out of trouble."

When Angel was 15, trouble found her.

Though her mother and stepfather had split up years prior, they were, as previously stated, still married. Her stepfather maintained a steady relationship with Angel's sister and oldest brother. He lived in Cicero, Illinois, a 15-minute drive from Chicago. One day he asked Angel's mother if she could swing by and help with his laundry.

"Unfortunately for me, that is not all that he wanted."

There was no history of any sexual abuse between Angel and her stepfather. But that day, things changed. That day, he raped her.

She was too scared to tell anyone what had happened. She even felt as if she had done something wrong.

"When it first happened, I thought it was my fault. I would always think there was some way that I could have prevented it from happening. Or maybe I was doing something that kind of… made me interesting to him, or whatever," she says.

She had always worn casual, loose-fitting clothes as a young woman – but now, those clothes concealed something she was desperate to hide.

She was pregnant.

Many in Angel's position might consider an abortion. She didn't.

"I don't believe in them for myself. I can't say if anybody else should, because I don't know their situation. But it was never an option." She knew exactly what she wanted to do and never swayed from that position. She decided to have the baby and give him up for adoption.

She was about eight months along when she could no longer hide her pregnancy.

Again and again, Angel's mother asked her, "Who's the father?"

"I was scared to say anything, so I just wouldn't tell her."

The situation came to a head during a drive home after an obstetrician appointment. Her sister was driving the car, her mother was in the front seat, and Angel was in the back with her aunt.

Angel's aunt – her mother's sister – besieged her with questions. "She was just hammering and hammering about who the baby's father was."

Finally, she admitted the baby's father was her stepfather. Everyone in the car flew into a frenzy.

"My sister almost ran into a fricking tree, because that was her father."

Her first instinct was to hide from the entire situation. She only remembers some of the chaos after they returned home. Her mother was furious. The situation grew violent.

"We came back to the projects and I think he was sitting in the kitchen. We walked in and my mother went for her knives. She tried to kill him. There was a struggle. I remember my aunt saying, 'Dottie, you can't do this. Angel's gonna need you.' And that was it. I don't know what else happened then."

Angel says she went off in her "own little direction" in an effort to escape.

After things had settled down and her mother had time to think, she offered her daughter an alternative to adoption. Not wanting to give up her grandchild, she offered to raise the baby as her own. Angel's response was a clear and resounding, "No."

"How confused would that kid be in that situation? He doesn't need that in his life."

When she was only 16 years old, she gave birth to a healthy boy and released him for adoption. For her, it was a hard, but necessary choice. She wanted her son to have every available opportunity to him, and that started with a life outside of the projects. Even though she never wavered from her decision, she would later hesitate, wondering if it was the right choice.

"You always have those questions as you go through life. I wonder what he's doing now? Did I do the right thing, giving him away? And wonder if he had a good life, if it was better than being in the projects, and stuff like that."

She left the door open for a relationship in the future. Before she let him go, she signed paperwork allowing him to contact her when he turned 18 if he wanted to.

The baby's adoptive parents named him Isaac. His new father was a pastor and his mother a music teacher. The couple sent Angel photos of Isaac up until he turned five. Even this limited contact with his family gave her some comfort that she had done the right thing.

But for now, it was time to move on. It was a process that would take years.

The ordeal left Angel with unresolved emotional issues. After the assault, her relationship with her stepfather was all but over except for a few loose ends.

"We were never in the same room alone or even in the same places."

What lingered was a strong sense of anger and resentment toward men.

"At one point in time I couldn't stand men, period. I didn't want anything to do with them. I was just happy to be by myself." Her mother strongly encouraged her to go to therapy, and she eventually did.

Her therapist helped her understand that the rape was not her fault in any way. She learned, "There are just some sick people out there. It gave me a different way of looking at it versus thinking that it was all my fault. Technically it had nothing to do with me. It helps to talk about it."

In later years she would find out she was not her stepfather's first victim. In fact, he had a history of abusing both males and females going back to the 1970s, including children as young as eight years old. He was eventually convicted for his crimes about ten years after his assault on Angel.

By the time she was 18, Angel had lived in an environment of addiction, fear, poverty, abuse and crime. She had survived a rape and the grief of giving her firstborn up for adoption. She was now at a crossroads. She either had to get out of the projects or risk being trapped there for life. She couldn't afford college, so she went into the military, serving as a cook.

"I joined the Army. That was it. I never looked back. You only have so many ways to get out of the projects," she says, "and it got me out of there."

She served for four years, spending the bulk of her time in Freiburg, Germany – a perfect fit with her German heritage.

"It was fun; I liked it. They have a lot of pretty churches, stuff like that. A lot of nice people."

While stationed in Freiburg, she became pregnant with her second child. At age 20, she gave birth to her daughter Ashley. This inadvertently kept Angel out of the Gulf War.

"Desert Storm was going on back then. They wanted me to send my daughter to the States and go to war, and I was not going to let that happen. My mother had to have a hysterectomy and was diagnosed with cancer the first time. She was in no position to care for herself. I did not know Ashley's father's parents well enough to give them my child, so I asked to be released," she says.

Her mother had since moved to Milwaukee, Wisconsin. When she left the Army she moved into an apartment upstairs from her mother.

Angelique

She raised Ashley alone.

Ashley's birth father is originally from Ohio, but he was stationed in Kansas prior to finishing his service in the Army. One week she brought Ashley on a trip to Kansas to visit him. While she was away, her old friend showed up on her mother's doorstep. His name was Walter.

"We both grew up in the projects. My mother's known his mother since she was pregnant with him. Out of the blue he just decided to look for me when I was in Milwaukee."

Angelique

"I always had a crush on him when we were growing up," Angel says, but things never panned out for the two. "I went my separate way – he went his separate way."

After she returned from her trip, everything fell into place.

"We started dating, then we lived together, got married – and 20 years later, we've got the kids and that's it." She says Walter is "the most amazing man."

The couple moved to Kenosha, Wisconsin – a midpoint between their mothers. They both started working for Pfizer in Skokie, Illinois.

Angel got her foot in the door as a temporary employee.

"I started working at the temp agency sewing uniforms." Next, she was running uniform services. "Then I did the glass washing services and slowly moved up. I got hired by the actual company in '96 in the chemical stockroom."

Angel's grit, intelligence and tenacity garnered her promotion after promotion. By the time Pfizer shut down several sites in the Chicago region, she had far surpassed many of her colleagues.

"When I left the Skokie area, I was actually a supervisor of all the areas I had worked in. So by that time all the people in those departments reported to me."

Pfizer transferred Angel and Walter to Michigan, where she did purchasing and scheduling planning for their manufacturing department – an enormous step up from where she started. She welcomed the change in position.

"I don't like repetitive work, because I get bored. As long as I can grow, then I'm good."

Sadly, just as her life was coming together, she lost several members of her family. Her oldest brother passed away from AIDS when Angel was only 22, followed by her mother when she was 23, and then her father at 26.

Soon she would gain a new member of the family. By the time she moved to Michigan, many years had passed since she gave birth to Isaac. When he turned 18 he wanted to meet his birth mother. In 2004, she received a phone call from the adoption agency asking if it was okay for Isaac to contact her. Angel said yes.

A strange twist of fate revealed itself when she learned that Isaac lived in Milwaukee – the very same city she migrated to after the Army.

"Yeah..." she says slowly and softly as she acknowledges the coincidence. A sly grin spreads across her face.

Angel and her family met Isaac and his parents at a McDonald's out in Milwaukee. "That's when we met face to face. He met his brothers and sisters and I met his adoptive parents."

She says she tried to make sure she didn't say or do anything to offend his conservative, religious parents.

"He is a pastor. Sometimes I can have a bad mouth." She laughs about her accidental slips, after which she would silently chastise herself,

"Damn, I swore!"

Despite the difference in their personalities, she was pleased to see her son had been raised by great people. "They seemed really down to earth. Really nice people."

However, meeting her firstborn also provoked painful flashes from the past. Isaac's strong physical resemblance to his father "brought back some of the memories," Angel says. Isaac's birth father had passed away years prior, but she couldn't help seeing him in Isaac's face. She also noticed other genetic links. Strangely enough, many of them were between Isaac and his half-sister Ashley.

"My son and my daughter learned that they have a lot in common. They both love Stephen King and heavy metal. The love for Stephen King came from my side. My mom loved to read Stephen King and V. C. Andrews."

The questions, doubt and uncertainty rattling around in the back of her mind were finally resolved 18 years after giving Isaac up for adoption. She could finally rest easy that the choice she made was a good one.

"It was a big relief for me because I knew that I made the right decision. If I kept him there, I'd probably still be in the projects. It gave him a better life." She continued to see her son on a semi-regular basis, sometimes for long-term visits.

A few years later, Pfizer closed down yet another region of operations. She was transferred to Groton where she and her family have lived since 2008. After the move she couldn't see Isaac as often in person, but she keeps in contact over the phone and through email or social media.

Angel's straightforward attitude toward life is clear and refreshing. "It's all about choice. There are people I grew up with that are still in those same projects. Just because you were born into it doesn't mean you have to stay there. I'll never forget where I came from, and it is what it is.

"It's all about the choices you make. If you choose to do something better with yourself, then that's what you do. I'm not saying I accomplished everything I wanted to accomplish, because there's always something different and I'll want to do something else. But it was my choice."

She stresses that people born in a particular situation are not doomed to a certain fate. "I've heard people say kids born of alcoholics are always alcoholics. I don't believe that. We could either learn from how we were raised, or you could stay there and not do anything with yourself."

She has strong opinions about those who don't choose to better themselves. "I believe there are people that truly need welfare. But I don't think once you go on welfare that's where you should stay. It's there to get you back on your feet and then you move on – not use it as a source of income for the rest of your life."

She acknowledges how her experiences have molded her personality and character. "I believe everything happens for a reason and I wouldn't be the person I am today if I did not go through the things that I have in life and overcome them. It has made me a stronger person."

Her advice to those who have suffered a sexual assault is to talk about it. "Don't internalize. Talk to people, because you can't just keep it in. It'll mess up your life. And don't believe what your head is telling you, because your head may tell you it's your fault."

As for forgiving her stepfather, she hasn't. The topic elicited groans and murmurs from both Ashley and her. Unapologetically, she explains, "*Pssht*. I've only wished death on one person in my entire life, and that was him. He died of –"

"Ugly," interrupts Ashley.

"Cancer or something," Angel clarifies.

Don't let her daughter Ashley's sarcastic sense of humor fool you. She is a registered CNA and has inherited her mom's compassionate and hardworking nature. When asked about her career, she says she likes it but, "It's hard, because you do lose people." She says she treats her elderly patients as if they were her own grandparents.

Her two sons are probably too young to understand everything their mother has been through. Her middle son has bipolar disorder and requires in-home therapy visits twice a week. His health is one of her top priorities.

"What I want to accomplish these days now is making sure that I raise my 12 year old, get him the help he needs to the point where he can be independent. It's been a lot of work for the past three or four years."

Despite working for a major pharmaceutical company, getting

the medications and testing he needs isn't always easy.

She talks about a diagnostic test he had done to determine which medications are best metabolized by his body. She had to save up for some time to afford the test's out-of-pocket price of $5,000.

"Insurance doesn't cover a lot of stuff. Mental health is very overlooked in every aspect."

Angel is a dedicated mother. "My life now is taking care of my children. When I became a parent by choice, I was 20. I'll get my life back when the last two leave. But I don't think that'll be anytime soon," she teases.

When talking about the future, she puts on a playful grin. "I haven't figured out what else I want to do yet, but you never know. Some people say I should open up a restaurant. But I don't have the patience for that either. It takes the fun out of it for me. I like cooking just to cook. I don't want it to be a daily job for me, because then it becomes redundant. So as long as I've got something new to do, I'm good to go. I get bored and then I'm like, 'I gotta go.'"

No matter what her next adventure turns out to be, she has proven that no matter what happens she will meet every challenge and come out of it a stronger person. Her amazing journey shows that even in dire circumstances, there is always a path out. She escaped poverty, trauma, and betrayal and created a brand new life for herself.

While her story may look like one of courage and survival, it is in fact a story about love. If you look at every choice she has made, they were all love-based decisions. Her love for her mother, four children, husband, and self was the primary motivation in everything she has done. While love does not always offer the easiest choices, as they say, it does conquer all.

Shannon

"I knew that I couldn't be quiet."

Bach, a beautiful golden retriever service dog, was the first to greet me at Shannon's home in Hartford County. He traipsed happily around, clamping a squeaky toy between his teeth. Behind him was Shannon, dressed in a strong primary color as she often does. Today it was azure blue, which nicely sets off her curly red hair and blue eyes.

Shannon lives in a spacious raised ranch with her husband and three sons. She has an undergraduate degree in Journalism and a Master's in Organizational Behavior, which she describes as "the study of how people interact with each other at a 40,000 foot view." After a successful career in several corporate positions, she changed gears to be a stay-at-home mom to Aidan, her firstborn son.

"When I stopped working, I suddenly went from a full-time job, which was pretty fast paced, to being home with an infant. They're very different worlds."

One evening over dinner, a friend asked her, "What do you want to do next?" Her answer would prove to be prophetic.

"I just want to find something that I'm passionate about." Shannon had no idea that her passion was just around the corner.

As a baby, Aidan suffered from constant illness. "He was sick all the time with chronic ear infections, virus after virus, and was constantly on antibiotics for the first year of his life."

Why Go On: Connecticut Residents Bring Dark Days to Light

By the time Aidan reached 18 months, Shannon noticed he was exhibiting atypical developmental behaviors, though admits most of these became apparent in hindsight. During Aidan's Kindermusik class, he would run around the room in circles while the rest of the children sat quietly. His communication development was also delayed.

"He had language, but it was things that he had memorized. It wasn't necessarily anything that would get his needs met. He could name all of his colors, he could count, he could do the alphabet, but he couldn't say 'I'm thirsty,' 'Get me a cup of juice,' or anything like that."

In the months that followed, she became more concerned. She brought the issue to her pediatrician who brushed off Aidan's behavior as the traits of a late bloomer or typical overactive boy. The doctor referred her to Birth to Three, a state-run program that helps toddlers with developmental delays or disabilities.

The Birth to Three therapists referenced a word no one had used

Shannon

to describe Aidan before: *autistic*. In response, she "balked and protested." She wasn't ready to believe Aidan could be autistic until her husband showed her something that changed her mind.

"I continued in my world of denial for a few more months until my husband showed me an article he had read in the *Financial Times* about autism and the signs of autism."

Her husband said, "I really think we need to look at this because this sounds like Aidan."

"We went for an evaluation at CCMC [Connecticut Children's Medical Center] and, in fact, the diagnostic criteria indicated he was on the autism spectrum."

Raw emotion flows across her face as she remembers this troubling time. "That was in December of 2003, when I was pregnant with our second child. Aidan was 32 months old when he was diagnosed with autism spectrum disorder."

Autism spectrum disorder (ASD) is a mental condition characterized by difficulties with communication, relationships and abstract concepts. Later, Aidan would be more specifically diagnosed with Asperger syndrome. Children with Asperger's can struggle with communication and can have significant challenges with social interaction.

"We see it more and more as Aidan grows older that he is just not wired the same way that I am, at all. Things are very literal to him. He's profoundly impacted by the world around him from a sensory perspective."

Shannon notes that autism "effects people differently, just like any sort of neuropsychological disorder would. I think all people on the spectrum have qualities and abilities that differ. It's not one-size-fits-all."

Now that she could put a name to Aidan's disorder, she felt a sense of relief "for about an hour." Soon, confusion took over again, "when we came home and realized very quickly that nobody had any idea what we were talking about. There were no clear paths to take, no support system. Then I was very sad."

She knew another woman with a child diagnosed with ASD, whom she quickly contacted. Unfortunately, Shannon and her husband found little other support. At the time, the recommended course of treatment was 20 to 40 hours of speech and occupational therapy, along with Applied Behavior Analysis (ABA), the only evidence-based treatment for autism. Her home became Aidan's treatment center.

"It was a black hole. It was one of the most depressing times of my life. I was pregnant with my second kid. We basically could not leave the house because we had therapists here all the time. I do not know how I got through the first year. My husband is tremendously supportive. He's even, steady. But I honestly do not remember the first year very well because it was so dark. There were no resources. I think what really spurred me into doing what I do is that in trying to get services for Aidan at the time they one, didn't exist, and two, if they did exist, insurance didn't pay for it.

"I started calling my state representatives and my state senator – and nobody really had anything to offer. They knew very little about autism, nor did they have any solutions."

Therapy and services for autistic children can cost an average of $80,000 to $90,000 annually. Shannon estimates the average family could spend anywhere from $50,000 to $200,000 each year for testing, therapy and medications. Back in 2003, none of these costs were covered by insurance, but for "a simple parity law, which was under mental health, and that really didn't touch autism," she says. Therapies like ABA, Occupational Therapy, Speech Therapy and Physical Therapy are critical.

"I knew that I couldn't be quiet. It was so inconceivable to me that there was something that could help my kid and I couldn't do it. We have this entire population of 1 in 68 kids on the autism spectrum, and a huge chunk cannot access medical treatment for their child because it costs too much money. That's shameful."

She first contacted Nancy Johnson, then Connecticut's U.S. Representative, and her eventual successor, Chris Murphy.

These initial efforts spurred something within her. "I started thinking to myself, *This is what I need to be doing*. I need to hold these people accountable because not only do they represent me, but at some point they'll also represent Aidan. They need to be accountable for his future as well. So that's where it all started.

"I just felt something in my gut – I still feel it – that this can change. This is my child. I can't sit here and let this happen to him. And I don't mean autism. I can't let society continue to shut him out, and I can't continue to stand by and let people excuse that behavior as acceptable, because it's not."

As ambitious, intelligent, capable and motivated as Shannon is, she admits feeling fear as she began her mission. Her technique for pushing forward through unchartered territory?

"It's one foot in front of the other."

Next, she reached out to autism organizations for support.

"I started looking for a national organization, and guess what? There wasn't much. There was a local organization called the National Alliance for Autism Research (NAAR.) But by local, I mean Boston. They were looking to start a chapter in Hartford County. Shortly after I discovered them, NAAR merged with Autism Speaks (AS), which was just forming at the time. At that point I had been working with a staff person in the Boston office to start creating the first fundraising walk in Hartford. So it was all coming together at the same time."

Shannon became a founding member of the Connecticut Chapter of Autism Speaks and served as its first Inaugural Walk Chairperson. The first year, she wasn't sure anyone would show up to the brand new "Walk Now for Autism Speaks" in Hartford.

On the contrary, thousands attended the walk and over a million dollars were raised in the first three years under her leadership. Shannon had mixed feelings about the event's success.

"It was an amazing experience, but yet bittersweet – and it gets more bittersweet every year. It's great that we all support each other, but there are still so many of us out there. Now, when I stand at Rentschler Field and I see eight thousand, nine thousand people, it's great. But to me it translates to: this many people need support and services. Where are they going to live? Where are they going to work? What about their education? What about their medical treatment?"

Those worries aside, she enjoys the day as a time when families have the freedom to be themselves. "Walk day is a day of celebration to me, because it's an environment where kids can be having their meltdowns and tantrums and it's like, 'Okay, here we are! This is what happens. This is autism.' It's a couple of hours of judgment-free existence, which is so precious."

That feeling of judgment is something every parent of an autistic child can relate to. Particularly in Aidan's younger years, she tolerated sounds of disgust from strangers and inconceivably rude comments. Comments like:

"That kid just needs a smack."

"That kid needs more discipline."

"You're letting him get away with too much."

It's not only the cruelty of the remarks that stings, but the timing.

"This when my autistic child is struggling so mightily, which is causing my other two children to struggle. Instead of offering help, people sometimes feel compelled to make you feel worse."

Shannon has learned to cope with these situations. Instead of reacting with anger or tears, now she can better manage her response.

"This just happened a year or so ago at a pool. Aidan likes to pace when we go to pools. At one point something happened and he started yelling and everyone started staring."

She briskly hurried over to Aidan from the far side of the pool.

"I was running to get to him and all along the way people were saying, 'Ugh, God. What is wrong with that kid?' I said to them, 'It's just a little autism, people. Move along.'"

She talks about the strange theories others have about ASD. "There are those who believe that autism is a punishment or is a result of bad parenting, and that's just ignorance. I think there are those who have minds willing to be changed, and then there are those who don't. I like to focus on the ones whose minds can be changed."

If changing minds was her goal, she has succeeded. After a promotion to the Autism Speaks' Connecticut Advocacy Chair, she worked with US Senator Chris Murphy, State Senator Tony Hwang and U.S. Representative John Larson to secure the passage of important autism-related bills regarding insurance, education, employment and housing – all with bipartisan support.

She also helped develop the Autism Awareness Bootcamp. This program is geared toward assisting newly diagnosed families and helps teach businesses and organizations how to better support the growing number of ASD children and adults. Bootcamps have been presented to Rotary Clubs, PTO's and regional businesses. The training helps employees understand how to effectively deal with ASD children to diffuse rather than exacerbate volatile situations.

In June 2009, Shannon helped make Connecticut become the 13th state to enact autism insurance reform. This means that instead of households paying thousands of dollars out of pocket, ASD treatments are covered under private insurance plans. In the next five years dozens of other states followed suit, with a total of about 40 states approving this type of coverage.

Every piece of autism-related legislation in Connecticut has her fingerprints on it. This includes bills providing a tax credit to businesses who hire people with disabilities and another to protect families against fraudulent behavioral analysts. Her help has changed the landscape of autism support in Connecticut. She's even helped introduce federal legislation, such as insurance reform for military families with children who have developmental disabilities such as autism.

Bipartisan agreement can be rare in modern times, but her successes also show just how important this issue is.

"In my legislative work, one of the things that I find the most pride in – other than, of course, passing legislation – is that we can have this conversation on both sides of the aisle. Can't have it with everybody, on either side, but there are some people who have stepped way outside of their party lines on both sides to stand shoulder to shoulder with us."

Shannon references Connecticut State Senator Tony Hwang as one of many legislators who have offered unwavering support to autism reform.

"I always say that there are supporters and there are champions, and champions know your kids' names. That's him. So we're very fortunate."

She encourages people to connect with their political representatives to enact social change. "I think having legislators as partners is the key. These are the people who are our voices in government and they should absolutely be a part of the solution."

She talks a bit about the unique dynamic among her three boys.

"It's a struggle for all of them. Aidan gets upset and he's yelling, which upsets the other kids and they don't understand why they're being yelled at. Then everybody's yelling. But they've never known anything different. This is how they grew up.

"Aidan struggles tremendously with social situations. He gets overwhelmed when there are a lot of people. He gets overwhelmed by a lot of language. He thinks very literally, so speaking in colloquialisms to him is frustrating."

Shannon is a highly intelligent, perceptive person, but these talents don't necessarily work with Aidan.

"He teaches me so differently. You can have intuition, you can read people – but I can't read him. Not all the time. I think that's one of the most hugely frustrating parts of autism. You have a child and expect to have a relationship that's like the relationship that I had with my parents. You say 'I love you' every night, you hug each other, you take family trips together. Those things are not part of the equation necessarily with autism. Emotion is difficult. Physical contact is difficult.

"It's a work in progress to see the other ways that we can connect. It doesn't have to be based on my assumptions, but it takes a long time to get there. It takes a long time as a parent to change your mindset and really start looking at your child as a differently-abled person."

Individuals with ASD perceive the world with a heavy focus on their five senses. "He experiences the world from a sensory perspective. He is driven by what the world around him smells like, feels like, tastes like. If I'm navigating based on sounds or taste or touch, they're secondary to me. To him, they're primary."

It's like being in Las Vegas during an earthquake – tumultuous and over-stimulating. "The way the world will feel to him from moment to moment is hugely anxiety producing. Not only the way the world feels, but you've got people talking at you, cars driving by, lights buzzing overhead, dogs barking… That is an assault on your sensory system. That makes me tense to think about it."

This anxiety bleeds out to the rest of the family. "We as a family absorb his anxiety. Autism affects individuals, but it's really about families. When he's having a hard time, we're all having a hard time. When he can't communicate, the rest of the family feels that angst."

Her younger boys, ages 10 and 7, wonder why Aidan can't participate in the same activities they do. "They're now starting to ask questions about why Aidan can't play on a typical soccer team, why he plays unified soccer [a Special Olympics program for kids with intellectual disabilities], or why he can't go to a school dance and have fun. In their own innocent way they don't understand why it has to be different."

On the topic of ASD children and sports, about five years ago she came up with a novel idea. A long time tennis player, Shannon pondered the favorable connection between tennis and those affected by autism.

"I came across an article about tennis and anecdotal evidence showing it was beneficial for kids on the spectrum. I was thinking out loud to a teammate of mine, 'You know, I get so much benefit out of this. It's so calming for me. It's rhythmic. It's not predictable, but I can control it.'"

She knew that Aidan could appreciate these things, too. "He wants to control the world around him, and tennis is exercise. There were almost no recreational or fitness opportunities for kids on the spectrum offered on a regular basis."

So she started a tennis camp for autistic children called Well Served Tennis Academy, the mission of which is to bring the lifelong sport of tennis to children with autism.

"We run the Academy for two weeks in the summer right out of the middle school here through their Parks and Rec. It was critical to me that our program be listed as something that you can register for through the town's recreational department.

"It was imperative to me that we keep the costs to a minimum. If I send Aidan to a camp, I have to pay the camp fee and then a paraprofessional to go with him. So, a typical Parks and Recreation camp might be $150 and then I'm paying another $150 to send someone with him. By then it's a $300 camp – which he may or may not get anything out of, because it's not tailored to what he needs. Our camp costs $25 for two weeks. No one will ever be turned away for financial reasons. We're entirely grant and donation funded.

"We employ a tennis pro and a behaviorist. We want the kids to be able to come away and say, 'I went to summer camp,' because they don't have that chance. 'Look, I got a t-shirt. Look, I made a friend, who I see in the halls at school.' And, 'I can play a sport and I can go out with my family on the weekend and hit a tennis ball around.'"

Shannon sees first-hand the profound improvements her camp inspires. She has witnessed children progress from sitting in a corner to lobbing balls back and forth with their coaches, squealing with delight.

"It's great. This year was our biggest year yet; we had 18 participants. Each kid has a one-to-one volunteer. It's just awesome. We're thinking about expanding to a satellite location."

In addition to her work as an advocate, she has volunteered in many other capacities. She's served on her town's Board of Selectmen and Economic Development Commission. She's been a liaison to the Aging and Disability Commission, and Task Forces for Tourism and Clean Energy.

She also hosts her own show on community access television featuring local women. "There are so many amazing women in this town who are doing amazing things or are going through incredible struggles and overcoming them, but nobody knows about it."

"One of my favorite stories is about a young woman in town whose daughter went through pediatric cancer and how she started to advocate for cancer causes as a result of that. We have a woman in town who worked with the state legislature extensively on passing laws to label GMO's. We have a local artist who travels the country showing her paintings. It's just been a fantastic opportunity to meet these people and be able to give them a platform and say, 'Hey, you're doing a great job, you should be recognized for what you're doing.'"

The show spawned a special event in town, which she spearheaded in conjunction with her local Junior Women's Club. In 2013, she held the first annual "Women's Forum," giving women the chance to hear informational and inspirational speakers on topics relevant to women's issues.

"Based on the premise of that show I wanted to create an opportunity for women to learn from each other." Lecturers spoke on issues such as the perception of women in the media, current legislative initiatives affecting women's issues, and a discussion about women putting themselves first.

Her educational choices as a young woman gave her the training necessary to embark on her many projects and initiatives. "Everything that I've done in my life professionally has prepared me for what I'm doing now. Just the ability to speak in public – which I do all the time – comes from my training in broadcast journalism. Being able to talk to the media: journalism. Learning how to work with various personalities on complex issues, that's legislative, relationship building. Everything I've done has brought me to this point."

Shannon feels there is much more work to be done. One of the biggest issues that needs to be addressed is educating people on the unique contributions autistic children and adults can offer the world.

"Each person on the spectrum has something to give. Whatever they have to give could be perceived by you and me as a small thing, but that ability should be recognized, nurtured and brought to light. It makes me very sad when people think that all autistic people should just go along in life and then go on disability. I think there's so much potential that is just not being recognized."

Her tennis camp is a prime example. "If people could take an hour, or a day, to come to my camp, they would see that each of these children can play tennis. They play it on different levels, they play it in different ways, but each of them can play it. If we give people the opportunity to be successful, they will be."

Her advice to families coping with a new ASD diagnosis is to utilize all possible resources out there to help. Thanks to people like Shannon, there is more available now than there was ten years ago.

"Don't hesitate to ask for help. One of the biggest mistakes I made early on is that people tried to help and I was like, 'Oh no, I've got this.' But I didn't. Take help."

She also has a suggestion for extended family members who want to give good intentioned, but unsolicited advice. Instead of pushing one's own opinions, show loved ones that you care, as that love is far more useful than any advice.

"Follow their lead. Let them teach you, let them show you, and walk with them. It's an overwhelming experience. Sometimes you just need someone to say, 'I've got you. It's okay.'"

Shannon continues to learn and grow, noting that Aidan "teaches me every day to see things differently. The world is not just the way I see it. The world is about sound, touch, and taste. I certainly would not have the appreciation for the intensity of the senses without him." She adds, with a laugh, "He's taught me patience."

Her outlook on the future is one of realistic optimism. "Life with autism can be extremely challenging. It's a physical, 24/7 vigilance. Kids wander, kids bolt, and kids have toileting issues. But in those challenges, there's success. If everyone would just give kids a chance. Look for the thing that's going to make them successful. They can do it. Just like anybody can, they can do it… but it takes work."

Shannon's path toward creating positive change would never have happened had it not been for Aidan. He, and the many other autistic children she has grown to know and love, helped provide the answer to

Why Go On: Connecticut Residents Bring Dark Days to Light

that nebulous question, "What do you want to do next?" With a lump in her throat and a thump of conviction in her heart, she acknowledges this.

"He and all of my kids have given me purpose."

Christine

"I'm just doing what I think needs to be done."

Christine lives in Rockfall, Connecticut with her husband, children, two dogs, and a lot of bras. In fact, we met in what she calls her "Bra Room." On the back of my chair hangs a pair of fluffy white "angel wings," reminiscent of the ones found on the shoulders of Victoria's Secret lingerie models. A batch of brassiere-clad dress forms are lined up in a row behind me like they're ready for some kind of busty battle.

But who are they fighting for? Breast cancer survivors.

Christine is everything you'd want your daughter to be. She's a devoted wife and mother who would do anything for her family. She's a responsible, sensible person with a huge heart.

After greeting me with a firm handshake, Christine led me to the aforementioned "Bra Room." She's tall, blonde, and speaks with a youthful, energetic voice.

She grew up in Wallingford before moving to Killingworth. She attended Stonehill College in Massachusetts before receiving a Master's Degree in teaching from Southern Connecticut State University. She's taught fourth grade at the same school for the past 16 years.

She originally met her husband Bruce in high school, but the two didn't really speak much. Bruce's father was transferred to Maine, and so he moved away in his senior year of high school.

Fast forward a few years to a random Saturday night when Christine and her friend Kelly were having drinks at Oliver's Taverne in Essex. The place was dead with the exception of three young men sitting at the bar. The guys started throwing peanuts at the ladies, accomplishing nothing but annoying them.

"What a bunch of losers," Kelly remarked.

The men ended up leaving the bar first, with the ladies not too far behind them. Unbeknownst to Christine, one of the young men hung around waiting for her, but he never had the guts to say anything.

Apparently he had made an impression on her, too. She made an offhanded remark about him to Kelly as they drove away.

"You know, I was probably supposed to marry that guy and we'll never find out."

The next weekend, the girls returned to the bar with some other girlfriends in tow. Unlike the previous Saturday, the place was packed. Christine spotted a familiar face.

"I looked over at the bar and I'm like, 'Oh my God, look it's Bruce, he's back from Maine.'" Then she realized that Bruce was, in fact, "the loser that was throwing peanuts at us the week before," she jokes.

The rest, as they say, is history. The couple married in 2001 and had their first child, Connor, in 2004. In 2007, she became pregnant with their second child. Bruce is a Physical Education and Health teacher, so in February of 2007, both were on a school break. A seven-months pregnant Christine and her husband went out for a nice dinner as a "last hurrah" before the baby arrived.

She remembers wearing a turtleneck with a purple and maroon striped maternity shirt. She felt an itch about two or three inches beneath her collar bone. Her whole right side had been itchy and irritated throughout her whole pregnancy, something her obstetrician wrote off as eczema.

But when she scratched her chest this time, she felt something: a lump.

"Wow, that has never been there before," she thought, immediately grabbing her husband's hand to touch the mass.

"Have you ever felt this?" she asked him.

Bruce shrugged off the lump as nothing. She hoped that perhaps it was just a clogged milk duct. Over the next few days she applied warm compresses in an effort to clear the blockage.

It didn't go away.

When she returned to work she asked the other ladies at school about the lump. Everyone said the same thing.

"It's probably a clogged milk duct," they echoed over and over.

After a week of trying to clear the duct, she knew something definitely wasn't right. During this time, she had been putting together a party for her son Connor's birthday. Though she was nervous about the lump, she put off calling the doctor because she already had a standing appointment with her obstetrician about three days after his party.

"I'm not going to ruin Connor's third birthday," she thought.

That Monday, about 2 ½ weeks after initially finding the lump, she went to her appointment at Dr. Flagg's office in Middletown. She mentioned the lump to a midwife.

"Oh, that's probably a clogged milk duct," said the midwife.

As she palpated the mass, Christine says, "Her face totally changed."

The midwife told her, "You're going to go for an ultrasound."

When she went for an ultrasound, the sonographer first brushed off the lump as no big deal, too.

"96% of these are nothing," the technician assured her.

"That's what people keep telling me," she responded, still hopeful for a good outcome.

As the sonographer looked at the scans, Christine notes, "Her face changed and she ran out of the room."

"This probably isn't a good thing," she thought to herself.

A radiologist came into the room and told her, "I've already called for an appointment with a surgeon tomorrow."

That's when Christine says she "lost it."

"I got myself together and drove home." Her mother came to her house and stayed over for moral support. The next morning, Christine and Bruce drove to the surgeon's office during a big snowstorm. A needle biopsy was performed. Now, all she could do was wait.

A few nerve-wracking days later the results came in.

"I got what they call the '5 o'clock cancer phone call,' when they want you to come in because everybody's left. I didn't know that at the time."

Christine is a strong woman, but if you listen closely, her voice cracks ever so slightly as she recalls the evening.

As they pulled into the office parking lot, Bruce tried to assure his wife that everything would be okay.

"Duran Duran was on the radio – Bruce loves Duran Duran."

She had a hard time mustering the courage to go in to get her results and, for a moment, craved an escape.

She said to Bruce, "Why don't we just go to Hartford and get on an airplane and just *go* somewhere, you know? Let's just get out of here."

Bruce kept it light, either being in denial himself or simply trying to ease his wife's worry.

"Oh, don't worry about it. Duran Duran's on the radio," he said, as if it were a good omen, "and everything will be fine."

She responded, "I really don't think everything's going to be fine."

When she received her results, they were not good. The doctor said she had the lab check the results three times to be sure.

"You have cancer."

Christine's initial response was a mixture of anger and shock. "You have to be kidding me," she says, in disbelief.

"I *wish* I was kidding you," replied the doctor.

And then, her world went hazy. "Everything after that was just like Charlie Brown," she says, mimicking the iconic brassy "wah wah wah" of Charlie Brown's teacher. "I didn't process or hear anything."

Within 24 hours a team of doctors was assembled.

"They had Dana Farber, a perinatologist [a special type of obstetrician] from UConn, Dr. Flagg, they had an oncologist – they had everybody you could think of." The group met right away to figure out the best course of action.

She was given two options: Option A would be to start chemotherapy in the hopes of shrinking her tumor. This would allow her to have a lumpectomy instead of losing her breast in a mastectomy. The procedure would be followed by radiation and possibly more chemotherapy. Option B would be to have a mastectomy first, followed by a course of chemotherapy and radiation.

Christine

Christine chose Option B. Because she was pregnant, she didn't want to do anything that might harm the baby.

"Take it. Cut it off. Let's just get it done," she explains frankly.

A week later she had her mastectomy, at which time they also removed about 20 lymph nodes. The nodes were surgically removed instead of performing a sentinel needle biopsy. A sentinel needle biopsy involves injecting the body with radioactive dye that makes cancerous nodes appear to glow. Because she was pregnant, this could not be done.

Of the twenty lymph nodes that were removed, three were malignant. The presence of cancer in her lymph nodes and the size of the tumor put her cancer in stage 2B.

"My tumor was 4 ½ centimeters by the time it was done, which is only a half centimeter from stage 3. It grew about a centimeter in only a week or so." Hormonal changes from her pregnancy contributed to the tumor's rapid growth.

Christine had much to live for, but first and foremost in her mind was her children. "I was determined to be here and be their mom. I didn't want anybody else to be their mom; that's my job."

Her main goal at the time was heart-wrenchingly poignant. "My first thought was I wanted to be around to put Connor on the bus for Kindergarten, because I figured that if I put him on the bus, he would remember who I was. That was my first goal. I figured, well if he was five and Chase was two, he probably wouldn't remember me, but Connor – at least *somebody* would remember I was there that first day of school and put him on the bus."

She never knew her actual prognosis for recovery – nor did she want to. "To be honest, I never asked for it. I didn't want to know, because unless you can give me 100%, there's no point. If you told me 95%, then there's still a 5% chance that it could all go wrong, so I didn't want to know."

She wouldn't let anyone tell Bruce, either. "Because if he knows, I'll know. He won't be able to keep it secret."

"Nobody's allowed to know except you what my percentages are," she told her doctor.

Five days after her mastectomy and eight months pregnant, she returned to work. School administrators kept her long-term substitute in the classroom with her, thinking Christine would only be able to work a couple of days. "We were there 2 ½ weeks and they decided to send her home."

"I told you I'm not going anywhere," she told administrators.

Two days after they released the substitute, Christine received a call from her doctor at 9 o'clock in the morning.

"Dana Farber called. You're having your baby today."

She replied, "I'm teaching math class right now."

After some back and forth, the two agreed she would report to the hospital at 5 o'clock – after the school day was over.

Her labor with her first child Connor had been quick and natural. He was born "almost in the back of Bruce's pickup truck." She assumed her second child would be just as speedy. "I didn't want the drugs or anything like that. I did it the first time, I could do it the second time."

She asked doctors to break her water and let her do the rest. They agreed and told her to "start walking." They gave her an hour before they would intervene with a dose of Pitocin to speed up the labor.

"They broke my water at 6:00. I made it a lap and a half around the delivery floor and I was in full labor. I had Chase at 7:02."

Everything went fine. She was now the mother of two beautiful boys. After a two-day hospital stay she went home. One might think that dealing with breast cancer *and* a new baby would be overwhelming, but the arrival of her new son brought something positive to concentrate on.

"I couldn't focus on me. I had to worry that he needed to be fed, take a nap, be taken care of – that kind of stuff. To me, that was a great focus."

Shortly after Chase was born, Christine was back in the hospital getting prepped for chemotherapy.

"I had my scans a week later and a port was put into my chest a week after that. We started chemo the Thursday before Memorial Day weekend, and I did that every other Thursday throughout the summer." During "off" weeks, she had shots to boost her white and red blood cell count.

"My last day of chemo was the day before the first day of school." She didn't miss a single day of work.

"I was there at the door to greet the kids. Then the middle of September I started my seven-week radiation every day, and a year of herceptin." Herceptin was a relatively new drug treatment at that time, which works to block the receptor sites of hormonal cells so they cannot interlock and become cancerous.

Her students were fully aware of what their teacher was going through. After chemotherapy caused her hair to fall out, she wore a blonde wig similar to her own hair for the first three months. When her hair started growing back in, the wig became itchy. She knew her autistic student might become uncomfortable with an unexpectedly bald teacher, so she met with him privately to get him used to it.

"I would hang out with him at lunch," she says. When he was comfortable enough, she took the wig off permanently.

As we spoke, Christine was a seven-year cancer survivor. She credits her strong willpower with helping her get through the experience.

"I'm more stubborn and I don't let things stop me from doing what I want to do. My personality, I think, played the biggest role in my recovery. We went to every family function, we went to Lake Compounce, we went on vacation. Nothing got cancelled because I was sick. We did everything that we were supposed to do. That was my big thing. The kids aren't going to miss out because I'm sick. We're going to go on with life, and that's how it is."

Throughout her treatments she developed a close relationship with the staff at Middlesex Hospital. "They were like family. Everybody knows your name, they know your family, they know your story, they know what's going on with you and they know how to help." At that time Middlesex had just started offering alternative therapies to patients.

"Middlesex had started dabbling in some integrative medicine modalities. They didn't have a department. They hired one person to do some reflexology." Reflexology is the therapeutic practice of applying pressure to certain points on the feet. Each point corresponds with a specific area, or organ, of the body.

The hospital used Christine as a guinea pig to sample their new services, sending her three or four times for free, asking her to "go – try it, let us know what you think."

The sessions rejuvenated her. She told hospital staff, "This is great. It makes you feel better, gives you more energy, makes you feel more relaxed."

Integrative medicine is progressively becoming an important element in health care. "They see the benefits with survivors and how much better they feel, ready to tackle what's next. I know a bunch of survivors that after they're done with chemo for the day they go for reflexology or massage. They book an appointment just to feel better."

The alternative care sessions became increasingly popular. "More people started to go. They started advertising, they started adding more people, they did some Reiki, they added acupuncture – they have a whole slew of things up there. You can just kind of get away, block everything out. You can focus on yourself. But it costs $60 a session. People going through chemo might not be able to afford it. They might be out of work. Insurance doesn't cover any of it."

Her next chapter began with a story in the newspaper. In the fall of 2007 an article in the New Haven Register publicized a support group led by a woman who had been diagnosed with breast cancer when she was pregnant, just like Christine. The group was for other young breast cancer survivors to meet over wine and cheese and have a girls' night out. Bruce and a friend from work both showed her the article, asserting, "You need to go to this."

Christine

The group was run by a woman named Melissa Burns. Melissa was raising funds for her documentary about young breast cancer survivors, titled at that time, "Life After the Storm." (It's since been re-titled, "Cancer? Seriously?") One thing led to another, and soon Christine was helping Melissa with fundraising. First, she helped organize a golf tournament. After that came "Art Bra."

Art Bra is a fundraising event that occurs all over the country, predominantly in the south. Melissa brought it to Connecticut. She asked supporters to submit extravagantly embellished bras to be auctioned off at the Art Bra event. The show featured 34 different bras, 30 of which came from Christine's friends and coworkers.

Bidding started at $20. Christine remembers Bruce's strong reaction to the event.

"This is the silliest thing I've ever heard. Who would buy a bra for $20?" he said.

Christine was more optimistic. "Let's just go with an open mind and see what happens."

In the end, she says, "That night we raised $7,000. So he ate his words on the way home."

Many of the bras sold for more than $20 – some even grabbing $100 apiece. After raising enough to fund her documentary, Melissa stopped fundraising and began production on the film.

Christine knew that Art Bra was a great opportunity to help people and decided to continue the event. In January of 2009, she became the founder and president of an official 501(c)3 non-profit charitable organization. She named her charity "After the Storm," an homage to the documentary that inspired it all.

Each bra has a special theme, often crafted by a cancer survivor or dedicated to one. Some are pretty or sweet, others wacky and wild, but each is immensely creative.

"Mosquito Bites" is an eye-catching garment featuring two giant mosquitoes poised on each of the bra's cups. There's "Deer in the Headlights," a camouflage number with two light beams guiding the way. One of Christine's favorites was made entirely from duct tape. Other humorous names include "Pat the Boobie" and "Treasure Chests."

Prodded by her husband, Christine created a bra of her own. She called it the "Bad Romance" bra, dazzling with Styrofoam hearts, pink feathers and dangling beads. Despite her passion for the cause, she was not enthusiastic about crafting.

"I can organize this whole thing. I cannot make a bra. I can't sew. I can put a button on; that's about it." She adds that the experience was "painful," though her final result is quite good.

Bruce had his own idea that turned out to be overwhelmingly popular. He spearheaded "the Man Show" segment, featuring eight male bra models. The man who once balked at the idea now revels in the attention of hundreds of screaming women as he steps out onto the runway. One year his outfit was called "Cherry Pie," replete with a bright red bra, billowy baker's cap, rolling pin, apron, cut-off denim shorts and work boots.

The event now features 8 men and 27 women modeling bras fetching up to $1,000 each. I ask her what the night is like.

Her voice sweetens quietly as she responds, "It's fun. It's a party. It's my favorite day of the year. It's better than Christmas."

Speaking at the event sparks a rush of emotions. She says, "I try not to cry. I get amped up seeing all those people that are there for this and where we've come from. It can be very emotional."

Art Bra is such a popular event she's had to change venue twice to accommodate the crowd. It is now held at the Oakdale Theatre's Dome in Wallingford.

After the Storm is in its sixth year, grossing an impressive $116,000 in total donations to date. Funds are dispersed to healthcare providers who apply through a grant application. Recipients have included Middlesex Hospital, MidState Medical Center and Griffin Hospital.

Patients at these facilities receive vouchers for complementary care sessions. For example, cancer patients at Middlesex Hospital receive vouchers for three alternative therapy sessions. Breast cancer patients get four. A wide variety of therapies are available.

"They offer reflexology, Reiki, massage, acupuncture, yoga, music therapy, art therapy, journal writing… they have anything you can think of that's holistic."

After the Storm also helps fund Middlesex Hospital's "Warrior Workout," a six-week fitness regimen combining exercise, mental exploration and meditation for full body and mind balance and training.

These treatments can make a world of difference for patients.

"There was one gentleman who was a friend of a friend of ours. He was stage 4 and terminal. At the end, with the money we donated, Middlesex was able to give him a lot of free services. His wife always said, 'You guys were a godsend. You helped him transition. To not have pain for even a couple of hours was a gift.'"

Christine hopes to keep expanding, though that might not happen right away. With a young family and a full time job, devoting enough time to everything in her life can be a challenge.

"To juggle the foundation, family, and my teaching job – somebody's always losing out. I can't keep them all in the air at the same time. We're just a small little grassroots effort. Sponsors are really what we need. It would be nice to have it grow, get big, and do it full time. It's a great dream and aspiration to have."

Art Bra has also inspired others to coordinate similar events. Over the past few years, other runway bra fundraisers have cropped up in Connecticut to support breast cancer causes.

Christine's efforts have not gone unnoticed by her community. In 2011, she received the Susan Campagna Survivorship Recognition Award and Anne Garland's Woman of the Year Award. A third award she received was close to her heart: the first annual Howard Kelley Community Award. She personally knew and cherished Mr. Kelley, whose own aggressive cancer ultimately took his life.

"I got a call out of the blue that I had received this reward. He was definitely a well-respected community member here and everybody loved him. And, he was a really, really nice guy. I was honored to receive that."

She has also appeared on local news programs hosting a mini-version of the runway event. She's been featured in various advertisements for Middlesex Hospital, including full-page glossy print ads, commercials and an interview.

What's amazing is that despite all she has been through, accomplished and given to others, she remains modest. While she could have easily simply returned to her way of life "before the storm," so to speak, instead she dedicated her time and energy toward helping others. When I asked how she feels knowing how many people she has helped, I expected her to respond with a sense of pride for her efforts. Instead, she deemed her hard work to be nothing out of the ordinary.

"I feel like I've been able to pay back what was done for me. I'm just doing what I think needs to be done. There's a need for these people to get these services and if this is something that I can do to fill that need, then I'm going to do it."

She then recounted all the help she received from her school, her community, and her hospital. She says she almost forgot how to cook because so many meals were made for her while she was ill.

If she could go back in time and talk to her newly diagnosed 30-year-old self, she would want her to know that everything will be okay.

"You're going to do this. You're going to get through this. This is just a hiccup – a 'blip' as my oncologist said – a blip on the radar, and then the rest of your life is going to happen."

Christine accomplished her goal of putting her son Connor on the bus – and now looks forward to "weddings and grandkids" in time. She feels that being a cancer survivor broadened her horizons in ways she would never have experienced otherwise.

"I do think that all things happen for a reason and this got me out of my comfort zone of wife, mom, and teacher. Maybe I was put here to do something besides just those things, and this is what I'm supposed to do."

She may never know whether or not this was her destiny. But for the hundreds of people she's helped, it doesn't matter. What matters is how her kindness, hard work and selflessness has brought comfort to so many individuals she's never even met.

Jan

"Patience, determination, persistence, faith and hope."

Jan closes her emails with the words, "Always Hope." She is petite, quiet and articulate. She glows with a positive energy that seems to radiate from her. Her electric blue eyes reflect both her kindness and tenacity. She and I sit at her dining room table, which has been delicately set with white porcelain coffee mugs.

Joining us is Bill, Jan's husband of over 40 years. Bill is a no-nonsense, blue-collar kind of guy hiding a heart of solid gold. The two are a perfect match – as evidenced by their enduring marriage, shared sense of humor, and ability to withstand one of the most horrific fates a family could face.

Their home is skillfully landscaped and beautifully decorated. Jan and Bill have an incredible ability to make others feel comfortable and welcome. The only exception to this is when the phone rings. Jan doesn't jerk or jump, but her tension is evident.

"This is every day," Bill remarks after the fourth or fifth call.

After one ring in particular, Jan gasps, "The tip line!" I can't decide whether my heart is sinking or beating with anticipation. I wondered if she has ever felt the same.

Jan is no stranger to loss. When she was seven years old her mother passed away, leaving Jan, the youngest, compelled to replace the family matriarch.

"I felt like I had to take care of the family for some reason. When my sister was out on a date I would wait for her to come home. Once everybody was in bed, I would go to sleep. We grew up real quick."

She is originally from Waterbury, but her family later moved to Oakville. She met Bill at Black Rock Lake in Thomaston when she was 16.

She smiles as she recounts the day. "We were on the beach and he asked me to come over and talk to him. Of course I said no," she says, bellowing with laughter. "I said, 'You come here!' I finally did talk with him and that was the start of our relationship."

Bill chimes in. "I thought she was a nice person, you know?" He pauses. "Kind of pretty," he says with a coy grin.

Jan adds, "I think once we started dating it was meant to be."

After they married, they moved to Bill's grandfather's dairy farm, which later became a beef cattle farm. It was a close-knit family atmosphere, with Bill's father living in one home on the farm and his sister in another. During the day, he worked for Pratt and Whitney as a jet engine mechanic.

Life on the farm was good. Jan says, "It was a nice way of life. We were self-sufficient. We had our own meat and vegetables, we canned, we had our own chickens – we had everything. It was a nice way to raise the kids."

The couple had two children. First came their son Billy, and three years later a daughter, Paula. Bill describes his son as "a tough kid on the outside – don't mess with him – but he was like a mush on the inside."

Young Billy and Paula grew up in an idyllic environment. Jan describes their childhood as one with many exciting adventures. Her son was especially full of energy.

"He liked jumping out of the hayloft and climbing trees. I was constantly keeping an eye on him. He loved sports, fishing, dirt bikes, snowmobiling, skiing, baseball... any sport. He was in the cub scouts. Billy was constantly going."

Paula followed in her brother's footsteps, zooming around the farm on her quad or riding on the back of her father's snowmobile.

In 1999, the family sold the farm after Bill's father passed away.

Jan

Now that their kids were grown, everyone went their own way. Jan and Bill settled in Cheshire, where they've lived now for the past 15 years. Paula married and had children of her own.

Billy, a 26-year-old bachelor, bought a home in Waterbury. If he was ever close to marriage, it was with his ex-girlfriend Mary Ellen, whom he dated for eight years. Billy and Mary Ellen had an amicable break-up and remained close friends. They even shared what Mary Ellen called "joint custody" of Billy's beloved German Shepherd named Harley.

Billy was a hard worker, sometimes holding three jobs to ensure he kept up with his mortgage payments. He worked as an HVAC technician, a tow truck driver and mowed lawns on the side. In his spare time he worked on his home and tinkered with used cars.

He worked as a bus driver for a little while. He met a fellow driver named Madeline and fell in love with her. The two started dating in 2003 when Billy was 30 years old.

Madeline was about 15 years older than Billy and only four years younger than Jan. She had five children and had been divorced three times. Her life was fraught with turmoil.

Billy loved Madeline and strived to be a father figure for her youngest son Jordan.

"Billy took a liking to him and used to take him fishing. I think he liked the responsibility of having someone to care for," says Jan.

After dating for about a year, Billy, Madeline and 12-year-old Jordan took a trip down to Florida's West Palm Beach to visit Jordan's older brother Tom. He asked his friend Mary Ellen to care for Harley while he was away.

During the trip, tensions flared when Billy caught Madeline on a phone call with another man, reinforcing his existing fears that she was cheating on him.

On Sunday, August 22, 2004, they arrived home. Billy confronted Madeline about her infidelity. By day's end, their relationship was over.

On Monday, Billy began a normal workweek at his towing job. That night he ran into Mary Ellen. They talked a little about Billy's break-up. Mary Ellen thought he looked sad, but okay.

Billy made a date of sorts with Mary Ellen as a thank you for watching Harley. He offered to take her to Six Flags Amusement Park the following Saturday.

His last words to her were, "Don't forget."

Even though Billy said he was through with Madeline, he was still angry. Shortly before 5 a.m. Tuesday morning he went to her house, tipped a ladder against the siding and climbed up to her bedroom window.

Madeline would later say that the two talked for about an hour, claiming he tried to rekindle the relationship. After the meeting, Billy went home and placed three phone calls to the reputed "other man," a married Woodbridge Selectman. In one message he threatened, "You better watch your back."

At 3:00 p.m. on Tuesday, Billy had lunch at Burger King and returned home. At 4:00 p.m. he told a neighbor he was going "up north" for three days to look at a car, despite already having half a dozen fixer-uppers sitting in his yard. His neighbor agreed to take care of Harley while he was gone. Billy said he would leave a key to his house outside, tucked in a shoe.

When his neighbor headed to the house to feed the dog the next day, the house key was nowhere to be found. He called Mary Ellen, who in turn called Paula, who called Jan.

The family went to Billy's house to investigate. His truck was curiously parked at the bottom of the driveway, near the road.

Jan called the Waterbury Police Department to report her son missing. But, because Billy had told said he would be gone for three days, police refused to file a report until 72 hours had passed.

Without any help from police, the family took over the detective work. They searched Billy's home. In the garbage they found the receipt from his lunch at Burger King the day before. On Thursday, they headed over to Burger King, hoping to watch a surveillance video for clues. Unfortunately, the establishment recycled their tapes each day, which meant that Tuesday's footage had already been recorded over.

They waited at the tow yard where Billy worked to see if he showed up for his 6:30 p.m. shift there. He didn't.

Billy had always kept in close contact with his family. He was the type of guy who would tell them what he was doing, where he was going, and who he was going with. The silence was deafening.

Jan

After he had been missing for three days, the family submitted a missing persons report. The family was assured that all officers would be apprised of his disappearance during roll call the following morning.

Later that evening around midnight, the family went back to his home and found the lights were on. They perked up, hoping Billy had come home. Instead, they found Madeline and her friend hanging out inside. Shortly thereafter, Bill Sr. changed the locks.

Police eventually questioned Madeline and the Woodbridge Selectman. They concluded that neither had any involvement in Billy's disappearance, nor was either individual ever considered a suspect.

A couple of days later, Bill and his brother headed back to the house to take care of Harley. As they got closer, they noticed his road was blocked off by police. Bill pulled over to ask an officer what was going on.

"A squirrel got fried on some electrical wires," the officer replied.

Bill said, "Let me ask you something. Do you know about my son, Billy? He lives here. He's missing."

"Who?" asked the officer, and admitted he had no knowledge of the case whatsoever.

This was not just one frustrating moment, but the foreshadowing of a maddening future.

Police did not provide any type of search team, so the family organized their own team of two to three hundred people. On a warm Labor Day weekend, volunteers searched high and low for three days in 90-degree heat.

Jan explains, "We saw where homeless people slept. Rats would be running by us. But we just kept on going through the brush and the prickers. When we were at Beacon Falls there was a foul smell off of the highway. Bill had to hang off of a rock to see what that smell was coming from."

It was a decomposing deer. Their immense search yielded no clues.

Paula arranged for D.A.W.G.S., a non-profit K-9 search and rescue organization, to help. D.A.W.G.S.' dogs faithfully sniffed their way through the woods every weekend until winter came. They too, found nothing.

The family was approached by a psychic who claimed Billy was bleeding on a riverbank and had hours to live.

"That threw us into a frenzy," Jan says. The lead went nowhere. Other psychics came forward, leading the family on more time-wasting goose chases.

After refusing them twice, the Waterbury P.D. granted the family a forensic investigation of Billy's home and truck two full weeks after his disappearance. During the search a detective found Billy's wallet and keys shoved deep beneath the seat of his truck – a sure sign of foul play. Jan had found a white rubber glove on the floor.

"What do I do with this?" she asked the detective.

"Throw it away," he replied.

"Now I know about DNA," Jan tells me.

Next, she had billboards put up on Routes 8 and 84 in Connecticut. Travelers on those highways anytime during the late 2000s are sure to remember these iconic signs. The words "MURDERED AND MISSING" appear above a photo of Billy wearing a blue plaid shirt, his hands clasped together as if begging for help.

Tips came in to police. Many were not relayed to the family or investigated.

The family printed missing posters and plastered them all over the region. Family and friends affixed thousands of posters to every inch of the Naugatuck Valley and beyond.

Suddenly, they started noticing flyers being torn down or mutilated. Some had "Who cares?" written on them. Bill conducted a stake-out to get to the bottom of what was going on. He placed a poster in one of the areas where they were frequently being torn down. He hid, and waited.

He watched in shock when he saw Madeline drive her school bus up to the sign, get out and rip the poster down.

The police told Bill they needed photographic evidence. This time Paula and her aunt planted a poster, hid, and waited – with a video camera. Once again, along came Madeline, who tore the poster off of the pole.

Even with videotaped evidence, police said they could not do anything about the vandalism. The incident further angered Madeline, who told police that Billy's family was targeting her neighborhood and workplace, saturating them with posters.

Jan and Paula headed to the Woodbridge Police Department to ask for help.

During their meeting, an officer dropped a major bombshell.

"I'm going to press five charges against you," he said. Among the charges were harassment and stalking.

Police offered to drop the charges if Jan and Paula don't go to the press with their video.

"I said to Paula, 'We're out of here.'"

Two weeks later, Jan received a phone call from a detective. Her heart pounded in her chest. *Maybe they found Billy.*

Instead, the detective said, "I'll give you two days to turn yourself in, or when you're in town you're going to be handcuffed and brought in."

Jan asked, "For what?"

"Criminal trespass, first degree – for hanging posters near school property." The charge is a Class A misdemeanor in the State of Connecticut.

Jan went straight down to the station to be fingerprinted and have her mug shot taken. At this point, she was the only person arrested since her son went missing. The arrest sticks with her to this day. The words, "You have the right to remain silent," still echo in her mind.

In court, the State's attorney read through the charges against her.

"Criminal trespass, disorderly conduct… this thing about the paintballing of the school busses really disturbs me."

"Paintballing of school buses?" she asked him, incredulously. "What are you talking about?"

It's hard not to laugh as she tells this story. A paintball gun is a curious weapon of choice for a June Cleaver type in her early fifties.

The charge had been fabricated.

At the end of the day, all charges were nolled. This meant she was relieved of criminal wrongdoing, but the incident would stay on her record for about a year. Having no previous history with the court system, she did not realize she was not fully exonerated from the charges.

"I should have pursued the charges being dropped, but I didn't know anything about court systems, and I didn't know about 'nolle,' I didn't know about anything," she says.

Years later, Madeline filed a civil suit, suing Jan and Paula (but not Bill) for emotional distress, defamation and punitive damages – and won. In 2012, Connecticut Superior Court awarded Madeline over $50,000. The family is in the process of appealing the ruling.

Bill and Jan have an inordinate number of war stories. Jan's DNA samples – taken to compare against human remains to determine if they are Billy's – were lost *seven times*. Two vials of her blood were also lost by police. Eighteen months after Billy disappeared, a Waterbury detective told an investigative reporter that he was probably "having a beer in Europe" and would come back when he was ready.

One of the worst blows came in April of 2007. Investigative journalist Andy Thibault helped the family obtain important documents regarding the case through a Freedom of Information request. The request uncovered a tip that had never been relayed to Jan and Bill by police.

Nearly two years after Billy vanished, a detailed tip came in on the Crime Stoppers hotline. The tipster stated that Madeline's son Shaun strangled Billy in his mother's apartment. The caller said Shaun, a grave digger, and his friend buried the body at an active construction site in Shelton. The next morning cement was poured over the site.

The police could not bring Shaun in for questioning because he had died a year earlier from a drug overdose. Police made no other efforts to follow up on the lead.

No matter how hard Jan worked to find her son, living or dead, she couldn't. The people she trusted to help, didn't. Nevertheless, this soft-spoken, demure woman was determined to bring Billy home.

After he first went missing, Paula acted as the family spokesperson since Jan was too devastated, perpetually clutching her son's photo and barely able to speak. She wouldn't even allow herself to go shopping, one of her favorite pastimes.

"All we had was one intention in mind: to find Billy," she says.

One day reporters showed up at Billy's house. Bill Sr. called Jan at home to say she needed to get down there to talk to them right away.

"I can't, Bill. I can't get in front of a camera," she told him.

Bill responded, "Jan, you're the mother. You're the only one that can do this."

She recalls, "I'm looking in the mirror as he's talking to me and I'm saying, 'Oh my God, I *am* the mother – and I'm the only person.' So I washed my hair, got the blow dryer out, went to his house, and that was a whole new transformation. I went from mom to… fighter, I guess."

Not only did she fight for her son, but for the thousands of other families missing a loved one.

Jan lobbied public officials to change the way missing persons cases are conducted. Among them included Congresswoman Nancy Johnson, Senators Joe Lieberman and Chris Dodd, but it was U.S. Senator Chris Murphy (at that time a U.S. Representative) who was the most receptive.

There are more than 100,000 missing persons in America. 40,000 unidentified remains languish in medical examiners' and coroners' offices across the country. In the early 2000s, information systems related to missing persons were in disarray. There were Federal, State, local and nonprofit data banks with bits of key information, but they weren't linked – rendering them ineffective. For example, if a missing person lived in Connecticut but was murdered in New York, data regarding their remains would only show up in New York's records.

In 2004, the only national missing person's database was the National Crime Information Center (NCIC). This FBI-owned database is only accessible to law enforcement agencies and related organizations.

In 2007, the National Missing Persons and Unidentified Persons System (NamUs) was first introduced. In 2009, NamUs was integrated with the NCIC to share unclassified information from the FBI's records, enabling everyday citizens to view missing persons data online. Families of victims can submit their own data to NamUs, including DNA records. Hundreds of cases have been solved using information from the NamUs database.

Jan contacted Rep. Chris Murphy to make him aware of these issues that sorely needed fixing. He then acted as her liaison with the FBI and Department of Justice. He returned to her with the "Help Find the Missing Act," more commonly known as "Billy's Law."

Billy's Law provides funding for law enforcement agencies to learn how to use NamUs and recommends specific procedures for law enforcement, medical examiners and coroners to best find the missing.

Rep. Murphy introduced the bipartisan bill along with Rep. Ted Poe, a Republican from Texas. Rep. Murphy introduced Billy's case as "tragic," and fraught with "systematic failures," "frustration" and "heartbreak." He described Jan and Bill's efforts to improve the system as "nothing less than heroic."

Jan personally testified before Congress in support of the bill. She lights up when she recollects the experience.

"Oh, it was *something*. It was nice. It was moving," she says.

The bill easily passed in the House, but it failed in the Senate. Subsequent efforts to enact the law have been unsuccessful.

In the meantime, many other measures have since been implemented. Standard policy in Connecticut for handling missing persons now requires law enforcement agencies to "accept without delay any report of a missing person. No law enforcement agency may refuse to accept a missing person report."

Jan helped create a new way to generate cold case tips in Connecticut. In the Gulf War, "Most Wanted Playing Cards" contained photos and information about the biggest terrorists in the region at the time. That idea later transformed into "Cold Case Cards," which highlight 52 unsolved homicides, missing persons, and unidentified remains cases. Cards are distributed in prisons for inmates' use, to generate tips. Jan heard about the idea at a conference in South Carolina and brought it to Connecticut, which is now the third state to use this effective tool.

She has been a keynote speaker at conferences in Texas, Washington State, Colorado, Florida and Maryland. She's been interviewed by Newsweek, USA Today, Discovery ID, WNPR, and countless other media outlets in Connecticut and beyond.

To say Jan has worked tirelessly to find her son and help others who have lost a loved one is an understatement. However, she has learned that although her heart compels her to keep working, she must prioritize family above all.

"Every time I went over Paula's house, I would go on the computer because it was always about trying to find Billy. My granddaughter came up to me and said, 'Could you watch *Cinderella*?' And I said, 'Sure honey, I'll be there in a minute.'" Fixated on finding Billy, she never left her computer.

Paula called the next day.

"Ma, I'm gonna tell you something," she said. "I'm trying to find Billy and I know you're trying to find Billy, but you also have family that's alive and you're pushing us away."

"That was like a slap across the face," Jan says.

She told Paula, "I'm sorry. You're right." Her eyes go blurry with tears as she recalls the conversation. "So when my family's here, I put everything aside. I shut that off," she says, pointing to her phone. "My computer goes down and it's family time."

Jan and Bill believe that if their son had not been an adult male, his case could have progressed differently, and speculate that had he been younger – or an attractive woman – his disappearance would have garnered more interest.

"It's sad because I always say – *everybody* is somebody," says Jan.

The astonishing number of pitfalls they have encountered begs the question, *Is there a higher purpose for all of this?*

Jan says yes. "I feel that we're put in this position for a reason. There are so many things that have happened that it's just surreal. Sure, we get angry, and there are times when we just want to go and scream. But it's not going to do any good. They're waiting for that."

Bill knows how to take a step back, too. He recalls a pensive moment spent in a doctor's office shortly after Billy went missing.

"I'm sitting there waiting for my turn and I see this father come in with this kid in a wheelchair and he's drooling. I said, you know what? Maybe I don't have it that bad, you know?"

Faith plays a strong role in Jan's life. "I believe you will get through certain situations if you accept being a soldier. I just have to carry through, you know? I'll go on my computer and, because I'm Christian, I'll ask the Holy Spirit to come down and give me the right words and the right situations and it seems to help. It always puts a person in my life who needs to be in my life at that time."

She has waited with bated breath while investigators searched four sites where Billy was allegedly buried. She watched as residential yards were dug up, septic tanks emptied, and dogs sniffed their way across acres of remote woods. The week after we spoke, Billy had been missing ten years to the day.

Why Go On: Connecticut Residents Bring Dark Days to Light

"I think it's faith that keeps me going. Without it I don't think I'd have anything," Jan says. "There's always hope. With negative comes a positive. Just look forward, because there are blessings along the way. There's always someone to take your hand and guide you. That's what I'm trying to impress upon people, to not think negatively. If a door slams in your face, it's not meant to be. Another door is going to open.

"Patience, determination, persistence, faith and hope," she says, pointing her index finger with each word, as if reciting a personal mantra.

I ask her if there was ever a moment when she thought about giving up.

The words have barely come out of my mouth when she responds with a deep and resonant, "*No.*"

She turns to Bill, smiling, and asks, "Have I?"

Bill, a straight talker who loves his wife unequivocally, shakes his head with comic resignation and echoes, "No."

"And you know, we're not dwelling on our issues. We're dwelling on other people's issues as well, and what changes need to be done. It's horrendous how it affects families. I have to do something positive every day because there's a force that's pushing me, saying,

Bill and Jan

Jan

'You can't take today off.' We'll go on vacation and I'll still work," she says, as Bill shakes his head again.

She reflects on the old days with a sort of wistful gaze that seems to question if they ever existed.

"I feel like I'm not the same person anymore. We were just a normal American family. We're not the same people we used to be. After all these years you've kind of lost your sense of who you were and you become a whole new person. I guess it's kind of like the new normal."

She tells me about an experience she and Bill had on their honeymoon; they were practically kids at the time. They had driven down to Miami Beach in Bill's souped-up Chevelle. On the beach, the two frolicked in the water, unaware that a hurricane swelled offshore.

"So we're playing in the waves and all of a sudden this undertow took us and flipped us," she says. They recovered, but they were all disheveled and covered in sand.

"We get out of the water, we go up to our blanket and Bill goes, 'My wedding band... where is it?' So we run back to the water. Now, this is a supernatural thing, I say. We go back to the water to search for the wedding band – and it didn't take us long, either – in the water was this shiny little thing under the sand."

Bill says, "The water was washing the sand over it and then every once in a while you'd see this little sparkle, you know? So I went over there and picked it up and there was my ring. Just like that."

Jan says, "We never thought anything about it, but now I'm saying, *Well, maybe this is a message.* Your life is going to be in turmoil, but you're going to stay together through it all."

I suggest it might also mean that they'll ultimately find what they're looking for.

Jan almost gasps and says with a look of excitement in her eyes, "Oh yeah, that's even better." She laughs, her spirit glowing with irrepressible optimism.

Ray

"From that moment on I dedicated myself to love, compassion and reality."

R ay is an old soul with new insight.

I met with Ray at his charming home where he's lived with his family for over 30 years. Built in the late 1940s, the abode exudes a cozy, warm feeling. From the rich wood flooring of the hallways to the cheerful checkerboard tile in the kitchen, serenity emanates from the ground up. The surrounding neighborhood is in a bright and friendly area of Meriden where the close proximity of houses feels more communal than cramped. On several occasions his neighbors waved happily as they walked or drove by. As Ray returned the gesture, he spread a friendly, genuine smile across his face.

Dressed in an oversized sweatshirt, jeans and canvas shoes flecked with paint, Ray offers a unique combination of mechanical know-how and dreamy idealism. He's soft-spoken, gentle, and sensitive. His salt-and-pepper hair exposes his age, but at 65 he exhibits no lack of energy. Looking into his bright hazel eyes, you'd never guess he died 40 years ago.

As he greets me on this unseasonably warm April day, his wife and two of three sons are outside propagating a variety of seeds for their extensive vegetable garden. An afternoon of peaceful tranquility was something Ray wasn't given, but earned. In fact, it was only through his own death that he was able to start over, discover his life's purpose, find love, and put a difficult past behind him.

We move from the sunny outdoors into Ray's office, a quiet room with calming energy.

"Rumor is I was born on Thanksgiving Day, probably late at night," he says. The lack of a precise birthdate immediately alludes to trouble at home. "My mother said that my father had a turkey sandwich," he says, implying that the late night snack acted as a mnemonic device.

Ray is the youngest of three, with two older sisters. His parents were two "good-looking people," he says, with his father resembling Clark Gable. His dad was a high-ranking state police officer, and the family lived comfortably – at least by way of money.

After his birth, it wasn't long before things went awry. His mother attempted suicide when he was just a baby. How, he's not sure, but he believes it was by slashing her wrists. This resulted in her institutionalization for the first few years of his life. During her absence, he and his sisters were raised by their father and several babysitters.

To help cope with loneliness and neglect, he had an imaginary friend named "Key." Key came to him as more of a "thick presence" than a solid apparition, but he felt very real to the young boy.

"I didn't think he was imaginary. He was very understanding and I could talk to him. He would play with me as an adult would." Key provided the comfort and care he so desperately needed.

He describes a feeling of confusion at age three when his mother was released from the hospital and abruptly reassumed her role as matriarch.

At this time his friend Key told him, "It is time for me to leave. You don't need me anymore." He remembers seeing his "new" mother sitting on the couch as Key disappeared through the front door, leaving Ray heartbroken. While this may have been the last time he saw his imaginary friend, it would not be his last experience with a celestial being.

The next visit from the Beyond came when he was around six years old. "I had jumped off a rock and shoved my leg about an inch into my hip. I spent weeks in the hospital." One day, he was visited by an apparition that resembled Christ.

"It was kind of stunning, you know, that everything in the room kind of froze and in walks this guy who, now that I look back, from the looks and everything, was Jesus."

Despite occasional visits from spiritual guides, his life became more difficult as time went on. His mother had a penchant for drinking vodka, swallowing valium and abusing her children.

"There were stages to it. She'd start walking around in a peignoir set. She'd get a glazed look in her eye and eventually wind up breaking dishes while my father tried to control things. Plenty of times it would wind up with her somehow attempting to commit suicide."

The home saw a revolving door of nannies, maids, and other help. They provided some degree of comfort and affection, but none of them lasted long. His mother routinely called for their dismissal, accusing them of watering down her bottles of vodka. Ray believes his mother was, in fact, watering it down herself in order to hide her own drinking. His father was forced to hire new help.

Because of Mom's knack for manipulation, Dad became the family scapegoat. Unable to control his wife, he unsuccessfully tried to control his children. Another struggle was in keeping his home life secret from his peers.

"Family problems did not happen to state policemen back in those days. That's one reason why we moved 11 times. I was always starting a new school. We moved mostly because of my father's desire not to appear to have *that* type of family."

When Ray was a little older, he was assigned the unpleasant task of saving his own mother's life when a vodka-valium cocktail sent her into unconsciousness.

"I was 11 years old and my father called me in. He was performing mouth to mouth on her, and he had to go outside and wait for the ambulance. He had told the ambulance to come without any lights and without any sirens. So, at 11 years old I was keeping my mother alive with mouth to mouth resuscitation."

Around 4th grade, his mother took him out of public school and began home schooling him in order to hide their dysfunctional home life from outsiders. Her lackadaisical efforts at educating him hurt him both academically and socially.

Looking forward to his later teen years, he sought escape through music and drugs. After all, "it was the '60s," he says. He had a friend John who lived just down the street. John had troubles at home too, so the duo bonded easily. He and John played music together, with Ray on guitar and John on vocals.

His guitar was his life, which he named Simon after the Bible's Simon of Cyrene, who helped Jesus carry the cross before his crucifixion. Music helped them cope. Drugs added color and chaos.

"I'm the one who started it," he says about their experimentation with drugs. "I got some pot and John and I started smoking. In Waterbury at the time there was a progression in how the dealer did it. There would be pot, then there would be no pot, but there was THC. That was the next step up. Then there would be no pot and no THC, but there would be speed. So, I went through the progression and ended up doing a lot of speed."

He shows me a photo of himself from around that time. He bears a strong resemblance to his current incarnation, particularly in his lanky body and long face, but with blonde hair substituted for the current gray. His face is serious, but not sad. His visage does not betray the loneliness he felt at the time, nor the complete lack of parental kindness or support.

Shortly before his life changed at age 21, he had a vivid lucid dream. He talks about it with utmost seriousness, as though he isn't convinced it was really a dream.

He woke up in his bed to find a faceless apparition rifling through his dresser. The ghost-like figure found a bottle of pills in the dresser and sat down on the edge of his bed.

The spirit struggled to open the tamper-proof bottle. He tried to kick the ghost off of his bed, but he responded by giving him a ghastly scowl before returning his attention to the bottle.

This guy is dead and he's still hooked, Ray thought, realizing in retrospect it was a warning against his own drug use. The dream then ended, but something more terrifying would happen a few weeks later.

His use of speed had damaged and weakened his heart. During a party at his apartment, he developed a persistent and peculiar cough he couldn't shake. He headed to the bathroom.

"I was kind of leaning on the sink and I was coughing. In retrospect I've learned what that is. It's called a cardiac cough. And very gently, black started to close in, like that," he says, creating a shrinking circle with his hands, "and I couldn't feel my heart beating. My heart had stopped. Everything was perfectly silent about my body. I started to go down, and wound up on the floor.

"Then, I found myself on the other side. It was mostly just darkness except there was a light. It was kind of a foggy light – like a light around fog or dew or something like that. And over here there was a male figure," he says, gesturing to the side. "Again, this male figure was more or less a thick presence – and he obviously was Jesus. Not that I was real religious or anything."

At this moment he had an epiphany. "The major thing was my conscience. It's the only thing you take with you when you go to the other side. And my conscience, of course, was not good. It was self-destructive, doing drugs, it was escapist – it was not maturing. I knew I

Ray

was dead and I just involuntarily said, 'Oh God, not this way!' I then found myself – it was a sensation of being poured back in your body – and I got up from the floor."

Ray was dead for no less than 10 minutes.

He immediately resolved to fix his state of mind. This revelation may have been the best thing that happened to him, but at his moment of rebirth he was in deep trouble.

"I was all sweaty," he says. "I got myself together and went out and found John to tell him what was happening. I started talking to him, and I was using words that I never use. There was something wrong with my brain."

Indeed, something was very wrong. He now had brain damage from a lack of oxygen and blood to his brain. He was unable to make connections between people, experiences and physical things. Humans are generally unaware of the magnificent mesh of innumerable associations the brain creates for a deep and meaningful life existence. For Ray, this all had disintegrated.

"Think of some item that you have that you cherish because it brings up thoughts of great and meaningful memories. A picture, a birthday card you saved, your favorite sweater, your favorite color, your favorite song, your best friend. One day you awake to have all that gone. It is as if these things have no meaning, no emotional connections, no connection to other memories – they might as well belong to some stranger that you know nothing about.

"Take a picture out of your wallet. When you look at that picture, you're looking at more than that picture. If it's a picture of your best friend, included in that picture you're also seeing all of the good times that you had; you're seeing what she wore at that time. This is all instantaneous and that's what makes the depth of the picture," he explains.

One could also think of it this way – if you read a story and find it engaging, chances are you've made an emotional connection with it. Conversely, if you find a story dull and uninteresting, you probably weren't able to find a way to make it relatable. In the first case, you made various emotional connections to the plot, the characters, or any bit of minute detail.

His own life became a story he could not relate to.

He even lost the bond with his constant companion: his guitar Simon. Although he was able to continue writing music (in fact, the depression enhanced his writing ability), the guitar itself no longer gave him comfort or familiarity.

"That guitar could have belonged to anybody. There was no emotional connection. I knew it was mine, but there was no connection, no memories behind it. It meant nothing to me except it was mine. I had to start dealing with that stuff and trying to figure that out."

His condition prompted him to move back in with his parents, who at first didn't seem particularly worried about his condition.

"They were not concerned with me. They just knew I came home, was depressed, and left me alone. I felt consigned by fate to a crippled life that had no chance of being normal and happy." Eventually, the point came where he had no choice but to look for help.

His parents made an appointment with Dr. Robert Notage, a psychotherapist in Cheshire. There, Notage performed a series of tests to establish his exact problem. The tests were "like an IQ test. MRI's were not in use at the time," Ray notes. After completing the tests, Notage determined that Ray had brain damage, which impaired his ability to perform tasks connected with associative memory.

Associative memory is the process by which one thought triggers another. It's the interrelationship between networks, including short-term, spatial, verbal and visual memory systems. Notage's diagnosis and subsequent therapy launched him into a mysterious journey of physical, emotional and spiritual recovery.

Though his brain was damaged, it was not irreparable. The brain has the capability to rewire itself through a phenomenon called "brain plasticity," also known as "neuroplasticity." Neuroplasticity is a term for the process of reorganizing neural pathways in the brain. To put it simply, it is the ability of the brain to physically change with mental exercise.

Neuroplasticity primarily occurs during two times: 1) during youth (pre-adolescence), when the brain is pliable and 2) while compensating for an injury to the brain itself. Meeting the characteristics of the latter, Ray immediately went to work. This began with a life-changing book.

Notage suggested he read *The Art of Loving* by German

psychoanalyst Erich Fromm.

"I took the book home and read it. What an eye opener," he says. It taught him about love, which he had lacked so sorely in his life.

"From that moment on I dedicated myself to love, compassion and reality," Ray declares.

Strangely enough, at the point when his brain was in its worst shape was when it was the most receptive to positive change and growth. Without the emotional distractions related to associative memory, he could absorb books without the constant mental chatter of associative memory.

The Art of Loving inspired him to start Zen meditation. He meditated not only to fix his brain, but also to make peace with his past.

"I was entirely broken. I had not been given any of the tools socially. I had done drugs and I was a wreck. I could not fit into normal society, period. I figured that the only way to get reprogrammed was through reality directly, because my thoughts on what I had been given were wrong, were broken."

He had a special meditation spot on a rock in his parents' backyard. At first, he says, he didn't know exactly what he was doing. In time he managed to achieve great mental states through regular meditative practice and experienced truly unadulterated feelings of bliss and enlightenment.

"Nirvana, the clear light, cosmic consciousness... I was drenched in it. Meditation gave me peace. It renewed my dedication to love and reality. I was able to see beyond the veil that other people live their lives behind and are so unhappy from – the veil that separates us from our own natural humanity."

He could finally shed the unattainable standards of perfection he felt the world wanted him to achieve. Liberated from this judgment, he could now devote his life to the practical application of Fromm's ideals.

Shortly after his near death experience, he took an impromptu cross-country trip to California, staying a few months in an apartment across from MacArthur Park in Los Angeles. He would often go out jogging, employing a silent mantra in rhythm with each step: "I'm not this body, I'm not my thoughts, I'm not my emotions, and I'm not what other people think of me."

One day, he had an experience similar to Dr. Jill Bolte Taylor's stroke, which she illuminated in her 2008 TED talk entitled "A Stroke of Insight." Only instead of having a stroke, his experience was more like he was being born again.

"I came in from jogging one evening at dusk. All of a sudden I bent down to untie my shoelaces and the smells that came in from outside were like… *Oh my God.* I could smell every flower and my vision was absolutely crystal clear. Colors, lights – this was not like being stoned. This was like every hang-up you ever had just dropped away. It was amazing." As he recollects the experience he stops to gather his emotions. "It was like everything is connected to everything in the world." He continued to have these experiences on and off for months.

These days, he doesn't think too much about his near death experience, but the concepts of reality and compassion are ever-present in his mind. "Two things are important in my life now. Most important thing is my conscience. I've been to the other side. I'm not going there again in that condition. And love. Real love."

His takeaway from spiritual texts of all kinds is that one should act in accordance to their own consciousness and heart, through loving and caring for other people. Though he came from a childhood environment of violence, denial and neglect, he was able to learn, after a massive crisis, how to be compassionate and kind. All he truly wants to do is get his message of love and compassion out into the world. He still plays music and meditates regularly.

Ray, raised Roman Catholic, often speaks using biblical terms and symbols, but he eschews the rigid laws of Catholicism or any religion. He now considers himself to be "mostly Buddhist." He believes that if one has a near death experience, they may not see Jesus like he did, but may see their own figures such as Buddha or Krishna.

The experiences of his early 20s are intimate and emotional. Death, transformation and nirvana are not topics of the faint of heart when you've experienced all three. Throughout his life, he has continued to have strange and beautiful moments that seem to happen only when he isn't looking. He's been repeatedly thanked by people who, at times, he doesn't remember helping. There is one occasion, however, that he remembers clearly.

While working in the maintenance field many years back, he supervised a gruff and unhappy man named Tom.

"A lot of people didn't like him," he said.

One day Ray was ordered to fire Tom, so he called Tom over to talk. Ray asked him flat out, "What's your problem?"

Few people could ask that kind of question without sounding rude, but perhaps it was Ray's compassionate presence that elicited an honest answer. In fact, Tom let it all out. He talked about his alcoholic parents, his troubled marriage, and how he feared he too might be an alcoholic because, "Every time I drive by a bar, I want to go in."

Ray consoled and advised Tom as best he could. The only thing he didn't do was what his boss asked him to do.

"I didn't fire him," he says, proudly. This decision could have jeopardized his own job. "I made my choice despite the probability of being fired. I made the choice to follow my conscience. I have made that choice several times in my life. It's harder to do in the beginning, but it's easier to do as the years go by."

Two weeks later, he saw Tom at a Christmas party and asked how he was doing. Tom said he was doing all right, and added, "I have to thank you." At this point in the story, Ray stops to collect himself before revealing Tom's next words.

"I was going to commit suicide that day."

Ray explains, "I have compassion for people. I don't let people fool me, but I have compassion for those that genuinely need help, whether it be psychological, spiritual or physical. If you can help someone who's trying to get out of a hole or needs to know what kind of hole they're in, do it, because you were in that position once."

One interesting way he helps people out of holes is in his participation with Thresholds, an organization that sends volunteers into prisons to teach inmates decision making skills. The program is designed to help felony offenders learn how to react, plan, and manage life events constructively instead of reacting recklessly.

Ray's life these days is free and peaceful. He met his current wife, Cathy, not too long after his near-death experience. They've been married for over 40 years.

Cathy is a delightful foil to Ray's airy, carefree personality. She is down to earth, perceptive and honest, but just as open and caring as her husband. While Ray is more of a "big picture" guy, Cathy is better suited at taking care of the details. The two go together in the best way that opposites can attract, each complementing the other without being obtrusive. Ray speaks highly of Cathy and values their differences.

Without his 10-minute brush with death, his life would have traveled a much different path. But this trauma sparked a valuable restoration of his brain, his wellbeing and his life's purpose. To observe him and his family engaged in something as simple as yard work on a sunny Saturday might simply seem like a "nice day," but it is truly an idyllic scene that he has earned through his own grit, kindness and courage.

Patty

"Is everything rainbows and sunshine? No. But you can't give up."

Patty is a whirlwind of energy, opinions and humor. She speaks quickly and smiles readily. Her nicely styled brown hair offsets her clear blue eyes. She wears sarcasm on her sleeve, and will not, under any circumstances, mince words.

She and I met at her home in Woodbury, Connecticut, a town known for its tranquil, woodsy landscape. She lives here with her family of five, two dogs and a cat. Tranquility is a luxury Patty lost long ago.

Patty grew up in Danbury. The youngest of three, she was a self-proclaimed rebellious child, "in probably every way," she says. Her twin brother and sister are eight years older.

"I was the rule breaker," she says.

She attended Henry Abbott Technical High School in Danbury before becoming a registered CNA. As any proper rebel would be, she was drawn to "guys that rode Harley-Davidsons." She often hung out at Danbury's now-closed Marcus Dairy, which for decades was *the* meeting place for thousands of bikers. She met her first husband and they had a son, Dylan, now 22. The trio moved to Florida and two years later she was pregnant again – this time, with fraternal twins.

Six months into her pregnancy things went very wrong.

"I was only 27 weeks pregnant and I got really, really sick. I ended up having toxemia and preeclampsia."

Why Go On: Connecticut Residents Bring Dark Days to Light

Patty

The illness forced doctors to induce labor, causing her daughters to be born three months premature. Alyssa weighed in at two pounds, eleven ounces, and Meagan weighed only one pound, six ounces.

Both girls suffered from an intraventricular brain hemorrhage (IVH), which is bleeding inside or around the ventricles of the brain. Meagan, the smaller of the two, had a Grade IV hemorrhage – the most severe grade IVH. It occurred on the left side of her brain, which controls things like logic, math and critical thinking. Alyssa's hemorrhage was weaker at a Grade III, and occurred in the right hemisphere, governing spatial perception, creativity and emotions.

The hemorrhages inflicted irreparable harm to the girls. "Even though the tissue re-grows," Patty explains, "the damage is there." They stayed in an intensive care unit for about three months before she could take them home.

At first, it was hard for Patty to reconcile having one healthy baby with two who had serious health issues.

"It was like, you had the flu and you go to the emergency room and from that moment your whole world flips upside down."

It would be several more months before she could see the true extent of hemorrhages' damage. Preemies naturally exhibit delayed development, so it was hard to gauge what was the result of the IVH and what was typical of a preemie.

Patty

By the time the girls were one year old, "nobody was walking or sitting up or crawling." Around this time they were diagnosed with cerebral palsy, or CP.

She explains that CP is "caused by a lack of oxygen to the brain, either during your pregnancy or when you're going into labor. Some kids have it because the umbilical cord was around their neck. It takes about ten seconds to have the lack of oxygen. It affects their muscles, their tone, their brain, their ability to do everything. It goes between spastic, or you could be a quadriplegic or a paraplegic. It depends on which muscles are affected and which parts, but it is all caused by whatever degree, I to IV, of brain damage."

She moved her family back up to Connecticut because she felt the medical care in the area would better suit her needs. Shortly after the move, she and her husband divorced. Despite this setback, she was determined to provide her daughters with the most loving, supportive childhood despite the challenges of being a single mother.

She rented a condominium in Woodbury owned by her uncle. Within a couple of years she met a neighbor at the complex named Roger and the two hit it off. She's been married to Roger now for 15 years. Roger grew to love Patty's daughters just as much as she does.

"He is a great guy and he has been *great* to my kids. That's what attracted me to him." She adds, "The whole handicapped thing doesn't faze him."

While she is passionate and intense, her husband is quiet and laid back. "I married the complete opposite and it works."

As Alyssa and Meagan grew older, their disparate disabilities became more defined. Now, at 20 years old, they exhibit different impairments.

"Alyssa, who was just a little bit heavier at birth, is in a wheelchair, but she can use a walker for short distances. Cognitively I'm not going to say she's 20. She's more like 17. Things just take her a little longer." Simple physical activities like getting a drink or tying her shoes are a huge challenge.

Meagan, on the other hand, is far more mobile. "She walks, but she has more than just cerebral palsy. She has a learning disability, an intellectual impairment and she's legally blind. So she has a whole unique, complex set of challenges."

Their personalities, too, are different.

"Alyssa is a really kind person. She's non-confrontational; not very aggressive or assertive. Her personality is like right here," she says, motioning with her hand to indicate Alyssa's even temper. "Very rarely does it go here," she says, raising her hand, "unless they are fighting."

"Meagan is kind and helpful, but she's an aggressive person. She likes to think she's a mini me. She likes to advocate and fight for the things that she needs."

She shows me photos of her son and daughters. The ladies are strikingly beautiful, with warm brown hair and eyes. Their faces fit their description. Alyssa carries a delightfully happy, innocent smile, while Meagan bears an equally loveable, but bolder grin.

One thing the girls had in common were identical surgeries, which they both had performed at the same times. Both had hamstring/heel cord lengthening, tibial derotation and rectus transfer surgeries at ages 3, 8 and 11, respectively. All three are orthopedic surgeries common to CP sufferers to help with mobility. Their recoveries were grueling.

"It was six-month recoveries. They were in half body casts and they couldn't move. They had pins put in their legs, so you couldn't move them wrong. And it was two of them. They would scream in pain and need morphine."

Thankfully, both recovered well and were eventually out of pain. But more adversity lay ahead. Patty's next challenge was fighting the school system.

The standardized treatment of special needs students caused constant problems for her daughters. Even CP can affect children in widely varying ways and therefore require different educational methods.

"It's either mild, moderate or severe. Everybody always thinks, 'Oh, she has CP.' They group them into a giant special needs bubble. In Woodbury alone I think we have 249 special needs students, everywhere from the low percent of Down syndrome to having cerebral palsy, to somebody with autism."

Patty constantly clashed with educators. Meagan attended a special needs school to accommodate her learning disability and Alyssa went to regular public schools. She had problems in both places.

"Every little thing you have to fight for." Alyssa struggled with a variety of issues that Patty believes should have been noticed and addressed. Things like: installing a push button door to the bathroom so she could use the restroom without asking another student to open the door, or, adjusting homework to match her capabilities.

"You can't give her the same amount of homework that you're giving everybody else. If you had a sheet with 200 things, you're not realizing that's taking her twelve hours. Why not pick ten questions on that paper and give those to her."

Meagan needed different modifications. She talks about one instance where Meagan couldn't read an assignment because the print was too small. "You can't hand something with 8 point print to Meagan." So, Patty asked the teacher to "blow it up."

"They blew up the *paper* the size of the table, but the font was still an 8. I'm like, no, I don't mean blow up the paper, I mean blow up the font!" she cries out, rubbing her face.

"It was a fight with every little thing. I know a lot of the special needs parents in town that are fighting for the exact same thing. They need to stop mainstreaming or look at each kid. It's like saying you have 249 special needs kids. No. You have Emma, Susie, Jake and Billy, and they're all different. Maybe Emma and Susie should be here, but maybe the other two belong in a private school. You're also wasting the child's time. They don't need to learn about the western movement. They need to learn how to write out a check, or how to go to the ATM. I'm the parent who's going to follow through and make sure she's treated right."

Through the years, Patty transformed into a shrewd, well-informed advocate for her children. "Sometimes you're sitting there with twelve people. I got to the point where it was the more the merrier, because that does not intimidate me. It took years of practice."

She became a fearsome negotiator. "You'll either learn how to work with me and we're going to come to a mutual agreement, or we're not – and then we're gonna have a battle. But somewhere you have to compromise. I would go in with a list. I'll ramble off fifty things that I want, but I know I'm going to get ten of those. It's like a barter system."

Her husband tried to convince her to let certain things go because the fight was too hard. Her response was quite the opposite. Telling her she couldn't do it was like "setting a match under me."

She says, "I don't take no for an answer. I always ended up

getting everything I had asked for, because I'll get you to the point where you're like, 'Shut this woman up and just give it to her.'"

Patty used to work caring for Alzheimer's patients, but she left the job to give her children the care they needed. "It's a lot of work. This is probably the hardest job I have ever had."

But, it's a job she'd never leave. "I would never quit on them. In the past, I would always quit something if I didn't like it, even if I needed the money. If I was waitressing – *eh*, I'm not going back there tonight. I would never give up on them. It's made me a lot stronger."

She gets some of her strength from talking to moms of other special needs kids, because they know what she's going through. In turn, new mothers of special needs children look to her for advice.

"I had a group of moms here a couple of weeks ago. A friend of mine had invited them. All of their kids have something different. I didn't know half of them. One of them is suing the school. One won. I can see how moms give up. We're not supposed to tell you, the school, what you're supposed to be doing and how you're supposed to be educating them. You're supposed to have the plan for us. There's so much anger."

She asked her friend why she wanted her to meet these women.

"She's like, 'I want them to see – are you bitter and angry? Yes. Is everything rainbows and sunshine? No. But you can't give up.' Like I never ever gave up."

Her advice for other parents is to be there for their children in every way they can – but also to help them become as independent as possible.

"You have to be their mom, their nurse, their advocate, their friend. You have to be their mom first, and then you have to teach them things. You have to stay on top of them, *for* them. I don't want my daughters to be weak young women. You have to push your kid into being the best and most independent person they can be. Definitely."

Because of their CP, Alyssa and Meagan had to miss out on a lot of the "fun parts" of high school life. When classmates headed out to see their boyfriends, go to the beach, the movies, dinner, or just drive around, Alyssa and Meagan couldn't.

"There's none of that. It's hard for me as their mom to see what they go through as young adults. To grow up and not have friends, to grow up and be bullied, to not ever be able to live the normal life of kids who are 16 and are getting their license and going off to prom. I would be *so* distraught if they didn't have each other. I hate when they get in an argument and fight. There are so many kids out there that are disabled and don't have anybody. At least they have each other to talk to or vent out on or go to the movies with."

She explains how difficult it was arranging prom night for Alyssa. "You have no idea what it took to organize. To have a handicapped limo, and then get kids to go with her that have special needs, and to have a specific table out of the way. Never mind the dress!" Alyssa had a good time, "but it's not the same experience. Everybody leaves and goes to parties and stays out all night, whereas they get picked up and go home."

Meagan is the first to express her needs, but Alyssa will not. Patty encourages Alyssa to try expressing herself through writing.

"I ask her, 'Why don't you write a blog for people that have special needs?' She has won some English awards and she's a really good writer." She encourages her to use the blog for making people aware of local issues that affect the disabled, such as listing retail stores that are not power chair friendly.

Patty's dedication to her children has become so ingrained in her daily life that it's like second nature to her. She says she doesn't ever get emotional and simply relies on her own assertiveness for motivation. She has to keep plugging away to get things done, because she's a "person on a mission."

Her children find it odd that they've never seen her shed a tear. "Nobody's ever said anything to hurt me enough to make me cry, and I don't know what would trigger that in me." She says she's more preoccupied with making life better for her girls than her emotions.

As tenacious and strong-willed as she is, you can see the warmth in her crystalline blue eyes, particularly when she talks about her daughters and the anxiety she has for their future. She admits her admiration for Alyssa's sensitive side, saying, "Alyssa has that personality of everything I would want to be."

She talks about the rare, fleeting moments of peace in her fast-moving, hectic life.

"This happened to me the other day. It's like that tree right there." She points to a tree in her yard just beginning to lose its green as autumn settles in. "It was after it rained, and it was so orange and the sun was hitting it. It caught my eye. I was like, wow. That is so beautiful."

She asked herself, "Who even enjoys that stuff anymore?"

She reminisced about the old days when she was more attuned to the beauty in nature. "When I was young I remember sitting outside my grandmother's house. You would lie on the grass and that was your Sunday. You would look up at the clouds and the trees. We'd take an eight-hour ride to Vermont when I was little. Now, to go from here to Kmart it's like, are you kidding me? It's 15 minutes away, 15 minutes back."

At this point her dogs became restless, so she lets them in from outside. She jokes that one of them, a chestnut shar-pei mix, is her "special needs dog."

"He has anxiety because he was from a puppy mill. I rescued him. He's attached to me, which is weird. The vet actually said, 'You two feed off each other.' Whether I'm gone ten minutes or five hours, he's hyperventilating in the kitchen."

Not once through our conversation did she ever imply that caring for two daughters with CP was a burden. Her love for these two young women is undeniable. In fact, she doesn't find raising them to be particularly challenging. It's their environment she finds a problem.

"It's not so bad having kids with CP. *They're* not hard. It's all that stuff around having CP that you have to deal with."

She jokes that her 22-year-old son Dylan is better at causing anxiety than her daughters.

"You know that commercial: 'It's 10 o'clock, do you know where your children are?' You know what? I do. I know where two of them are."

She sees her rebellious young self in her son. "He's me at that age. I was wild and rebellious and you weren't going to tell me when to come home and what to do and who to go out with."

But Dylan, the super popular ladies' man, has a heart of gold just like his mother. "He wants to be a doctor because of his sisters," Patty says.

Though she envies other families with children so perfect "nobody even wears a pair of glasses," she readily acknowledges things could be worse. She's met several other moms who are dealing with even tougher scenarios. She sees other children and young adults, some as local as Woodbury, with disorders or diseases that carry a short life expectancy. CP is not fatal.

"I always tell my friend, 'Our kids are not terminally ill.' Her son has Down syndrome. I could never handle the death of one of my children and take care of the other ones and try to move on. That's like, the hardest thing."

Her biggest concern is ensuring her daughters have a good future. Right now both of them are in transitional programs that help ready them for the workplace.

"It's all job shadowing. So you pick a few things that you would be interested in doing, and then you're set up with a job coach. Hopefully, it will help them get ready for a job."

Alyssa is a voracious reader, so her dream job is to work at a bookstore. Meagan works in a bakery. While the transitional program bolsters their résumé, there are no easy routes to future employment. State assistance provides limited help but is often too backlogged with cases to be beneficial.

In the future, Alyssa and Meagan will be able to live independently with some help. "Together they're like one. Because what Alyssa can't do, Meagan can, and what she can't do, Alyssa can. But they would still need someone because neither one can cook. Alyssa can't get her shoes on and somebody should be there while they're taking showers in case they fall. They would still need a personal care assistant here and there."

Thoughts about the future create an uptick of anxiety – something Patty says is a common problem for parents of special needs kids.

"Most people have kids who graduate, go off to college, get a degree, have a career, get married and have kids of their own." When a typical child reaches age 18, or perhaps graduates from college, parents can let go to a good extent. "It's a time when you say, 'Okay, I raised a good kid that can now make their own choices and successfully survive as an adult and go out and live life to the fullest.' As parents our job is done, in a sense. Then you sit back, watch them succeed and wait to be grandparents someday."

Watching your children leave the nest, however, isn't always easy. She says of her son Dylan that she's "extremely proud of him in every way," but at the same time views his upcoming college graduation with "excitement and fear, but in a good way."

With special needs children, it's not that simple. "I always get overwhelmed with the thought of *later*... in life, I mean. Most parents retire, live on their retirement and social security, and get some freedom back. They get to enjoy the rest of their life and happily become a 'couple' again. When you have a special needs child who cannot live or survive on their own, or can't work a full-time job to support themselves, you don't get that."

As time goes on, Patty says, "The stress and worry gets stronger. It's a constant in my head every day, every moment." When she makes retirement plans, she has to provide funding for her daughters' care well into their retirement, too.

"It's not excitement, just fear. Fear of the unknown. You can't live on the hope that everything is going to be okay. It's more like I live on the panic of how am I going to make it okay for them. Life is full of the unexpected – it's the unknown that's the scary part."

When asked how she manages to cope with her own anxiety, she sighs and says with a coy lilt, "Pinot grigio?" She then laughs, quickly suggesting another option. "Lots of coffee?" All joking aside, she admits that coping is just something she has learned to do over time.

"It took me a long time to live in the moment. I don't know what's going to happen tomorrow or ten days from now. But that's really hard for me. I really need to know."

One of the ways she finds relief is in having trusted friends to confide in. She recommends other parents of special needs kids find the same.

"I think it helps to have one person to vent to. I wouldn't make it your husband or your wife, or your mom, or family. Pick a best friend, or a friend that you know is going through something. Not the 'perfect' person; not the friend who gets Tiffany jewelry at Christmas. Pick that person that can listen and relate. Find somebody that's not going to judge.

"I want that person I can call at 10 o'clock in the morning and just rant about everything that sucks. And they're just going to laugh on the other end. 'Okay, I'll call you later...'" she jokes.

After I asked about her personal goals, she lets out a quick, but heavy sigh. "I don't know," she says. "To live on a beach and drink something tropical."

Her next answer was more serious. "Peace. Just to have a moment of peace. My future is hopefully happy. If they're happy, I'm happy. To have a future plan that would give me some peace to get over the anxiousness of the unknown. That would help me. If I could sit back and breathe because it's all planned out and written out. I'm sure that's how other special needs moms feel."

One of her main objectives is to change the way people look at disabilities of all kinds. Over a quarter of a million people in the United States are diagnosed with some type of CP. Each of those individuals has their own unique daily challenges. She would like people to show respect for these challenges in even the smallest ways. This includes refraining from staring or taking handicapped parking spots in crowded shopping centers.

"I will admit that I have gone on a rage in the mall," she says, guiltily slapping the table.

She hopes for "more awareness for all the disabilities, not just CP. Everybody has something. Nobody's perfect. If you meet that perfect person, let me know. I don't like the way people are treated. It drives me crazy."

If she could have foreseen her future 20 years ago, would she feel she was capable of handling the challenge? She answers with a decisive "yes."

"I can honestly tell you from the bottom of my heart, I would've chosen to have them, because they are the sweetest, kindest people. To watch them go through it is what's hurtful." She adds that they've taught her to become a nicer person, "like them."

When asked if she's able to see the good in herself, she humbly responds, "I guess."

Patty would never get too touchy-feely about being a loving, devoted mother who would travel to hell and back for her kids, but she is – and she has. The lesson of her story is that no matter how high the obstacle or heavy the weight, with love one can overcome anything.

Greek philosopher Epictetus said, "It's not what happens to you, but how you react to it that matters." We may not be able to choose what happens in our lives, but what defines us is how we choose to live. Patty has chosen to stand and fight for her beautiful daughters. She reminds us that life isn't all "rainbows and sunshine," but if you live to make a difference for the people you love, you'll never regret a thing.

Salvatore

"I'm going to be thankful for everything I have, with every footstep that I take."

Sal's home bears the mark of a woman's touch, even though he lives alone. With a chic sunburst mirror here and a crystal chandelier there, a feminine presence lingers everywhere. He speaks to me from the comfort of his love seat, which is upholstered in a unique book motif. In fact, books peek out from every corner of his home.

Sal is a calm, mellow man with a wise, educated mind. He's tall and lanky, his bright blue eyes gazing from behind rimless glasses. His childhood was spent in the Bensonhurst area of Brooklyn and later Dix Hills, Long Island.

He describes himself as a quiet kid. A bad bout of asthma at age 10 nudged him into introverted hobbies like reading and listening to music. He grew up in a Catholic family but sought more spiritual concepts as he grew older. He enjoyed reading books about Buddhism and classics like *A Course in Miracles* by Marianne Williamson.

"I knew no organized religion was going to work for me. I had a deep-seated unhappiness at the time. I was trying to find my way and become who I am. I was lost and I just started reading different things."

Next came a deeper exploration of music. His college roommate introduced him to a broad new spectrum of artists, including Prince,

Tears for Fears, and other '80s English synth bands.

"I was really absorbing everything. Music is the number one love in my life."

In school, he majored in Economics and History. After graduation he steadily moved up the corporate ladder, eventually landing a job with Goldman Sachs. He ultimately found a career in commodities trading and support, a field he has worked in for the past 20 years.

When he turned 30 he moved to New York City. The Big Apple coaxed him out of his shell and opened him up to new people and experiences. He found a church where he felt truly comfortable. He joined The First Church of Religious Science, also known as the "Science of Mind" church after its founder Ernest Holmes' books of the same title.

"It blew my mind because I was anti-church. I thought it was a meditation center. I sat in the back for a month. I thought, 'It's kind of interesting, and they're not pushing it on people.' And I saw different types of people; I saw gay people and different ethnic groups.

"The church was about changing your consciousness, changing your viewpoint to change your life, and that's how I started on the path. That was a big moment for me. I finally found something."

Then, at age 34, he signed up for tango lessons. Tango was in his blood. "My grandfather danced tango in the '30s," he says. At his grandparents' 50th wedding anniversary, Sal remembers watching a group of seniors gather en masse to tango, and says it did something to him.

"I don't like dancing at all," he says. "I think as a shy person I was looking for ways of expression. Tango to me is not dancing. It's almost like playing twister. You're not jumping up and down like salsa and those other things. You're pivoting and there's all this torsion from your upper lower body. I took a whole gamut of salsa, the hustle, swing – but tango appealed to me because I had started listening to the music.

"The classes were very challenging. It's not spoken of enough how spiritual it is, compared to sensual. Because for 10 minutes, for a three-song set, you get this incredible bond with somebody if you're moving well together. It's like nothing else out there. You're just moving as one. That's why I don't look at it as dancing. I look at it as this beautiful way of connecting, which I was looking for."

In 1998, a particularly stunning woman walked into class. "I remember her dark beautiful eyes that were very expressive. That's what really drew me in. I was sitting with a friend and I saw her walk in, wearing this red dress. I just looked at her eyes and I was taken."

He points me toward some photos of Ket (short for Kethrin) on his mantel. In one she looks strong and passionate, with Sal looking blissfully happy next to her. Another shows her standing outdoors, smiling sweetly with her head cocked to the side. In contrast to Sal's mellow demeanor, Ket's energy practically jumps out at you.

Ket's childhood was one of upheaval. Her family, including eight siblings, escaped war-torn Laos in 1975 toward the end of the Vietnam War. She was only 11 at the time. Moving from her home country to Bridgeport, Connecticut was a "huge adjustment," Sal says, but nothing she couldn't handle. Her family no longer enjoyed an affluent lifestyle, and faced the challenge of learning a new language in a country quite unlike their own. Nevertheless, she was resolute to make a life for herself.

"She really had a drive that even her siblings didn't understand."

Ket graduated from UConn with a Bachelor of Arts Degree in Graphic Design. "She went to New York and was determined to succeed in something," Sal says. After working in the advertising field for a while, she started her own graphic design business in 2001.

Sal believes she was drawn to tango in search of connection, just as he had been. Though her family was kind and loving, the strain of surviving in a new country detracted from the individualized attention she craved. Through tango she found that attention and a whole lot more.

Sal and Ket began dating. They spent blissful evenings dancing the night away. When they weren't dancing, they were going to jazz clubs, the symphony or spending weekends away together.

"We had a two-year period that was just wonderful. We were in New York City, the city everyone would love to live in, and dancing tango till 1 o'clock in the morning. It was a romantic time period, just enjoying everything and having someone to do it with."

Following a six-year courtship, the two married when Sal was 40. They later moved to Stratford, Connecticut. Three years later, Ket started hormone treatments in preparation for having a child via in vitro fertilization. Because she was over 40, she had testing to determine her body's viability for pregnancy. Results concluded she was not capable of bringing a child to term. The news was devastating, but not as devastating as what was to come.

During the testing, doctors discovered a mass in her colon. Ket was diagnosed with colon cancer, the same kind of cancer that had killed her father years earlier. The family history of the disease, Sal speculates, could have been related to exposure to toxins during the war.

She had surgery to have the mass removed. "It was a brutal experience as far as the way they cut her, because she's very tiny. She's like 100 pounds. They basically cut her below her breast down to just above her vagina. So think about a horrible scar, how it feels and how it looks. My wife got cancer six months after she found out she couldn't get pregnant, so it was a double whammy."

Nevertheless, she quickly bounced back after the surgery. Doctors prescribed a round of routine chemotherapy, which Sal says, "really sucked the life out of her." During treatment "the cancer exploded into her ovaries – which I felt was an emotional death of her child bearing ability."

Ket was rushed into surgery to remove her ovary. Once again, she recovered – but with a caveat. She would not take chemotherapy again, no matter what. Sal encouraged her to try alternative therapies, including the Budwig Diet, an anti-cancer diet named after its creator, German biochemist Johanna Budwig.

Her illness initiated a new sense of intimacy for the couple. They shared spiritual readings and vacationed together in San Francisco, Martha's Vineyard and Argentina. After the second surgery, she had a clean scan. Things were looking up.

Sal's friend Becky, a practitioner at the Science of Mind church, had been praying for Ket. Sal told her she didn't need to pray anymore, thinking the worst was over.

"Oddly enough it was right after that that she started getting ill."

Ket's cancer returned with a vengeance. Her other ovary had to be removed. During surgery her ovary ruptured, spraying cancer cells everywhere.

Her doctor relayed the bad news to Sal. "I've seen this before. It's not good. You can't even go in there and clean the cancer cells up." He gave Ket a prognosis of five years to live.

"I basically collapsed and was crying on the floor of the hospital by myself. There was nobody else there."

Her recovery from surgery was excruciating. "I'll never forget her recovering from surgery, lying on a table screaming because of the pain. The whole ordeal really left its mark on me."

The cancer spread to her liver. At the end of a nearly three-year battle, she remained at home under the care of her devoted husband and hospice nurses.

"She could only drink juice out of a straw, no solid food. She was basically forced to starve to death and I had to sit by and watch it."

Ket resisted death. "She wasn't ready to go. She didn't want to leave. She said she wanted to live to 100. No one can imagine her not being here. But, it was written."

One evening in June of 2011, a hospice nurse told Sal that it would be her last night on earth. She lay dying on the very same couch where Sal sat before me.

"On the final night of her passing I told the nurse, 'I don't know why, I feel like reading something out of this book.'"

Sal pulls the book out from a pile on his coffee table. It's called *Change We Must* by a Hawaiian mystic named Nana Veary.

"I found it at the Science of Mind church. The author used to be a Science of Mind practitioner in the '40s. She came from the old Hawaiian culture where her grandfather would talk to the rocks and the trees. You'd ask permission to cut down a tree. You had a connection with nature. Everything was spiritual. I was reading a chapter a night of this book to Ket in her final week.

"I just started reading this one paragraph:

About eight years ago I stopped giving classes in metaphysics and began holding silent retreats. I changed my emphasis from talking to God in prayer to listening to him in silence. In silent retreats, which last several days, you can go deeply into your consciousness. The purpose is to free yourself of anger, guilt, resentment, discouragement, disappointment, worry, all the negative thought patterns buried in the subconscious mind. In silent retreats you clear your channels so life can be fulfilled. Silent retreats give you spiritual dignity.

"As I read those words, the nurse was saying, 'She's going, she's going.' I knew it as I was reading. And these were the *exact words* she needed to hear. She took two or three deep breaths – and then left."

Sal, like a spiritual guide, helped her transition to the other side with a healthy state of mind. The book helped release some of the emotional baggage she carried. "I was so moved because she had a lot of anger, resentment, and guilt inside of her."

Ket passed away at the age of 46.

Sal and Ket's family crafted funeral services that combined Catholic and Buddhist traditions. A cremation funeral service was held, wherein the family accompanies the deceased to the crematorium.

"She had the most beautiful funeral. We did this ceremony where all the women in the family had these beautiful flowers they would put in the casket. Then we had a string that I held around the casket with her oldest brother and her mom. When we cut the string, she was no longer bound to the family. It sets her free.

Salvatore

"It was a beautiful ritual. Then 100 days after her death we had a party to celebrate her life and another offering we made. That meant a lot to me. I understand the value of religion for those events."

Sal's parents stayed with him for about two weeks after his wife's death, providing much needed comfort and distraction. But after they left, he descended into a deep and unrelenting phase of grief.

"When I was finally alone, it was horrible. It was the most

unimaginable pain. You just let everything go, let it all out. It was devastating. I spent that year really grieving hard. I forced myself to face it, head on. There's no turning away from it. I cried, collapsed on the floor at times."

Sal tried an array of methods to conquer his grief.

A month after Ket passed, he joined a bereavement group. "That was really helpful to me." Most of the predominantly female group had also lost someone to cancer. Sal was the youngest member.

In a way, Ket was part of the group, too. Sal says, "I saw this woman who was consumed by anger and refused to cry – and I remember I said [in my mind], 'Ket, put your arms around her, help her cry.' And she started crying."

It was a place where he could be himself without any pressure or judgment.

"Family moves on – you don't. It's the only place, when the rest of your family doesn't understand, you can let it out."

He also saw a therapist, had acupuncture treatments, and tried Reiki and journaling. "I was just interested in whatever I could do to move through it."

One day while organizing a bookshelf in the living room, he found something he never knew existed.

"For whatever reason, I decided to go clean the top of the bookcase and this thing came down. I looked at it and saw it was a diary. I saw what was in it and I said, 'Oh my God.' It was my wife's cancer diary. She wrote it in the last year and a half of her life. I didn't know about it till I discovered it.

"I had told her, why don't you write to help deal with it? And she goes, 'I am writing, I am.' You can even see in her writing at the end that she barely had the strength. I don't know how she had the strength to write." Finding the diary had a profound effect on him. "It just really messed me up."

Sal's friend Becky from church, the one who had been praying for Ket while she was alive, had often spoke of a medium who had connected her to her late husband.

"I was even trying to get Ket to go to the medium when she was alive." She eventually *did* see the medium, but from "the other side."

"It's easy to be skeptical. I didn't talk for the first 30 minutes – I wanted to see what she had to say."

"There's somebody here," said the medium. "She's been waiting for you about 10 minutes before you got here. Her name is like a c-word, or a k-word, right? Like Cat?"

Ket wanted Sal to know she was fine. "The first thing was to assure me that she's okay and she wants me to be okay. Her personality came through. She was thanking the woman endlessly. She said things like, 'You did not want to be on my bad side.' And I'm like, 'Wow, that's definitely someone she was.' And she kept asking for forgiveness."

She apologized to Sal for her behavior toward the end of her life, saying, "I was mean to you at the end. I was always mean to you."

Sal is convinced of the medium's authenticity. "I made contact with my wife. No doubt about it," he says.

The medium told Sal something that vastly comforted him.

"The reason that we met is I gave her this unconditional love. That kind of helped me really start to heal. Once I heard those words, it made sense. I felt like she was there with me."

Through the medium, she also said, "It's so easy to connect with you through certain songs." Sal said he'd often hear a song during times he was really hurting that expressed exactly what he needed to hear.

He asked about the diary.

"I found your diary and I don't know what to do with it. I don't know whether I should burn it or show it to your family."

The response was, "I think you should turn it into a book."

He then spoke with the medium about Ket's final moments.

The medium told him, "When you spoke those words, you gave her unconditional love. You gave her something that was the whole purpose of her life."

"That validated the whole medium experience for me, helped me move forward, and I needed to because I was in such a bad state."

Sal shared the encounter with his bereavement group, which prompted others to visit her as well.

"When they came back, they went from constantly crying in the meetings to sort of having this inner glow. They just had this change in them."

Then he reconnected with another former love: tango.

"It was a perfect way to deal with grief because you get the connection with your partner. I hadn't danced since we met. When I was kind of numb from grief, I needed that to get me out."

A year to the day after Ket died, Sal lost his job.

"I was really in a tough place. I was depressed. I lost the best job I ever had. I lost the best woman. I was just sleeping. I couldn't do anything. I didn't have any motivation."

He decided to fly to Sicily, where he joined a tango festival.

"It was in the town that my great grandfather came from. It was a wonderful time. I was lonely, but I met some good people."

When he returned to the states, he met a special new woman named Daniela, but it was still too early to move into a new relationship.

"When I started to go out and date again I wasn't really ready. I felt like I was ready, but I was talking about Ket too much."

He says Daniela is "a very gentle spirit. She had been by my side during that time."

He told Daniela he couldn't see her anymore until he was able to straighten his life out. He was facing possible foreclosure on his home and was still reeling from the past few draining years.

At the end of 2012, 18 months after Ket's death, Sal slogged through his second Christmas alone, feeling desperate and confused. In a moment of despair, he asked Ket for help.

"I was in bed and I just kind of screamed out, 'I need your help. I need help with my life, I need to get a job, and then this book… If you really want me to write it, I want a clear sign and I want it now.'"

He laughs as he says, "I never thought I'd get one… just having a moment."

A day or two later he found an envelope in his mailbox from a woman named Gladys.

"I opened it up and a picture of Ket fell out from when she was 20 years old or something."

The letter read, "I've been meaning to write this letter to you for several months. I met you at Ket's funeral. I was her best friend in high school. I have all these letters your wife wrote to me when she went to UConn. If you ever want to talk, if you ever want to see the letters, give me a call."

"That really blew me away. That was the sign I asked for." He immediately called Gladys.

"We started meeting every couple of weeks and I started writing the book. I read all the letters from her college years." Sal didn't meet Ket till she was in her 30s, so by reading her college letters and speaking to Gladys he was able to see an entirely different side to his wife.

"I put some of the letters in the book, so it's this messy mix of a diary, a memoir, college letters, and me having discussions with Gladys. This woman really was the catalyst for me finishing the book. It would not have been written without her." He is still putting the book together, with the hopes of getting it published in the near future.

Each of these events was a steppingstone in his recovery. He slowly, but surely, was becoming fed up with his grief and had the strength to move forward.

"I reached a point where I knew what I had to do. You know how you have something you always want to do but you don't do it, you don't act on it, you don't want to take the work that's necessary? I have spiritual books all over the house."

He said to himself, "You've read every book known to man. You have the tools necessary to get out of this. It's not just going through the motions. You have specific methods that you can use to move out and move on. You know it's just a matter of changing your mindset."

He started an online meditation series that focuses on the concept of gratitude. This initiated a vast expansion in his consciousness.

"I did these meditations in the morning. Every day there was a unique twist on gratitude. I'd be in tears listening to the person talk."

The video meditations posed questions like, "Do you know how lucky you are, just to have clean drinking water? To bathe in clean water? To have a roof over your head?"

"I said, I'm going to do this every day. I'm going to be thankful for everything I have, with every footstep that I take. I started to shift."

Opportunities immediately began manifesting. A friend texted Sal with a perfect job offer – ironically, for a different employer, but in the same building with the same coworkers as his last job.

"Blessings upon blessings have come to me, and I owe it all to this change. I continue to use the habits as much as I can. I wake up and I give thanks every time I take a shower and I give thanks when I get out of bed and try to take that through my morning. Things didn't change just by sitting around being miserable. It didn't change by me being more active looking for work. A lot of those efforts are good intentioned – but it's really what's going on inside that brings it to manifest."

It also helped him reconnect with Daniela.

"I gave her this blown glass in the shape of a heart – partly out of friendship, partly out of, 'Let's try again if you're willing to let me give you all of myself instead of part of myself.' She's been the best thing to happen to me since Ket."

For others who are grieving, Sal says, "You definitely have to face it. There is a tremendous gift in grief that people miss out on. We're here to experience emotions. You need to look at it and embrace it and feel it. You need to feel all of that pain until you don't want to feel it anymore. You reach a point where you don't want to cry anymore. You have to get to that point. That's why I danced tango for a little bit. Then the grief calls you back. It's a see-saw. But that's part of life. I still have moments. I cried last week about something, but it doesn't affect me the way it used to. The best thing you can do is gather with other people who can understand, because you need somebody to talk to."

"When I look back on my marriage, I was so busy living my life. You take things for granted and you don't enjoy the moments with that person."

On special anniversary dates he will drop a single red rose into the ocean, or sometimes just display the flower in his home for a couple of days. It's something he learned from Ket, who did the same after her father passed away.

"That was a thing I saw her do. I think those rituals are something that your soul needs."

He recommends opening up to communication from loved ones who have passed. "When you're driving you could see a truck with some writing on the back of it and it's a message for you. It could be a commercial you see when you're changing channels. People are reaching out to us all the time – or maybe it's our spirit guide just trying to say: pay attention. You're never alone. I think there's a perception we're always alone and disconnected – we're *always* connected.

"I think a lot of us are trying so hard to find peace and contentment and to have what everybody else has – but it's in our relationships. That's the reason why we are here. I have the skills necessary to do my work well, but that has nothing to do with why I'm here. For me I find relationships, love, the way I process reading and music – I think it's all connected."

He believes he and Ket made a karmic pact before they were born.

"We had this short time together and I think there was something I needed to learn and understand and it was something she needed as well – and we gave it to each other. I'm not the same person that I was. Her experience with cancer has taught me a lot. I can deal with a lot of things much more easily now."

As for his new job and relationship with Daniela, he is excited about where both are headed.

"What I've discovered is love kind of takes you by surprise. The feelings grew over time until I was ready to have my presence with her. I'm thrilled about the future. I'm working in a place I'm so grateful to be working for. I absolutely love it there. I'm really grateful and happy."

Sal's story is powerful proof of the soul's ability to heal. He shows us that we can find gifts in grief and wealth in a glass of water. His experiences can teach us that we are never alone, for we are always surrounded by love. Most importantly, he reminds us that the key to happiness is in gratitude for all that we have.

Christina

"Take a deep breath. Breathe. Focus. Listen to your heart."

I met with Christina at her early 20th century home in New Haven County. She and her former husband renovated the structure to a breathtaking finish, which features beautiful wood flooring, stone accent walls and cathedral ceilings. Two large paintings of nudes hang on opposite walls in the living room. In each, a pale body starkly contrasts a dark background. One is accented by whirls of red, the other, blue.

We stepped outside in order to appease her puppy Rosie, a tan pit bull-whippet mix. Christina has been working on easing Rosie's separation anxiety. Plied with treats, sticks and a generous length of run, Rosie was kept distracted and happy enough for us to talk a while on a bench a few feet away.

"You do carry me through," she tells Rosie. "She really does. Animals, I believe, are so therapeutic. And I saved her life."

Christina has a slim figure, short curly brown hair, and enchanting light green eyes. Today she is dressed in a blue and white polka-dot jumpsuit, red beaded earrings and red leather thong sandals. Her voice is high in tone and often takes flight in a singsong cascade at the end of a sentence.

She talks a little about her parents' separation when she was six, and their eventual divorce. The situation was confusing for her.

"I didn't understand. No one explained divorce to me. It was that era. It was a time when divorce was shunned upon."

Her parents' relationship problems triggered problems for her in school.

"Because of my parents' conflict, I suffered and had to repeat a grade. I had language problems in second grade. I was put in a special remedial class. I also had to go to a reading specialist."

This caused her great anxiety. "I felt really bad because I had to be separated from my colleagues. I remember having severe trouble with it."

When she was eight, she, her mother and younger sister moved in with her grandparents. Christina started going to therapy because she was "acting out." She was temporarily prescribed tranquilizers, but after vehemently protesting she was allowed to stop taking them.

Her mother prioritized education above all. "She always pushed me to succeed in school; that really saved me. She enrolled me in St. Thomas's Day School in New Haven." The school is an Episcopal day school with a rigorous curriculum. "I excelled in French," she says, noting she won the French Award. "Then I went to Hamden Hall. I had to take entrance exams. I was so terrified about taking tests."

Despite her progress and accomplishments, she continued to have issues with language.

"I still was recognized as having weak English language skills. I had to take Latin and German, because they were both related to English, and I did really well. Then in 9th grade I had to choose a foreign language to study for the next three years, and I chose German because I excelled. I was an A student."

Her aptitude for the language gave her the opportunity to become an exchange student in Germany for her senior year. After high school she pursued a degree in German Literature at Bard College, located in Annandale-on-Hudson, New York.

"I loved studying languages and it came easily to me. It was a creative outlet, in a way. So I just pursued it."

Christina has an innate attraction to the dark and mysterious side of life. For her senior project she translated poems by Ingeborg Bachmann, who was a bit like Austria's version of America's Sylvia Plath. She felt a strong connection to Bachmann's work.

"She was a very depressed individual. She was addicted to

barbiturates and fell asleep while smoking in bed. She died from her burns at a very young age. I really connected with that, with the darkness. My advisor in college said, 'I don't understand why you'd want to translate her. This is so bleak.' And I was like, 'I dunno, I *love* it!'" she says excitedly.

Among her other favorite writers were Paul Celan, Heinrich Heine and Franz Kafka. She pronounces their names with a sugary lilt, melting any stereotype that German is a harsh language.

Translation of foreign poetry presents a unique set of challenges. "It's a very tricky thing about translation, because there are subtleties, idiosyncrasies, idioms that are different, and the best you can do is to get the literal meaning as well as the subtleties. With poetry it has a rhythm or rhyme and it's hard to incorporate it all."

Apart from teaching, language majors often have a limited range of career options.

"I imagined translating German literature, creative writing, poetry. I thought that was what I wanted to do. That's a weird, really small, strange niche. They didn't really prepare me for the working environment, like how to sell yourself or integrate yourself into the working world. There wasn't really a call for translators of German literature," she says, laughing. "Maybe the best I could do was work for the U.N., but that wasn't me. I'm more of a creative person."

She was a work-study student at Bard while living in Red Hook, New York. Most of her jobs were in child care. When she graduated in 1992, she was still "stuck in Red Hook. It's very rural. In the boondocks."

An old friend invited her to live with him in the Boston area. It was a perfect area for her, combining the charm of New England with the excitement of urban life.

She worked the odd job here and there, including temporary jobs in stuffy offices with harsh fluorescent lighting. But, they weren't jobs where a free, imaginative spirit could flourish.

By the time she was 26, she met the man she would later marry. From the way Christina describes him, the two are like night and day. Though they shared some interests, like appreciating fast sports cars, he was more of a business-oriented type while she was more creative. With degrees in law and business management, his budding career kept him on the road. This left Christina with a lot of time by herself.

While he was temporarily living in Maryland – they were only dating at this point – he asked her to move in with him, but she declined. After that, a black cloud moved into her life. Her world began to darken and grow quiet.

"I just had a difficult time all of a sudden when he was gone. He was working out of state and the reality of my situation was: 'I have these student loans. What am I doing in my life? What kind of career? How can I build anything? What am I doing? What can I do?' I studied German for all of these years, thinking I could use it as a skill for a career and it's not happening. I didn't know how to make it happen and I felt like everything was falling in on me. I was being buried and I didn't know what to do. One day felt like I couldn't even express myself. I couldn't even speak."

Her tumultuous relationship with language was now failing her in a very basic way. She had literally lost the ability to talk.

"I found myself not even able to put sentences together. It wasn't until years later that I learned the word aphasic, but that's what happened to me. Something was really wrong. When people would call I couldn't really speak."

"Aphasia" is a term used to describe the inability to communicate, whether it be through understanding or verbalizing, due to a dysfunction in the brain. The word is often associated with brain injury or stroke patients who have lost the ability to talk, but for Christina, the phenomenon occurred in concurrence with depression.

Depression, she says, feels like a "dark hole, going nowhere. It's a tunnel, a totally dark tunnel. It's not like you think, 'oh, there might be a light.' Or you just don't know what to expect. You don't know. It's like you're sinking into something that you're not familiar with. It's very scary."

The culmination of a difficult childhood, a sense of aimlessness, a genetic predisposition to depression, and mounting debt triggered these feelings of insurmountable despair.

"I had never experienced it like that before. I was always sort of a dark type of person. Pessimistic. But all of a sudden I was paralyzed. That's what it was, with the language: paralysis of speech. I was just so scared. I was afraid of myself and the world and I guess my body just sort of shut down. It really frightened me because I studied languages before and I've been writing poetry since I was a teenager and I could not express myself. So I was like, I have to do something. Even though I was reluctant to take drugs, I was desperate."

In 1995, at 28 years old, she left Boston and went back home to live with her mother. There, she could figure out what she was doing with her life. She enrolled in a study on depression with the Veteran's Affairs (VA) Hospital in West Haven.

For six months, Christina visited the VA Hospital every week to have her vital signs checked and receive a dose of medication. At first, she didn't know whether or not the pill was a placebo. Staff asked her a litany of questions about how she was feeling. The pill, as it turned out – was Prozac. She says it helped her feel only "slightly better."

Then she started seeing a new therapist, whom she has been seeing for the past 19 years.

Most importantly, however, was her new career endeavor.

Back at Bard College, Christina remembered seeing postings for artist's models. These gigs paid double what other work-study jobs offered. As a self-proclaimed "wallflower," she shied away from these opportunities.

"I felt self-conscious and insecure doing that in front of my peers," she says.

But now, wanting to pay down her debt and also make a contribution to her mother's household, she thought, *You know what? Maybe I could do that. That's something where I don't have to interact with people and I don't have to speak.*

She applied at Paier College of Art, her father's alma mater, and was accepted.

"I began a career, basically. I'm very creative, so I relate to artists. It's not a vain thing. I just felt like I wanted to do something, I wanted to earn money and not have to interact with people in an oral way. The model coordinator for Paier is a wonderful man. I'm still friends with him today. He got me lots of jobs. I got connections all around the state. So I worked for Yale, Lyme Art Association, Lyme Academy College of Fine Arts, and various art associations around the state. Then I branched off to private people that I met through those groups. I did it for years."

She posed for painters, photographers, and even sculptors. Her work was generally done in the nude, but not always. She recalls her first class.

"I felt like – oh my God, what's it going to be like to disrobe in front of a class? I basically just had to do it. It was October or November, and was kind of chilly in the cement room. There's no way to do it, but just to do it. So I went behind a screen, took off my clothes, walked out onto the platform and asked them what they wanted me to do. They may have told me, 'We want you to have a contrapposto pose,' or something." Contrapposto is a type of standing pose.

She instantly fell in love with her new career, and word of her talent spread quickly. She scored more and more gigs and achieved real success in the classical art community. She was well liked not only for her ability, but her reliability.

"People liked that I was very focused. I guess a lot of artist's models are unreliable and don't show up. I was always on time and focused and willing to do what people wanted."

As she speaks about these experiences, her demeanor changes. She becomes more intense, confident and enthusiastic.

"It's a collaborative process. I was a muse to these people and I felt like I was really contributing. I was part of the work. It was very exhilarating to be part of this creative, beautiful process. I didn't care what the thing looked like. It was just like, 'What do you want me to do?'"

To better explain the process, she reads a piece she composed for a writing workshop. She pulls out a notebook filled with her swirly scrawl. The entry describes how a session will start with a "quick pose," lasting one, five or seven minutes. That's seven minutes of sitting, standing, or reclining, utterly motionless. It may sound easy, but it isn't.

She writes, "For longer ten to twenty minutes poses, a kitchen timer is required. I bring my own, which I've painted with golden paint." The shorter poses help both her and the artist to warm up.

After the sequence of ten to fifteen practice poses is complete, she descends into the final pose. She will remain in that pose for two to three hours, with breaks. She poses on a platform, "under carefully positioned spotlights with tensed muscles and a firm, but relaxed gaze."

Modeling worked as sort of a practical meditation. It helped lift her out of the dark hole she was living in. She became part of something larger, something more productive, and something positive.

"I got to focus on something that was creative, and it got me outside of myself. I was thinking more about these people. It gave me a purpose."

"Fire" by Judith Reeve

Christina says while she can intimately relate to artistic minds, she herself is not skilled at creating visual art.

"I'm a very literate type of person, but I don't have a good connection between my mind and my hands. I can't draw, paint, or sculpt. But I've worked for those types of artists, because I appreciate it. I think that comes from my dad." Her father is a glassblower.

"It was thrilling and fulfilling to be part of that process. I did it as long as I could physically do it." Her modeling career lasted eight years, until she was 35.

The aforementioned nude paintings in her living room were modeled by Christina herself. The two are part of a series by artist Judith Reeve based on the four elements: earth, air, water and fire. She shows me "Fire," which depicts her kneeling, partially enveloped by a thick band of scarlet.

A smaller portrait leans against the fireplace, one of her favorites. It was painted by a different artist, who lives just down the road. It portrays Christina wearing a kimono, holding a mug of coffee and reading the newspaper, her face serious and determined.

She most closely identifies with the water-inspired painting entitled "Maelstrom". The word maelstrom represents either a powerful whirlpool or, more figuratively, "a situation in which there are a lot of confused activities and emotions."

The word makes a second appearance in some of her writings from the late 1990s, when she collaborated with fellow artists in a literary magazine named *Azimuth*. Azimuth is a navigational term used to describe a point in relation to true north, or 0° Azimuth. She uses the word to explain how she was able to return to an identical position day after day, sometimes for months, using azimuths.

"You take a point of reference. So when I posed, I would be looking in a certain direction. My head had to be tilted this way and I'd be looking at that point and see this from that eye and this from that eye." She explains the process by extending a straight arm reminiscent of yoga's warrior pose.

"They would tape me, too. It was always a rigorous thing to get in that exact position again."

She worked for three hours at a time, with periodic breaks. Larger pieces would take months to complete. "That's why the azimuths are so important."

The *Azimuth* magazine included lithograph sketches of Christina posed in ethereal postures. The journal also includes some of her poetry. A verse in her poem, "Punkte" (German for "points"), reads:

> *Help me understand*
> *this emotional Maelstrom*
> *that plagues me now!*

Another poem from *Azimuth*, entitled "Pecadillo" (Spanish for "a small sin"), alludes to her turbulent emotions:

> *Sight of an everpresent tower was obscured by*
> *The sedating movement of cool air.*
> *I protrude.*
> *Am I dying or just waking to life?*
> *Somebody help me decide!*

While her work as an artist's model helped her emerge from a deep chasm of darkness, it would not be her last foray into the shadows.

Sixteen years ago, she tried to commit suicide. Her husband was away traveling at the time.

"I had a BMW Z-3, a little sports car. It was parked in the garage. I just went down there and put a tape in the deck and I was playing it, listening to music, and thought that was it. I sat in the car, running, for I don't know how long. For hours."

Fortunately, the attempt didn't take. "It didn't work. The garage was leaky and the car was too efficient. So I woke up, you know? And I'm like, 'Sh—.'"

After realizing her suicide attempt was unsuccessful, she simply went on with life. That meant heading out to a modeling job later in the day.

"I had a date to work, a gig to do. I was hoping I would just die and not show up. I was like, I'm awake, I'm alive, and I'm not brain dead. I survived. I had to go. So I drove to Oxford where I had my job and I just did it. I just proceeded with the day."

After getting a second chance at life, she resolved to keep living. "I have to be here for whatever reason and I can't do it – I can't take my life."

Suicide is now the 10th leading cause of death in America, with the highest rates occurring in adults aged 45-64 and 85 and older. Men are four times more likely to die by suicide, but females attempt suicide three times as often as males. For Christina, the key is in knowing there are ways to reach out for support. There are options.

"The bleakest thing is to think that you are alone, but you're not."

These days, things like meditation, yoga, exercise, and helping others have enabled her to stay centered. One of her main focuses now is her dog Rosie.

"For many years, even before my depression set in, it was recommended to me to relieve stress by going for walks, at least 30 minutes a day. That's when I began the habit of walking. I did it throughout the depths of my depression. When my husband left I got a dog so I would have a companion to walk with."

Rosie gives her a sense of responsibility, purpose and connection to other people. "It's put me in touch with people, like at the dog park, with other dog people, and it's broadened my social sphere in a certain way that's unexpected."

Interacting with others can be a source of stress, but with Rosie it's far more manageable. "I'm happy to socialize while with a dog. They bring you out. It's just another dimension."

She offers simple, but sensible advice to others prone to depression.

"First of all, breathe. When people reach out to their friends, it's always in a state of panic. One of the first things I say is, take a deep breath. Breathe. Focus. Listen to your heart. Don't feel you have to do what society tells you to do. If you have a passion, pursue it. For me, I never really thought of myself as a creative writer. But if I apply myself and send positive energy toward that endeavor, I can create something. Get in touch with the community. Whether it's a faith-based thing or creative, or if it's a volunteer type of thing, be in touch with people. Really, it's people. Or animals," she says with a laugh.

"You're here, we're here, and it's manageable. It's not ever going to be perfect or idealistic necessarily. But you can strive for something. I was a very, very shy person." She speaks of her involvement in her ex-husband's business activities. "I had to force myself to do these corporate things – really uncomfortable, really not me at all. But it did teach me to interact socially and be professional. But these things, they're lessons.

"What I've learned is to go on. Don't give up. There is a solution. There's always something. It might not be a complete solution, but there are alternatives. There's always a different perspective. Even if you don't see a light at the end of that dark tunnel, there's something else. Another little trick, toy, *something* that can spark curiosity that you want to check out. Something to go on."

As for her faith, Christina believes in God, but she doesn't adhere to any specific dogma. "I consider myself a Christian. And I pray. I pray a lot. I've also been doing some Buddhist meditation recently."

She strives to make life easier for others. "Every individual can contribute something, whatever it might be." She does things like help a hearing impaired neighbor go grocery shopping, or she visit a mentally ill friend in a psychiatric hospital.

One of her current challenges is being there for her father, whose health is rapidly declining. "That's a big thing for me, being able to be here for that. Not that it's pleasant, but I have to be here."

As for creative pursuits, these days she's writing. For the past seven or eight years she's been part of a New Haven writing group that inspired her to hone the craft. Her next goal is to write a memoir, currently under the working title, "Azimuths of an Artist's Model".

Before I leave, she serves me homemade iced tea made from the flowers of her proliferous hibiscus plant combined with the buds of dried nettle. After that, she plucks the blossoms from a nearby spirea bush and gives them to me because they match my outfit. She walks me to my car, where we chat for a little while about random things like chewing tobacco, meditation, and the recent death of Robin Williams. ("It's hard to even believe, it's almost sickening," she says of his suicide.) All the while, Rosie lets out several barks to remind us that she has been inside and alone for at least five minutes. Christina dutifully excuses herself.

During our talk, she stressed that her work as a model was not "fueled by any vain motivation." She proves this point when she asks that I photograph her paintings instead of snapping a shot of her that day.

"I don't really feel photogenic," she admits. Though I'd prefer to capture her in "real time," her idea does make sense. A portrayal of Christina in paint is more appropriate because it's here that she becomes most confident and alive.

While words may have betrayed her in the past, she is now an articulate and expressive woman. Her affinity for the term "azimuth" is an important one. Within the word is a valuable principle: always be aware of your focus. During her depression, her main focus was on darkness. To escape the darkness, she changed her focus.

For better or worse, our focus, passions and priorities, define us. Spanish philosopher Jose Ortega y Gasset said, "Tell me what you pay attention to and I will tell you who you are." Re-establishing a connection with a particular azimuth, or finding a new one, can turn a life around – or even save it.

Stan

"Above all, maintain a sense of humor."

Note: Some of the material in this chapter may not be suitable for sensitive readers.

S tan was 21 at the time. He wasn't in any danger. He wasn't ill. He had no financial strain, relationship problem or other crisis looming. Nothing in his life was in jeopardy – except perhaps his innocence.

Stan and I talked about his experiences at the Bethel Public Library. He hands me a paper bag containing two heavy round objects, saying, "That's for you."

I feel the bottom of the bag, trying to guess its contents. Knowing the topic we were set to discuss, I fear it is some kind of spooky souvenir related to the subject.

"It's garlic," he clarifies, as I sigh with relief.

Stan is tall, standing over six feet in height, with a mustache, broad shoulders and piercing blue eyes. Today he's wearing a royal blue t-shirt tucked into his jeans. He's an affable guy who laughs easily and often, but at the same time he does not suffer fools gladly.

He was born to German parents in Javorník, a small town in the Czech Republic (then called Czechoslovakia), close the Polish border.

He affectionately refers to his homeland as "the old country." His father was a game warden and his mother a crane operator. He lived with his parents, grandmother and two brothers in a happy, hard-working household. To Stan, the cycle of life was a natural thing.

"We slaughtered a pig every fall and had a lot of turkeys and chickens. We would have chicken once a week and one of us would go out there and behead the chicken. It was part of the farming life," he says.

Stan grew up in a devout Catholic family. He attended Mass every Sunday and was an altar boy along with his older brother Heinz, often serving at funerals and weddings.

His migration to the United States developed through a fascinating cluster of events. After World War II, Stan's paternal grandfather became entangled in a forced labor camp along the African shoreline.

"He decided to escape. He ended up being a stowaway on a ship, not knowing where he was bound. He ended up in New York. Once he came to New York, he was processed and got himself a working visa and stayed here for many, many years. In '67 my father reconnected with him."

His grandfather obtained a visitor's visa for Stan's father, who then came to the United States for a couple of years before the rest of his family joined him. His father found a job in Ridgefield as a caretaker for the estate of a prominent industrialist, who later built Stan's family a home and sponsored their immigration.

The kids' transition to the U.S. was difficult. "We were pulled away from a normal childhood. We had to abandon all of our friends and the rest of the family. I haven't seen my cousins since 1969." With the exception of one trip in 1999, Stan has not been back to Javorník in 45 years.

The boys struggled in the new land. Their biggest challenge was learning a new language. They already knew German, Czech and Russian, but they now had to learn English, which Stan refers to as a "disaster of a language." He cites the usual complaints about dual meanings and words that aren't spelled the way they sound.

To be clear, he has no trace of an accent whatsoever. But at the time of their arrival when Stan was 12 years old, he and his brothers knew only a few key phrases like "thank you" and "you're welcome."

"I was lucky because I got piggybacked with a German-speaking student in Ridgefield and we became very close friends. We managed to stumble through it."

Shortly after arriving in the United States, his mother was diagnosed with ovarian cancer. For nearly three years, Stan's father tended to his wife's health with the utmost of devotion. He shuttled her back and forth to Danbury and Yale New Haven Hospitals for doctors' trips and cancer treatments. At home, he was her nurse.

"They would actually give him a box of glass ampoules with morphine in them and he would inject her. There was no IV – he actually injected her."

His mother had two last wishes. The first one was to see Niagara Falls.

"My father knew she only had a little bit of time left, so he converted the family station wagon into an ambulance. He hung curtains in the back, folded the seats down, put a mattress in the back, and he drove her to Buffalo to view Niagara Falls." Thanks to his father's kind heart, one of her last wishes was fulfilled and she was able to see the falls.

Her second goal was to live to see her 41st birthday, which she did. Shortly thereafter she passed away when Stan was only 14.

His mother's death was difficult for the whole family, but it hit his father particularly hard. "It left a void in our life, but it destroyed him." Stan's father died in 1983 at only 50 years old, never having properly recuperated from his wife's death.

After he and his brothers finished school, all three worked in civil service positions. Stan's younger brother Peter served in the Navy and Heinz was a police officer for almost 30 years. Stan loved airplanes, so he gravitated toward the Air Force.

"I knew Basic Training was in Texas, and to me Texas was always farm country and beautiful farmer's daughters." At age 18, he and his best friend from high school signed up for the Air Force, not knowing that once enlisted he would feel like "a caged animal."

"Once you sign up, they put you on an airplane, they fly you out there and before you know it, you're on a bus and they bring you to a base at 2 o'clock in the morning. They shave your head and give you some clothes, and for the next three months you're just beat up. I didn't see any farmer's daughters," he jokes.

He had wanted to become a pilot, but a problem with his eyes prevented them from being corrected to 20/20 vision – a non-negotiable requirement of the Air Force. Instead, he chose the next best option and became an aircraft mechanic.

After Basic Training he was stationed at Dover Air Force Base with the 436th Military Airlift Wing from 1976 to 1979.

"I started on the B-52 bomber, went to a C-130, C-140, and a C-5 Galaxy, which is one of the biggest transports in the world."

He shows me a photo of himself with about twenty other young men with whom he attended Aircraft Training School. He is blonde and baby-faced.

Two years into his military career, terror was brewing 2,500 miles away, as the crow flies. Cult leader Jim Jones and nearly 1,000 of his followers had created a new settlement called "the Peoples Temple," also known as Jonestown, in the jungles of Guyana, South America. Jones' followers emigrated to the remote land with the hope of living in a multi-cultural utopia under the guidance of what they believed was a compassionate leader.

California Senator Leo Ryan, a plucky, fearless man, flew to Jonestown in search of answers on behalf of his constituency, as many of Jonestown's residents were California natives. Along with his aide, other government officials, concerned relatives and a few journalists, Ryan embarked on a courageous fact-finding rescue mission.

Ryan's visit put added strain on what was an already tense situation. Jonestown was beyond capacity, and its residents lacked sufficient food and water. His followers toiled tirelessly on Jonestown's farms, and were deprived of sleep – allowing them to be easily controlled.

A drug-addled Jones was becoming apprehensive and paranoid. Ryan's interviews with defecting Temple members and Jones himself proved that the situation was dire.

In the early evening of November 17, 1978, Ryan, along with 14 Jonestown escapees, was set to flee. While waiting on the airstrip to depart, Temple devotees opened fire on the group, killing Ryan, three journalists, one defecting Temple member and wounding nine others.

The next day Jim Jones delivered a final speech to hundreds of devout followers. In a 44-minute long rambling diatribe, Jones declares his plan for "revolutionary suicide," glorifying death as a sacrifice for the greater good.

Vats of purple Flavor Aid (a drink similar to Kool Aid) poisoned with cyanide, Valium and sedatives were prepared prior to his speech. The toxic brew was first given to the babies, trickled into their mouths with a syringe. Toddlers and older children received the poison next, dispensed directly by their parents. Finally, the adults drank their portion, and in only a short time, the community of Jonestown was gone in one horrific mass suicide.

Jones didn't "drink the Kool Aid" himself. Rather, he was found dead from a gunshot wound to the temple. Some debate remains as to whether the shot was self-inflicted, performed as a favor, or an act of revenge. Most of the evidence points to suicide.

Meanwhile, nearby at Temple Headquarters in Guyana's capital of Georgetown, disciple Sharon Amos and her three children, Leanne, 21, Christa, 11, and Martin, 10, found out what had happened in Jonestown.

Sharon wanted to join her peers and bring her children with her. She began by cutting the throats of her two youngest. Her oldest daughter Leanne is believed to have done the same to her mother before turning the knife on herself.

Over 900 people perished that day. It was America's greatest loss of civilian life in a non-natural event until the terror attacks of September 11, 2001.

Home to the largest military mortuary in the country, Dover Air Force Base was chosen to receive and process the bodies. By the time the deceased were moved from Jonestown, they had languished in the hot Guyana sun for three days.

Stan remembers his superiors explaining what had transpired during the morning roll call. They asked for volunteers to help transport and identify the bodies.

"Not too many volunteers, if any, stepped forward during their first attempt," he says. "On day two they were more insistent."

"We really need help here," they said. "You guys gotta step up." Air Force personnel could not issue an order forcing reluctant recruits to assist because they knew the task was so gruesome that many would not be able to handle it.

After their second request, Stan volunteered.

He didn't expect the detail to be a big deal. After years of living on a farm, he was no stranger to death.

"My thought was – I'll go back to my childhood – I was an altar boy, so I've seen a lot of dead folks as a young kid. I was the son of a game warden, so I've been helping my father gut deer, wild boar, elk and all that. I was there, you know, sweeping guts out of the deer. I'm thinking, if I could've done that when I was 12, I could do this when I was 21."

The next day they still needed more volunteers. "On day three they became a little more insistent. Ultimately we got a crowd," says Stan.

Stan

Volunteers were given an aptitude test that required viewing the body of a deceased airman, displayed unclothed and badly wounded.

"There was a crashed airman, a captain, who came down in an F-4 into the ocean, but he never bailed out. He was displayed on a stainless steel operating table. He was there, just broken terribly, all backwards and bruised up. All kinds of pieces were missing."

Many of his peers had never seen a dead body, but claimed they could handle it based on how many scary movies they'd seen.

"But when you put them in front of it, all of a sudden, whoa –

this is something different. Especially because it's not a regular funeral type body, you know? If you didn't survive that viewing, then you weren't part of the detail."

Viewing the airman's body proved too horrific for some, and many dropped out. Stan and a group of about two dozen volunteers continued on. They had no idea the horror that awaited them.

For the first two days of the detail, Stan's job was simply to carry the bodies off of the aircraft. The crew was first trained on how to respectfully carry the bodies, particularly because they were being filmed by news agencies on a daily basis.

"For about six hours they taught us how to goose-step with coffins." The formal march was short-lived.

"There were so many of them we asked the cameras to leave because we had to drag them off by the dozen."

After all bodies had been accounted for and brought to a processing facility, he was upgraded to assistant to the FBI.

Next, he helped FBI officials with more intricate processes. This assignment required full surgical gear to prevent exposure to disease.

"My job was to go get a body, drag it out of the truck, put it onto a stainless steel gurney and bring it into the facility. It was a very large room with shower heads, stainless steel tables where you would perform an autopsy, drain the blood out of people, things of that sort."

He would remove the deceased's clothing, shoes, and search their pockets for personal effects. Many were brought in without any ID, so determining the identity of each individual was a mystery, which, in many cases, was never solved. The deceased could certainly not be identified by sight alone.

"The bodies were in the sun for three days, some longer than that. They were heavily bloated. The skin was very, very brittle. The bodies really had no color. You couldn't tell what color or race they were. They were all kind of a purplish color. A lot of them were kids. I think about 30% of them were kids from toddlers to the age of 15."

While the mere thought of 900 decomposing bodies may sound gruesome enough, the devil is truly in the details. It is difficult to relay the situation inside of those bags without sounding utterly grotesque. Maggots were everywhere. The bags leaked a gelatinous substance.

Stan's initial reaction to unzipping the first body bag was, "What in the hell kind of a mess is this?"

He helped obtain fingerprints from the bodies, which was difficult due to their partially decomposed state.

"In some cases I would actually have to peel the skin off and print the skin because you couldn't roll it. The fingers shriveled up like if you were swimming for a while. In many cases they would actually just cut the fingers off."

Another aspect of the nauseating process was the odor. "The smell was just – you can't believe the smell. You've probably smelled a dead deer on the side of the road – it's much stronger than that."

He recalls processing the bodies of Sharon Amos and her two youngest children. He remembers their gaping wide neck wounds in an image "that lingers."

"Talk about a desperate scene, huh?" he comments. While the other bodies shared a homogenous, purple hue, Sharon Amos was visibly white. Her children were of mixed race, so their skin was slightly darker. "You could see they were fresh," he says.

Stan helped process another body of significance.

He opened the body bag and emptied the man's pockets just like everyone else who came through. He, too, did not appear purple or bloated like the rest, but "he was definitely a mess. I think he got popped in the head or something. I didn't know who it was.

"The guy had some kind of jacket on and I saw a piece of paper sticking out of the jacket. I left the body there, and I went to the FBI guy. I didn't even read it. I said, 'Listen, I found this piece of paper.' It was all folded up. I don't know if it was in an envelope or not. Ultimately he came back to me and he says, 'You found a very important note.'

"To this day, I believe I found one of the suicide notes, if not *the* suicide note from Jim Jones himself."

The days he spent on this detail, he says, "became like a fog. You do one or two or three or four, and then it's lunchtime. Well, how do you eat?"

He subsisted by submerging himself into a state of denial.

"To me it was firewood. After a while I became numb to it and it didn't bother me. I didn't look at them as people anymore. To me they were objects. They were lifeless objects. Sure, they had families and extended families; a lot of them had their own kids there. But I didn't piece that together. To me it just didn't matter anymore.

"There was a lot of discomfort. A lot of guys quit after two days." Those that stayed bonded while choking down dinner in the chow hall. "We'd sit in this dazed little group and compare notes."

Stan forged on. He considered quitting, but he persisted and completed the task.

In the years that followed, he didn't think much about the event, nor did he talk about it. While stationed at Dover AFB, he drove home every weekend to visit his family in Ridgefield – with the exception of those ten hellish days in 1978. The next time he saw his family, he didn't speak much about it.

"I just described it as a casual event. Beyond that it was nothing spectacular." He went on with his life – though that is not to say it did not affect him.

In 1981 he met his future wife, Mary, whom he describes as a "brilliant" woman. When the two married in 1985, Mary's extended family became his family, too. This helped fill the emptiness after leaving behind so many relatives in Europe.

The couple vacationed in tropical locations like Hawaii, Jamaica, and Antigua, a benefit from Mary being the manager of a travel agency. Later, Mary gave birth to three daughters, including a set of identical twins.

"They're the love of my life," he says.

Nature played a large part in their family life. They often enjoyed activities like apple picking, cutting their own Christmas trees, and hiking.

Stan says he had no problem adjusting from growing up with two brothers to living with three daughters. "I'm incredibly close with them. I think they fill a lot of voids from the past. I always wanted daughters. Maybe that's the way I missed my mother."

Within his household lingered a few small, but significant reminders of his history with Jonestown.

No Kool Aid was allowed in the home. "It makes no sense, but it just ties it to the event." He also refused to watch horror movies or even fictional sitcoms with the family.

"I've seen the scariest movie you're ever going to see. I don't waste my time on violence or scary movies," he says. Instead, he prefers watching comics, especially his favorites Steven Wright and George Carlin.

The most significant change in his life has been his attitude towards religion.

"I'll still go to church on holidays with my wife and kids, but it's a function to me. It's not reality."

Disillusioned by the hell he'd seen, he found it hard to comprehend that a loving God would allow these events to take place, and he doesn't believe in an afterlife of any kind. "Personally, I think there's a dead end, which is okay."

Referring to Jonestown and other tragedies, he says, "If God's allowing this kind of activity to happen on this scale, he must not like too many of us. There were a lot of innocent kids who died. I saw that as a broken promise."

That being said, Stan is not without divine inspiration.

"My church right now is Vermont," he says.

After leaving Dover AFB in 1979, he found a job back home in Ridgefield working as a quality control inspector in the field of aerospace, and then later as an assembly foreman.

"After several years the owner asked me if I could represent the company as a sales engineer or a salesperson. So I took that on and traveled all over the place and have been in that role ever since." His career sent him on business trips to 30 countries and nearly every state in the Union.

When he was in his early 20s and still working as a quality control inspector, his shop foreman became a close friend and personal mentor. The foreman organized a men's hunting trip at his cabin in Rutland, Vermont, which Stan attended. Ever since that trip, he has been addicted to Vermont. Through the years he has continued to regularly visit the cabin for hunting and golfing trips.

The cabin has been a permanent fixture in his life for over 30 years now. He heads there once every two or three weeks during the summer season.

His voice softens like a man in love when he speaks about the site. "It's very remotely set up on a mountain. It has electricity, but no running water – you get it from a beautiful spring up the road. It has a kitchenette and bunk beds, but it's just really remotely set. There's always a nightly bonfire. I'll go up there with a gun, because there's some interesting critters always sneaking around, have a glass of wine, sit out under the stars. You get time to think and reflect."

He shows me photos of the cabin and campsite. The nearby trees surround a lake that is curiously bluer than the clear sky above it.

"It's a very special place."

He says he likes this environment because "it's quietly predictable – unlike society."

Stan adds to this predictability with his own habits. "I get some local foods, like a Vermont goat cheese with some crackers, bring it up to my camp, get my water and get settled in. The next morning I'll go for a hike, go off swimming down at the gorges, and it's very satisfying.

"That's my place of thought, my place of reflection. I come back very refreshed from Vermont. My twin daughters love going up there. They ask about it all the time. They've brought friends up there and it's just nothing but a good time."

As for his wife and eldest daughter, they're inclined to take a pass on using an outhouse. He also notes his wife's skepticism that Stan is as okay about what happened in 1978 as he says he is.

"My wife keeps telling me, 'This really bothers you.' I say no, it doesn't. It never bothers me. It never did."

Yet, as he gets older, he finds himself thinking and talking about the event more often.

"I think I've realized my mortality. When I was younger I was too busy to think about it. When you're younger you tend to be a little more daring, a little more careless, a little less sympathetic or empathetic." Between working and raising three daughters, what he witnessed at Dover Air Force Base had been blocked out by the rigors of daily life – until recently.

"I tend to look at life differently since that day, because it is a fleeting moment. Why cut it short? To me, I've developed a sense of humor to combat some of the ugly stuff. I like to laugh, I like to make people laugh and I think it came from that. The benefit is to appreciate what we have, because it just happens too quickly.

"I look at it as motivation to stay around – but you never know. You'll stroke out, you'll get cancer. Certainly, my mother died early."

He affords me a tiny glimpse of his own personal pain when he mentions a recent death in his life. He casts his eyes downward and fixates on a spot on the table, saying, "My friend just died of cancer. Actually, he was the first friend that I met when we moved here from the old country. He was a neighbor in Ridgefield. Nice guy."

Briskly changing the topic, he says, "So, yeah. My motivation is to stay around, enjoy my family and friends, smile, go to Vermont, sit at a campfire drinking wine and eating goat cheese."

He most appreciates "the simpler things. Nice things. I like to garden. I like sports cars. I like to see the nicer things in life. I don't want to see ugly anymore."

When asked when he's been the happiest, he answers, "Now – because everything has kind of fallen into place." In a few months he celebrates his 30th wedding anniversary. His eldest daughter is now 25 and the twins are 21. His daughters are intelligent, hard-working women who have grown into "superb young ladies. I couldn't be more proud or happy."

The tragedy reminds him of how fortunate he is. "Little moments are that much more positive. You open up the newspaper and you see ISIS is executing 13-year-old kids. You know what? Things are pretty good. It is always sort of a benchmark, a sanity check. Things could be that bad, but they're not. Life is actually good."

Through all the bumps in life, his mantra remains, "Above all, maintain a sense of humor."

It's a tangled journey from the tropics of Guyana to the woodsy outdoors of Vermont. At times it's difficult to reconcile living in a world where both divine and wicked acts occur, but it is a truth nonetheless. The point is to live in spite of it. We share the same soil with those who may wish to destroy us, but we never lose the power to make our own choices and think for ourselves.

Stan chooses not to follow man, but nature. Nature may play on polarities, but in the wild "good and evil" does not exist. There's no certainty why, or how, man has distorted "survival of the fittest" into a nefarious undertaking. Nevertheless, perhaps many more should follow in Stan's muddy footsteps for an occasional journey into the cleansing depths of nature to reconnect with the purity of our souls. Or at the very least, seek pure joy in laughter.

He shows me a certificate given to him in commendation for his help identifying the 900 bodies of Jonestown. For a piece of paper from 1978, it's in pristine condition.

He says, with a sort of humble pride, "I keep it in my safe with my few valuables in life."

Tom

"Helping people is the best thing."

Tom is a collector of many things: records, model cars, ephemera, memories and romances. He and I spoke at his apartment in rural Pawcatuck, Connecticut. His place is brimming with vintage collectibles, all lovingly curated behind glass and wooden shelving. A hummingbird feeder affixed to his window offers a breathtaking view of the tiny creatures just a few feet beyond his living room couch.

This morning he is sporting a black polo shirt embroidered with the words "Books and Things with Tom." His wavy gray hair frames his wide brown eyes and charming smile. He looks about ten years younger than his age, if not twenty. He's notorious for wearing a cowboy hat, though today it is noticeably absent. A self-rolled cigarette habitually hangs between his fingers.

Tom, born of Portuguese descent, says he was a fairly shy kid "right through high school." He missed much of middle school due to health issues, including a bad car accident in seventh grade that left him relatively immobile.

"I was laid up with a cast on my chest down to my ankle. It was very difficult to move around. The principal came over and tutored me on Saturday mornings for an hour or two a day."

His younger brother Greg was in a dangerous car accident also. "My poor mother went through 30, 40 years saying, 'I almost lost my two boys.'"

He describes his father as a "very intelligent man. He would sit at night and read, so he was very skilled at what he did. He was a machinist, first class. He was a hard working man." His pronunciation of the word "hard" reveals his childhood spent close to the Rhode Island border in nearby Mystic.

Tom married for the first time at age 23. The relatively brief relationship lasted nearly four years. Ironically, he met his second wife on his way home from finalizing the divorce from his first.

"I stopped at a restaurant in downtown Mystic and she was working there as a waitress. I met her; she was cute. We laughed and joked. We got married and had my son."

Tom's son Todd was born in 1973. Todd was a happy, sociable, laid-back kid with lots of friends and female admirers.

"He was a great kid. Very outgoing. He was a nice kid at home and basically gave me no problems."

There was one evening though, he recalls, when Todd did give him a problem. Technically, two.

Tom worked in retail sales for many years. He and his second wife had divorced by the time Todd was 14. Todd lived with his father and split weekends between his parents. Tom, a newly single father, would often work until 8 or 9 o'clock at night. One evening he called home to say he'd be a little late.

"Yeah okay, Dad, no problem," his son replied.

When he came home that evening, he peeked into Todd's room to make sure he was okay.

"I opened the bedroom door and he was fast asleep in bed. I closed the door." No sooner than he had turned around, he had the feeling something was awry.

"Something's not right," he thought. "A parent knows when something's not right."

He opened the door and flipped on the light. Three heads poked out from under Todd's blanket.

"Two girls were in bed with him," he says. "All were fully dressed," he clarifies. He quickly corralled the girls and drove them home. One of the girls asked him to shut his car lights off before he pulled up to her house.

Tom

"You're lucky I don't blow the horn!" he barked.

Tom married his third wife, Marcia, when Todd was 15. He and his son continued to enjoy a close, loving relationship. One day, the happy-go-lucky young man had a rare melancholy moment.

It was just before Todd's high school graduation. He and his dad were sitting on the deck when Todd started crying. He said he was worried about where his life was going now that high school was over.

"Dad, I don't know what I'm gonna do. I'm so scared."

"Everybody is," he assured his son. "You'll find a job; everything will be fine."

Tom recollects, "Next thing I know he tells me he enlisted."

In 1991, at the tail end of the Gulf War, Todd enlisted into the army after being inspired by several other friends who had done the same. His army photo sits atop a glass shelf in Tom's apartment. He looks dapper in his military uniform and cap, but his expression is one of terror. Despite his fear, Tom says his son became "a good soldier."

His absence wasn't easy for his father.

"Oh God, it broke my heart. Everything he did broke my heart, damn kid," he says, only half joking.

Todd served for two years at bases in Germany and Louisiana. By 1993 he had moved back home with his father, Marcia, and her two children.

Unfortunately, this was the beginning of what Tom calls "five years of hell."

The first two blows came in April of 1993.

"I got laid off. Three days later, my mother died."

He had no luck finding a new job, so he pursued his dream of opening a record store, utilizing inventory from his extensive private collection.

In December of 1993, his 1,000 square foot store in Gales Ferry was ready to go and things were looking up. He and Marcia toasted to the New Year in January of 1994 with high hopes. Their optimism was short-lived.

In February of 1994, his father was so badly injured in a fall he would never walk again.

In the spring of 1994, Tom filed for bankruptcy.

By late June of 1994, Todd had been dating his girlfriend

Stephanie for a couple of months. He sat his father down in the living room to deliver some big news.

"I really did it this time," Todd said.

Stephanie was pregnant.

Though it was a shock at first, Tom was excited to welcome a new baby into the family.

There was soon another new addition to the family. After Todd's truck died, he went car shopping with his father for a new set of wheels.

At the dealership, a sleek black Mazda caught his son's eye.

"Look at that!" said Todd.

"No. Don't even think about it," his dad responded. "That'll kill you."

"Oh, Dad," Todd whined. At the end of the day, he bought the sports car anyway.

A few weeks later, the family was enjoying a gorgeous Sunday morning at home. It was the type of weather that made it feel "great to be alive," Tom says. It was July 3, 1994.

He was up early mowing the lawn. Todd was sleeping in after a late night out with friends, but would later attend a Fourth of July picnic with Stephanie's family.

The air in the room changes when he starts talking about that day. He lets out two labored, choppy sighs full of tension and anguish. Twenty years later, his pain is still palpable.

Todd eventually crawled out of bed to wash and wax his new car before he left for the picnic. The vehicle was down at the bottom of their steep driveway, so Tom drove it closer to the house as a favor to Todd.

He says, "I banged my head on this little knob on the top of the windshield where the safety belt swings into it. I smacked my head on there and it hurt like hell."

Before Todd left for the picnic, his father gave him a warning.

"Be careful of that car," Tom said. "It's very fast, it has quick steering, and I banged my head on it trying to adjust the seat."

"I banged mine, too," Todd admitted.

It wasn't unusual for him to hug and kiss his son goodbye or tell him he loved him. Today was no exception, but he felt the need to go a little further on this beautiful summer afternoon.

"I told him what a great kid he is, that he's a good looking boy, and he's got a lot of friends. I said, 'You've got it all. You're the cat's ass.'"

"What does that mean?" Todd asked.

"I said it was an old saying. Sometimes you try different sayings because they don't listen to you," Tom says, laughing. "And that was it."

Breathlessly, he says, recalling his son's face, "God, he was a handsome kid."

Todd faithfully arrived home every night by 11 p.m. If he couldn't make it home by that time he'd give his father a quick call to let him know he'd be late. That evening, he rushed home to make sure he arrived on time. This last act of devotion to his father would cost him his life.

At 11 p.m., Tom was waiting up for his son when he first heard the sirens. From his window he saw police cars, fire trucks and an ambulance screaming down the street. He called his brother Greg to find out if he had heard anything on his police scanner. Over the scanner, Greg heard there was a car accident near Tom's house.

Tom

Why Go On: Connecticut Residents Bring Dark Days to Light

The words "it's Todd," dropped from Tom's lips, as his stomach turned sour. He continued trying to convince himself that his son would be okay as he waited for him to arrive home.

Restless and concerned, he called Greg again. From his side of the phone line he heard squelched voices on the scanner.

"White male. Age 21. Cardiac arrest."

Tom immediately drove to the scene of the accident.

He approached the fire police who were directing traffic. He recognized one of the officers and asked him if Todd was involved.

"I don't know," responded the officer. He was told he could not drive closer to the wreck, so he left the car and walked over.

On the walk over he noticed some of Todd's friends standing on the side of the road. They had been at a nearby party and walked over when they heard the crash.

"Is it Todd?" he asked.

"We don't know," they answered.

He walked on until he reached an overturned car in the middle of the road. His heart sank.

It was Todd's.

In the meantime, Todd had been transported to Lawrence & Memorial Hospital in New London. Tom's mind scrambled with confusion and anxiety. He went home, picked up Marcia and headed to the hospital. The 12-mile car ride was mostly silent.

At the hospital, Tom and Marcia waited to hear of their son's condition. Tom was in a frenzied haze but tried to keep calm. A doctor appeared. He uttered the phrase no one ever wants to hear.

"I'm so sorry. He didn't make it."

The words hit him like a sledgehammer, and he felt like he was going to collapse. Nurses sat him down in a chair. He was desperate to see Todd one more time. A few minutes later, nurses led him into a room where the lifeless young man lay on a metal gurney.

"He died of blunt trauma to the chest or the head. He had a big red spot in the same place I banged my head that morning." He had also slammed his chest onto the steering wheel.

Todd had been speeding and lost control around a curve. He hit an embankment and flipped his car only three-quarters of a mile from home. He was killed instantly.

Tom

Tom hugged and kissed his departed son, wishing that somehow the two could switch places.

When asked how it feels to lose a child, the typically loquacious man became quiet, unable to find the right words.

"There's no – you can't describe it. You just... Your life ends, right there."

Then, he is silent for a few moments.

That night, Marcia said she heard the sound of Todd walking down the hallway and into his room. The following night, Tom saw a light on in the bathroom and thought he heard Todd inside.

Upon seeing the light, he says, "I just kind of felt peaceful and went back to sleep. Of course, the light was out later."

A huge outpouring of community support began at 8 a.m. when friends and family started calling. By 9 a.m. they were stopping by. His home was never empty. "Adult" visitors streamed in during the day with arms full of food. At night, Todd's younger friends hung out in his room and grieved.

He received hundreds of sympathy cards, which he still has today. "I don't know what I'm going to do with them," he admits.

Todd's friends erected a 4' X 2' metal cross, which they set into concrete at the site of the crash. The funeral procession was comprised of over a hundred cars. Five hundred people attended. His former employer, the Mystic Ramada Inn, graciously offered to hold a reception at the hotel at no charge.

Tom knew of an old superstition that a clap of thunder after a funeral heralds the deceased's entry into heaven. On that hot summer day, there was no rain – but after the burial, he heard thunderclaps.

In the months that followed, he sank into a deep depression. At the record store, he'd find himself crying when friends came to check on him. He dreaded going home knowing his son's empty room lurked just around the corner. For the first six months he visited Todd's grave two or three times per day. He felt uncomfortable doing anything he enjoyed, including eating.

"No matter what I did I felt guilty. I even stopped cooking. I used to cook for him all the time. I stopped cooking because," Tom sighs, "he wasn't there to enjoy it. I felt guilty enjoying anything. When somebody tells you a funny joke, you don't want to laugh. But in the end, laughter is what helps you out of the depression."

There was anger, too. One night he found himself grabbing a friend by the collar over a disagreement at a Lion's Club meeting. Today he can't even remember what the quarrel was about.

"I was going to punch him – and that's not me. I don't think I've ever punched anybody. But I wanted to kill that guy."

Evenings were especially difficult. "You feel so alone. Nighttime was horrible. Darkness comes over and you can't function. Not properly, anyway." Despite his debilitating depression, he chose to abstain from anti-depressants and other medications.

"I wanted to experience the whole thing. It's the same reason I don't go out and get drunk. I don't like that feeling of not knowing what you're doing." He knew he would eventually have to face the grief anyway.

Holidays were a nightmarish blend of anxiety, grief and dismal reminders of lost love.

"Oh God, his birthday's in two days," he'd think every February, "and you cry for two days."

In January of 1995, Todd's son Cody was born. He describes the birth as the only uplifting thing during this time, but it was also a stinging reminder of his heartache.

"It's just bittersweet because I kept looking at him and thinking of my son. He reminded me so much of Todd. I could feel myself wanting to cry every time I'd touch him. But I loved him."

Tensions in the home were building. Marcia and her children came to terms with Todd's death. Communication between family members was strained, with everyone isolating themselves in their own area of the house. Tom spent more of his time alone.

In February of 1996, Tom's father died at age 80. He was buried on February 12th – Todd's birthday.

Business at the record store was sluggish. He fell behind on mortgage payments again and lost his home in January of 1997. He and his wife moved into an apartment. The couple separated about six months later and eventually divorced.

He moved into the back of his record store. He had lost his son, his job, his house, his wife and his parents. A weaker man might have thrown in the towel, but not Tom.

Tom

Living in the back of the store was surprisingly easy. It gave him a safe place to be himself.

"It wasn't bad. Nobody bothered me. I was comfortable. I had a little room in the back where I did my cooking. I had a little refrigerator and a George Foreman grill. At nighttime I'd sit in my office, watch TV and work on the computer, get in chat rooms."

Tom lived in the store for two years until a heart attack in 1999 forced him to move in with a friend, where he slowly recuperated. Around the same time he entered into a new long-term relationship, which ultimately lasted twelve years. The romance helped guide him through the shadows of anguish into the light of hope.

His path to healing was a slow and steady one. Looking back, there was no distinct remedy that brought him back to life. Instead, he slowly gained strength through the years by ever trudging forward and never surrendering to his sadness.

He gradually rebuilt his life by simply going out into the world and trying new things. Some efforts made him feel better, others didn't. He just continued trying to heal and uplift himself. It was difficult at first to find someone to help.

"When Todd died, there was no hospice bereavement. There was nothing. There was no one to turn to."

He went to therapy, which gave him the opportunity to express his grief freely.

"People lock it up inside. I found the more I talked about it, the better I was able to talk. At first I couldn't say anything. I would cry. But you talk about it and get used to it and then it's easier."

He met with psychic mediums. One psychic said Todd was with a friend named Stephen or Scott who had just passed away. Todd's friend Scott had died a couple years after him and was buried only four plots away.

One day at the grocery store Tom ran into his friend John, who said he really needed to talk about something.

"Your son is driving me crazy," John said.

He explained that Todd had been coming to him in his dreams. "He says he can't get through to you. He's been coming to me and telling me, 'You've got to talk to my father. Tell him I love him.'"

Tom thanked him for the message.

"Maybe now he'll let me sleep," John joked.

After that, John said, Todd never appeared in his dreams again.

Three years after his son died, Tom started writing a book called *My Son Todd and my Guardian Angels*. His original intention was to give his grandson Cody a written history of his father's life. Instead, it turned into a healing experience for Tom and his readers.

"I had no idea how or why I wrote it. I was told by a medium that Todd helped me write it. I think he did. I remember writing the first few chapters on the computer and crying so hard I couldn't see what I was writing. The next morning I read it and said, 'Wow. I wrote that?'

"A therapist that read it said she was surprised that I was able to put two sentences together, let alone write a whole book because I was so depressed. That's why people read it and they feel it, because it's raw."

He wrote the first part of the book three years after Todd died. Then, three years later – after the worst of his depression was over – he wrote the second part. Another three years later he wrote the third part. He added a final chapter on the tenth anniversary of Todd's death.

The book is surprisingly detailed for being written years after the events took place. *My Son Todd* not only details what he went through, but it also offers advice to others who have lost a loved one. He describes his mood swings, his confusion, his methods of healing, and what he's learned. One passage about his personal transformation reads:

> *I have become more mellow, more interested in other people, and I have a sensitivity for other people's feelings that I never had before. I have a totally different outlook on life… I also feel closer to God and my son than ever before.*

Tom has sold his book everywhere from the Big E to people who hear his lectures about the grieving process. He gives each of his customers a warm embrace.

"I love to hug. To me, hugging is essential for people who have lost a child."

It's not only parents who have lost children that respond to the book. He shows me an email from a British reader who recently lost her beloved husband. The last line of her email reads:

Your thoughts and writing about your son helped me get through the night.

Easing others' pain makes Tom feel better, too. "I think helping people is the best thing, because it takes your problems away and helps others."

My Son Todd makes reference to the virtues of helping others:

I have learned that life here on earth is precious and we should learn from the experience of being here. Help and love others.

After finishing *My Son Todd*, he kept writing. His second book, *Mystic in the 1950s: Growing up in a Small Village*, pulls readers back into the simpler times during which he was raised. Today, he is working on a third book, designed to further help readers navigate the grieving process. It reveals everything he's learned in the ten years following the publication of *My Son Todd*. One of the things he's learned is how to release attachments to the past.

"I've gotten out of it because I've made new memories. You don't forget about it, you just push it aside so it doesn't hurt so much. And that's what I do. I just create new work for myself."

He is now the chairman of the Southeast Chapter of the Connecticut Authors and Publishers Association, or CAPA. The organization helps new and established writers succeed, offering guest speakers, webinars and marketing opportunities.

Two years ago he started a brand new endeavor with a cable access program called *Books and Things with Tom*. Tom invites regional guests such as authors, politicians and musical artists to discuss their latest ventures.

He credits part of his recovery to his guardian angels.

"They come as spirits or they come as people. They're there all the time. They are the ones that tell us right from wrong. Guardian angels keep you out of trouble."

Tom advises those who are grieving not to attempt skipping the process entirely. Many may look for the fastest way out of their misery, but it's a progression that needs to run its course.

"Bear with it. People try to get through this as quick as possible.

I had one lady say, 'Tell me what the grieving steps are so I can get through them.' I said it's not going to happen. You've got to step through each one before you can get to the end. You've got to go through it all: the hatred, the jealousy, the guilt. You can't possibly sidestep any of them."

When asked if he thinks there was a higher purpose to Todd's passing, he sighs thoughtfully and replies, "I think more the other way around – that there was a higher purpose for him to be here. He served his purpose," he says, implying that his life objectives were fulfilled during his short 21 years. "I think we're sent down here for a reason and when we've accomplished our jobs, we go back."

He says his son comes to him every once in a while, in dreams. It's a time he can check in and ask "what it's like up there."

Todd always answers, "It's wonderful."

"Every time I've dreamed of him, I woke up in the morning feeling like I've had a hug, feeling that he was there, and not sad about it," he says. "I've woken up with a smile, thinking that was so nice for him to come and visit."

When asked why he never gave up, he responds, "I think sometimes I'm driven, and if I give up I won't know what the end is. I'd rather stick it out and find out what's going to happen next."

Todd's memory will never truly disappear, and part of him will live on through his son Cody. For Tom, creating new memories means writing, collecting, and helping others. I suggest the notion of perhaps finding a new love, too, since he is a bachelor these days. He says he is reluctant to marry again.

"But you know," he says, taking a deep breath, "I like women."

Tom's "five years of hell" took a great toll on him, but through self-awareness, inner strength and perseverance, he was able to mend his broken heart. By doing so, he found a level of compassion and love for others he never knew before. Then, through his writing, he used this newfound compassion to help others through their own losses. At times, grief can seem like an unfair burden, but Tom transformed his heartache into a gift.

When asked what he would say to Todd if he could see him again, his answer is remarkably sweet.

Tom

"I'd probably want to know what he thinks of me after what I've done in helping other people."

In response, Todd would surely say, "You're the cat's ass, dad."

Gary

"When you're down 20 and there are three minutes left, you still play your heart out."

"There are two things that really keep me going," Gary says. The first is his apartment's incredible view of New Haven Harbor. The second is "her," he says, pointing at his toy fox terrier named Sarky. The pooch happily bustles around, searching for something to chew on or chase. At one point Sark drops a rubber toy and it tumbles to the ground beneath the deck. I offer to retrieve it and Gary accepts.

"Depending on how tangled I am, sometimes I can reach it," he says, referring to the long and unwieldy tubing of his oxygen tank.

We spoke on the rear deck of his apartment on a warm, pleasant day in August. Our chairs overlooked the great New Haven skyline extending out from beyond Morris Cove. Boats bobbed silently in the glistening water. The tranquil scene is reminiscent of a beach house getaway. But for Gary, his life is no vacation.

He was born in New Haven. He was an athletic kid, excelling in sports like tennis and basketball. He led his basketball team at the Jewish Center of Greater New Haven and was captain of the Hillhouse High School tennis team for two years. When he moved on to college, he played tennis for the University of Connecticut.

Growing up in a racially diverse area, his high school demographic was comprised of 75% African American students.

"There was a very heavy black influence in my life growing up. My father owned a pharmacy in the heart of the ghetto, but it was one of the nicest pharmacies in New Haven. Some of my ex-girlfriends were women of color. Many of my friends growing up were as diverse as you could get."

His mother's friend one remarked, "Boy, when you look at Gary in the backyard, there's a bunch of little black kids and a bunch of little white kids running around together."

He adds, "This was in the early sixties, which you didn't see too often. One of my best friends, Willie, growing up – we used to get stares when we were riding on the same bike together. My friends used to tease me when I was a teenager, saying that if I ran for mayor I would get the white vote, the black vote, the Jewish vote – so I would have been covered."

Gary drinks from a seemingly endless glass of diet coke on the rocks, a lifelong addiction inherited from his father. He bears a distinct resemblance to actor Dennis Farina, with neatly styled salt and pepper hair, moustache, strong nose, deeply tanned skin and rich brown eyes. He wears a necklace upon which two charms hang: a turtle and a set of lungs.

"I've been called Turtle since seventh grade. My friends call me Turt." He jokes, "My nickname has a nickname." He says there are a few reasons why the moniker stuck, but he never reveals one of them.

As a young adult, he never figured out exactly what he wanted to do with his life, but that didn't stop him from trying just about everything. He is a free spirit in many ways. He's fearless, determined and creative.

He briefly considered taking after his father and becoming a pharmacist, but soon realized that "chemistry – that wasn't for me."

In college he studied marketing and advertising, a suitable fit for this quick talking, fun-loving guy with a sharp wit. Gary himself admits it's something he "should have pursued."

Instead, he took the state's civil service test to see what opportunities opened up to him. "I got a few calls for different things, but none of 'em interested me. Then I got a call and it had the word 'investigator' in it. Sounded pretty cool, to be honest."

He became a Child Support Investigator. "I got a promotion and worked for the Superior Court as a Child Support Officer."

Gary started the job with marked ambition. "The first couple of years there I set records for how many cases I did. It got to the point where no matter how much work I did, the person sitting next to me might have done nothing – but they still got their raise when I did. I got disillusioned, so I left."

Later he bartended at clubs from New Haven to Waterbury, including some establishments where he was the "only white guy in the building." He managed clubs and Showcase Cinemas. He ran a duty-free division for an import/export company at Bradley Airport and the U.N. Plaza in New York City. He also sold wine for many years, asserting he helped one company get "on the map."

"I get bored and move onto something else," he says.

Eventually, he utilized his marketing degree. In his kitchen hangs a glossy advertisement for a Greek beer, with an eye-catching layout and an amusingly lewd tagline. "Shows my sense of humor," he admits. In addition to the ad, he worked on some television spots for the lager with an equally cheeky message.

His salesmanship skills helped him squeeze onto Yankee Field the day before the World Series Game when Reggie Jackson earned the nickname "Mr. October." He shows me a photo of him giving Yogi Berra a double handshake with a broad, proud smile on his face.

Gary breached Yankee territory by pitching a product his brother Alan came up with.

"This was back in the pet rock days. He came up with the idea of a security blanket. The tagline was, 'For the man or woman who has everything.' It came with a little booklet on how to use it, with pictures of me in a dentist's chair holding it. I talked my way into the Yankees to give them all the security blanket."

He was leading a life of many adventures, but something would soon hold him back. In his late thirties, he started coughing up phlegm and rapidly dropped a lot of weight. He thought he maybe had chronic bronchitis and went to the doctor to get checked out.

"It doesn't sound so good," his doctor said, listening to his breathing. "Let's send you for an x-ray."

The x-ray revealed some spots on his lungs, but it was nothing overly concerning to his doctor. He was prescribed antibiotics and given a follow-up appointment in two months.

"I do the course of antibiotics. I have some weeks where I feel a little better, I have some weeks of not feeling so good," he says.

At his follow-up appointment, a new x-ray determined the spots had completely disappeared. That was good news, but he still wasn't feeling well. His doctor set him up to return for another check-up in two months.

Eight weeks later the newest x-ray revealed a devastating picture.

"There are spots *all* over my lungs. The doctor came in and he said, 'Gary, there are four times as many spots as there were.'"

His doctor conveyed four possible causes for his condition.

"It could be tuberculosis. It could be lung cancer," Gary says, counting off each illness on his fingers. Next, the doctor asked him if he ever did any drugs using hypodermic needles, as the third option was HIV.

"No, no, no, no, no – it's not that," Gary told him.

The doctor gave him one final possibility. "The last thing is something called sarcoidosis. I want you to root for sarcoidosis."

He had never heard the word sarcoidosis before. "In fact, I asked him to repeat the pronunciation a few times," he says.

He went home and talked to his pharmacist father, who in turn called "a couple of his buddy doctors. This was pre-internet, so it wasn't like I could go home and Google it. It wasn't in the World Book Encyclopedia I had at home," Gary says, with a laugh.

"My doctor made an appointment with a pulmonologist – supposed to be one of the best. When he reads the doctor's evaluation, he looks at me and says, 'To be honest with you, I don't think it's sarcoidosis.' Now I'm thinking, 'All right, it's lung cancer.'"

The pulmonologist set him up for a bronchoscopy, which meant having a scope inserted down his throat. A tissue sample was taken to be biopsied. After a week of nervous anticipation, he returned to the pulmonologist for his results.

"Well, I was wrong," the doctor said. "It *is* sarcoid."

Sarcoidosis, commonly known as sarcoid, is a rare disease that causes scarring on the lungs, effecting about 25,000 people in the U.S. The good news is that in 90% of cases it goes into remission after three to ten years. Others can suffer more serious complications from the disease, which in rare cases can be fatal. Sarcoid can potentially ravage the brain, heart, lungs, nasal passages, lungs, skin, or virtually any organ, depending on the case.

Gary has now lived with the disease for more than 20 years. He's fortunate it never moved to his brain or heart, but its slow and brutal attack on his lungs has been debilitating. Chronic onset of his disease was initially gradual, but once it gained traction it unleashed a fast and furious onslaught that has nearly killed him.

"I have groups of cells that form granulomas on my lungs." A granuloma is a small area of inflammation. "What happens is these granulomas end up causing scarring, also known as pulmonary fibrosis. So my lungs are full of scars. There's no elasticity left in my lungs."

Sarcoid is typically treated with a corticosteroid such as prednisone to reduce inflammation. His prolonged use of the drug has caused considerable damage to his body. He was spared the side effect of weight gain, but he suffered many others.

"These are my battle scars," he says, showing me the top of his arms, which have become mottled with dark brown blotches. "I have paper thin skin now. Nobody should be on prednisone 23 years like I have been. Plus, after a while it can have a lot of psychological effects, effecting my mood big-time. Whenever I would have to go up on higher doses I would warn my bosses, people I worked with, my then girlfriend, whatever. I also deal with chronic pain. A lot of that is from the steroid use. The steroids have killed my bones."

In total, he takes over a dozen medications, some of which cause a constant tremor in his hands.

To this day Gary does not know what caused the disease. He didn't smoke until he was 26. Earlier in his life he was an enthusiastic non-smoker, even encouraging girlfriends to quit. He eventually submitted to the lure of cigarettes due to working in a nightlife environment.

"It was a bad habit I picked up, really. It was everything against what I always believed in."

Regardless, sarcoidosis has nothing to do with nicotine use. "As a matter of fact, it's often called 'the non-smoker's lung disease.' The etiology of sarcoid is unknown. They believe there are two things that you need: the genetic factor and the environmental factor together. But no one knows what causes it. That makes it difficult. I wish I knew why."

One of the ironic aspects about his disease is that it most commonly strikes women of African American descent. In fact, it hits black men eight times as often as white men, and is twice as likely to affect black females as black males. Referencing his affinity for African American culture, his father's friends quipped, "Gary, how far you gonna take this?"

For the first ten to fifteen years of living with the disease, Gary led a relatively normal life. For a long time he appeared to be perfectly healthy, which he says is a negative aspect of the illness.

"One of the things people talk about on a lot of the sarcoid websites is that you don't always look sick. That can make it tough for some people. It's like, 'Boy, they don't believe me.' I don't think if I'm walking around without this," he says, tugging his oxygen tubing, "too many people would think I'm dying.

"I had gone through many times where I got worse, I got better, I got worse, I got better – but I was deteriorating." By 2005, he was told he would eventually need a lung transplant or "that would be the end."

By 2009, seventeen years after he was diagnosed, he was walking four miles per day – an amazing feat for someone with only 50% of their lung capacity.

"In 2010 is when it all started to go downhill. This is when I'm going to interrupt you and tell you let's go inside," he says, abruptly.

After talking outside for about 30-45 minutes, the warm, humid air became too heavy. He, Sarky and I retreated into the air-conditioned apartment. After letting out a relieved sigh, he says, "I'm not used to running my mouth all the time."

We take a seat at his kitchen table, next to a few binders filled with information about lung transplants. During the intermission, he gives Sarky some attention and a treat. Gary adores his dog. He radiates happiness every time he speaks about her.

"I can't stress how important she is," he says. "I always wanted a dog," he says. "Since I was a kid I used to cry for a dog. One year my parents gave me a parakeet. You can't walk a parakeet."

When he finally decided to get a dog a few years ago, he

thoroughly researched breeds to find which were compatible with his sarcoid, and decided on a toy fox terrier. The next debate came in deciding what to name her.

"People with sarcoid are known as sarkies [alternatively: sarcies]. I was thinking, 'Boy... would it really be *nuts* to name her Sarky?' I was berated by a couple people for even thinking of naming her Sarky."

"How could you name a dog after the disease?" they growled.

Gary's response replaces their disapproval with levity. "I use humor. That's how I get by."

His friends in an online sarcoid chat room understood what he was trying to achieve. His fellow sarcoid sufferers fully supported his name choice and even suggested that it might help raise awareness about the disease. The perky pup has been Sarky ever since.

After his Sarky break, Gary resumes telling me what happened in April of 2010. Doctors said his health was "spiraling downhill at an alarming rate." He enunciates these words to show how profoundly they impacted him.

One of his best friends, Theresa, visited him one day when he felt particularly ill. Around 10 p.m., he asked her not to leave.

"I went into the bedroom and I lay down. My breathing was getting worse and worse."

Late that night, he yelled out to her, "T, come here! We gotta call 911."

"I was rushed to the hospital. That was my first time on a ventilator. I remember the ambulance ride but then I really don't remember much until I was kind of coming out of it."

After he regained consciousness, his brother told him he had been on a ventilator for three days.

"I was on *machines*?" Gary says, remembering his disbelief. "I was in the hospital for a week that time, and then I went to rehab for a week."

This was the first time he had been hospitalized due to sarcoid complications, and it changed the way he lived. He was placed on an oxygen tank, making him less mobile and more uncomfortable in public.

"Being on oxygen was not fun. Having to go out wearing this is really quite a blow."

In the following months his health stabilized. He started researching his viability for a double lung transplant. A lung transplant will not cure his sarcoid; it will only refresh him with a new set of healthy, unscarred lungs.

"We knew that I didn't have too much time left – or so they thought."

In September of 2010 he was rushed to the hospital again, where he remained for nearly a month.

"The nurses wouldn't tell me how long I was on the ventilator." It had been two weeks. Patients without a tracheostomy are generally not kept on a ventilator beyond fourteen days due to the risk of developing pneumonia and other concerns. A tracheostomy is a procedure wherein a tube is inserted directly into the windpipe to assist with breathing.

Gary

"They couldn't take me off. They tried. I wasn't going to survive." Despite coming within inches of death, he rallied. He enunciates his words again, quoting his doctors as saying he has "an uncanny propensity to bounce back."

After his release from the hospital, he resumed testing for a potential lung transplant with New York Presbyterian Hospital. Going out of state was a necessity because Connecticut does not perform lung transplants.

While 2010 was a stressful year, 2011 would be worse. He pulls out a piece of paper on which he jotted down the dates of his ER visits in 2011 alone. In the months of January, April, May, August and September he was rushed in separate incidents to the hospital.

"These are a lot of hospital rides," he says.

In fact, he rode in an ambulance eight times within 18 months. He refers to his September 29, 2011 visit as "the big one."

As he desperately gasped for air in the back of the ambulance, an EMT told him, "Gary, I might have to intubate you." By this time he had been intubated twice in the past, but never in the back of an ambulance.

He describes it as a "very scary" experience. Fortunately, the EMT was able to facilitate his breathing with a CPAP machine to delay intubation until they arrived at the hospital.

Gary shows me his tracheostomy scar. It's probably not as noticeable as he thinks it is, but it is certainly visible. He was put on a ventilator for three weeks this time. Doctors shared a grim prognosis with his family. If – and that was a big if – he became well enough to be discharged, there was a good chance he wouldn't be going home, but would instead be sent to a nursing facility.

"I started to show my bounce back."

He awoke to a tracheostomy tube in his throat. These can be inserted for temporary or permanent use – and up until now it had always been removed.

"As I started doing better, the doctor said 'Gar', we're probably going to have to leave you trached.'" This was the last thing he wanted to hear. He couldn't imagine cleaning out a trach tube or the embarrassment of going out in public with the device.

The fear was short-lived. While recuperating at Gaylord Hospital in Wallingford, he heard the good news that they would remove the tube.

"Ah," he says, laughing, "just hearing that was fantastic."

Against all odds, he made another miraculous recovery and felt better every day. He avoided being transferred to a nursing home and was allowed to return to his own apartment.

"Doctors were amazed at what I could do. They still are. In

certain offices they call me 'The Mystery'. They call me 'The Cat' with how many lives I have. They didn't think I would be here right now without a transplant. I proved them wrong." He had to continue using an oxygen tank, but remained relatively healthy, considering his lung capacity was only about 32%.

On February 10, 2012, Gary got "listed." Three months later, on May 12, 2012, "The Call" came.

"Everybody who's waiting for a transplant talks about 'The Call.' It's what you live for. You hope you stay alive long enough. I always dreamed that the day the call came, the first words out of my mouth would be 'Oh, thank God.' Well, the day the call came, the first words out of my mouth were, 'What the f—?'"

He explains that deciding exactly when to receive a lung transplant is a critical and delicate decision. His transplant doctor recently lost four patients within a year of their transplants.

"One was two weeks after transplant, one was three months after transplant, one was a year after transplant, and one was just over a year." Gary himself had heard mixed reviews from people he's met. One man he knows said he's lived "a great life" with transplanted lungs for the past 11 years. Yet, another woman said she never would have done it if she "knew what she had to go through."

"A double lung transplant isn't like a liver transplant. It's not like a kidney transplant. It's a much different thing."

So when The Call came, he wavered. "I grabbed my bag, which was packed, ready to go. I called my ride. I'm sitting here, well I shouldn't say sitting... I was pacing back and forth. I just didn't know what to do."

He didn't have much time to make a decision. He only had a four-hour window between receiving The Call and when he would need to arrive at New York Presbyterian Hospital.

Gary weighed the pros and cons. His body could immediately reject the new lungs, but if he waited too long his health could deteriorate too much to accept the new organ. His rally since getting listed could be used as a justification to get the transplant, because his body was healthy enough to adjust. Then again, it could also be used as a justification to *not* get the transplant, as he wasn't in such dire need.

He ultimately declined the transplant. According to the National

Heart, Lung, and Blood Institute, the median rate of survival for a double lung transplant is about six and a half years. To put it simply, Gary says, "50 percent make it five years."

"I kept telling my friends, 'I just want to get through the summer. At that point I never thought I'd make it a few years.

"It's a very tough thing to handle psychologically. I often think had I done it, I could be living without needing an oxygen tank, maybe. I could be working. But you don't know."

With all of the "could bes" and "maybes," one fact remains. "I've extended my life three years already by saying no," he says.

His primary care doctor agreed with his choice, telling him, "Gar', I think you made the right decision."

He is now in the process of getting relisted. He's optimistic, but he knows a challenge lies ahead. He borrows a sports analogy to illustrate his resolve.

"When you're down 20 and there are three minutes left, you still play your heart out. You still do what you can. You strive to do a little better."

Sometimes that's easier said than done. "When you see me at home and I'm in my comfort zone, it's one thing. When I exert myself is when I have problems."

In fact, at this moment he looks fatigued and flushed, his eyes growing bloodshot. Though we had been sitting comfortably for about a half hour, he looks as though he just went for a mile long jog. He asks for another break, this time to use his nebulizer, a motorized device that delivers medication in the form of a breathable vapor. The nebulizer hums and hisses for about five minutes before we reconvene, with Gary looking completely refreshed.

One benefit to his experiences living with a chronic disease is seeing the kindness in others. "I gained a whole new respect for nurses and CNA's. What they do is phenomenal. I made some friends with people that have taken care of me."

Sarcoid helped him "see that there are some really, really nice people out there. People have gone out of their way to do things for me. It is really very humbling."

His brother Alan and sister-in-law Sally have been an invaluable source of strength. "If it weren't for them, it would be much more difficult. I've got a great brother, but I've got an even better sister-in-law. She is fantastic."

It's not just family, but friends too, who help him through. A couple of years back, shortly before he found Sarky, he spotted a woman walking a dog near his home. The two started talking, and before long he became fast friends with Leah and her husband Frank. Frank and Leah now come to his house every day to take his dog on a play date with their own.

Back when he was recuperating at Gaylord Hospital, one of the hospital volunteers stopped at his hospital room door. He stared into the room for a few moments before stepping inside.

"Turt?" the man asked.

Gary didn't recognize him at first, but the visitor was Burt, one of his best friends from childhood, whom he hadn't seen in years. The two reconnected and Burt is now a vital part of his support system.

Another old friend named Curt, who lives in Virginia, calls about once a week to see how he's doing. "He tries to lift my spirits," Gary says. Yet another childhood friend, Paul, accompanies Gary to virtually every one of his required seminars for the transplant program, and to his medical appointments in New York.

"My buddy Paul has been unbelievable. We talk pretty much every day."

Gary was surprised but impressed to learn that his friend Paul is signed up for the organ donor program. Paul joins 100 million registered organ donors in the U.S., but the fact remains that 18 people die every day waiting for a transplant. He shares a thought-provoking quote about the topic:

Don't think of organ donations as giving up a part of yourself to keep a total stranger alive. It's really a total stranger giving up almost all of themselves to keep a part of you alive.

One of his main goals is to remind people of the importance of becoming an organ donor. He urges people to think about the issue and discuss the pros and cons with their family before deciding what's best for them.

He also wants to create a greater awareness of sarcoidosis.

"Nobody really knows what sarcoid is. Most people have never heard of the word." He stresses though, his chronic sarcoid is not the norm.

"I'm the exception to the rule. If you do hear the word, don't think you're going to need a lung transplant." Only 10% of sarcoid cases will become chronic. He lists a few celebrity sarcoid sufferers, including: comedian Bernie Mac, basketball player Bill Russell, actresses Tisha Campbell and Karen Duffy, and football player Reggie White.

One of Gary's major motivations to keep going is his 91-year-old mother. He lost his sister to emphysema less than a year ago. He used to tell his sister, "I am not going to die before Mom. I don't want her to go through that."

In response, his sister joked, "Well, Mom's gonna live another twenty years."

One of his favorite quotes is the motto of The V Foundation for Cancer Research, created by famous basketball coach Jim Valvano.

"Don't give up. Don't ever give up."

These days, he keeps himself busy with doctors' appointments and a trip into town every day. He might drive over to Krauszer's Food Store in East Haven, or get the paper and read it at the diner. The point is to make sure he gets out and stays busy.

"I try to keep the carrot in front of me that my best days are ahead," he says. It's difficult to reconcile the two Gary's: the one who is full of life, humor and strength with the other who is tragically ill. Most would agree it's the Gary with a resilient spirit to never give up who is the only one that really matters.

Gary never had children and is currently single. Another one of his goals is finding someone to share his life with. "It's that much tougher going through things alone."

There are several lessons to be found in Gary's story. First, be cautious when judging someone's disease by their outer appearance. Many might be grievously ill but appear rosy-cheeked and optimistic. Second, be aware of those around you who need help. Even just a few words of support can provide much needed motivation.

Finally, doctors inform their patients to the best of their ability. However, there are many "cats" out there who far outlive their prognosis.

Gary's sense of humor has helped him cope through the past twenty years. Perhaps the most important moral of his story can be summed up in the words of Yogi Berra himself. For those who are fighting a long and arduous battle it is not only essential to laugh, but to live by these six little words:

"It ain't over till it's over."

Cjet

"Something changed in me that night. I stopped crying about me and started feeling for someone else."

C jet (pronounced "chet") rolls up on a moped sporting a pink helmet and pink wayfarer sunglasses. Clipped to her grey denim jacket are two round pins: one of Charlie Brown, the other, a rainbow flag. Standing on the sidewalk of Branford's lovely town green, she and I searched for a place to grab lunch. We decided on an Indian restaurant, one she calls "our favorite," referring to her wife and two daughters.

Cjet, a tall slender vegetarian with a super short pixie haircut, is charmingly polite. She appears happy and content, but her softly downturned eyes betray an inner world of layered, deep, and complex emotions.

In a sense, I felt like I already knew Cjet after reading her book called *Dear Diary: I Think I Said Too Much*. The book is a collection of entries from journals she wrote when she was 13 to 16 years old. It's not the typical diary of a teenage girl complaining about schoolwork and obsessing over romantic crushes. *Dear Diary* offers a meticulously documented account of a young woman's anguish and confusion growing up in an abusive household.

There's no specific day it began. As far back as she can

remember, home was an abusive environment that, for a long time, didn't seem out of the ordinary. What started as physical abuse from her father developed into sexual abuse when she entered puberty. Her father, a former navy sailor, mocked young her developing body, teased her about poor performance in school and called her ugly. He would make her stand for hours in a corner as punishment for the smallest disobedience. Under the guise of "tickling," her father would forcefully pinch her breasts and ridicule their size and shape. He would peep at her while she was getting undressed. Certain passages in the book quietly allude to more severe sexual abuse.

Her parents rarely hugged her or said, "I love you." Her mother was torn between her husband and daughter, but ultimately chose to live in denial.

"Her component was neglect. She wasn't abusive physically, but she didn't stand up for me. She didn't stop my father and she didn't protect me," Cjet says.

During her early years, she tended to take her aggressions out on other kids at school. "I was a complete brat. I got in trouble a few times for pushing or getting mad and yelling. I slapped a girl once. She was a good friend of mine, so it wasn't totally aggressive, but stuff was flying inside of me and I must have reacted to something. I got in trouble with my teachers for calling out and being obnoxious."

Part of her sixth grade curriculum included a course about behavioral issues such as bullying and abuse. The class made a huge impression on Cjet. It alerted her to her own behavior, while planting the seed of awareness to her own abuse at home. The course instructor, who was also Cjet's guidance counselor, was Mrs. Lobo, a woman who would change her life.

Mrs. Lobo also taught a health class that included some of the usual topics: recommendations against pre-marital sex and lessons on the life-changing implications of pregnancy. She offered the students a chance to write down an anonymous question for her to answer. One unusual question amongst the bunch read, "Do you have to have sex to have a baby?"

Cjet says, "I think somewhere in me I was feeling like I wanted a family, but I was not into the sex thing. I knew my father had a penis and I hated him."

Cjet

After class, Mrs. Lobo casually asked if her question had been answered, knowing that Cjet might need some extra attention. Soon Cjet would start seeking out Mrs. Lobo on a daily basis.

She connected easily to her teacher, and was always met with an open ear and sage advice. Mrs. Lobo suggested that she start keeping a journal – which eventually turned into the book she'd publish many years later.

From page one of *Dear Diary*, Cjet's exhaustion is evident. Her writings are not the bewildered musings of a mistreated child, but the battle cry of someone who has reached their breaking point. The first person she confided in was her friend Abbie, a kindhearted girl born of a picture-perfect family. Abbie knew there wasn't anything normal about Cjet's home life and encouraged her to tell someone.

Cjet gave her father one last opportunity to settle things quietly. After years of silence, she told him to stop pinching her breasts.

He didn't. She'd had enough.

"I knew I needed to tell so it would stop," she says.

At age 13, she summoned the courage to speak up. Accompanied by Abbie, she went down to Mrs. Lobo's office. After some initial nervousness, she blurted everything out. Abbie was excused, leaving Cjet and Mrs. Lobo to discuss the matter alone.

At first, it was strangely serene. She felt relieved. Mrs. Lobo coolly stated that she was required to report any abuse or neglect to the Department of Children and Families (DCF), and the police might call in a couple of days. It was done with such finesse that she thought, "Okay, cool, this is easy. I should've done it a while ago."

Sure enough, the police called later that evening. Cjet's mother brought her to the police station for questioning. She was asked to explain in detail about how she was touched, for how long, and how she felt about it. Her mother was questioned at length also.

Meanwhile, her father had been the first of the three to meet with police. Surprisingly enough, while Cjet left out the details of more severe abuses, her father confessed much more to DCF's social workers.

Her father was angry and resolved to punish her for "telling on him." He completely ignored her. He took away her TV. He turned her photos around in the house. He wouldn't let her eat in the same room. He held his hand up to his face, blocking her from his view. He wouldn't let her participate in any extracurricular or social activities.

When he eventually started speaking to her again, he called her a "big lying idiot," "worthless child," and accused her of ruining his life forever.

"Everything was suddenly my fault," she says. "Anything that he felt or dealt with, any anger or frustration, were because I told on him."

Her parents argued about the matter while she was in the room, making her feel invisible and unloved. The physical abuse had stopped, but now verbal abuse was constant.

"I felt like that was harder than the abuse was before. That's when emotions were introduced to our family, and we hadn't really had those before."

Her mother was initially sympathetic, but as the situation deteriorated, she took her husband's side. She was resentful that Cjet didn't talk to her about the abuse before going "outside," and blamed her for the tension at home.

Cjet had opened up to her teacher because it felt safer to confide in her than in her own mother. Daily visits with Mrs. Lobo kept her sane.

Her diary illustrates the mixed, swirling emotions she was feeling at the time. She knew she did the right thing, but her self-esteem took a deep hit. Her father's verbal attacks and her mother's weak or non-existent support made her feel alone, rejected and suicidal.

About three weeks after his initial interview, her father was arrested and subsequently released on a $10,000 bond. His charges were three counts of fourth-degree sexual assault, a Class D Felony when the victim is under age 16, and one count of risk of injury to a minor, a Class C Felony that, at the time, carried a maximum sentence of 10 years in prison and a $10,000 fine. He would never serve time for his crimes.

Court ordered counseling was fruitless. Her father maintained that everything was Cjet's fault, while her mother dwelled on the fact that she didn't come to her first.

Months passed. Court hearings came and went. Cjet had never thought about foster care before, but it became clear that she could no longer live with her parents. As she became closer with Abbie's family, they invited her to move in with them. Her court-appointed lawyer worked on getting her placed with Abbie's parents, Mr. and Mrs. Jones.

When her father learned that she was moving out, his reaction was, "If you think you have that many problems with us, fine."

Five months after her initial confession and shortly after her 14th birthday, a judge determined there was sufficient evidence to award an Order of Temporary Custody. Cjet was given permission to live with her best friend Abbie. It was a memorable day.

With a broad smile, she says, "That was my liberation date."

Her friends and teachers immediately noticed a marked difference in her demeanor. She was smiling and happy. Abbie's house was comfortable and safe. There was no cursing, disrespect, fighting or unkindness. It was an ideal environment for a young woman badly in need of love and support... at first.

About three weeks after she moved in, the Jones' went on a previously planned vacation. They were not allowed to bring Cjet along because they were not fully licensed foster parents yet. She was sent to stay with another family in a nearby town until the Jones' returned from vacation.

The Marsh family had several children, including two other foster girls, ages six and nine. The father cozied up to Cjet right away, chatting her up and showering her with compliments. One day Mr. Marsh took her for a stroll and spoke to her for a very long time about very adult topics.

He told her graphic stories about his sex life. Cjet was repulsed, but she kept quiet out of confusion and fear. He tried educating her in grotesque detail about sexual topics, even asking disturbing questions about her experiences with her father. He said that many women choose to stay with their abusers, as if he were setting himself up for that role in her life.

"That was not pleasant. He was so gross. I didn't stop him or tell him this wasn't okay, because I didn't have strong enough conviction. I was brand new in the foster care world." Fortunately, this was only a temporary home and she was soon back with the Jones family.

When Cjet graduated from middle school, she had to say goodbye to her guidance counselor and friend, Mrs. Lobo. She shares the poignant moment in her book:

It was sad saying goodbye to the one who was closer to me than my mother, but I did it. And it felt good that I was able to initiate the hug. When we let go, with a really strong and firm voice I said, "I love you," while she held my hands. I choked then, and didn't know what to do, so I smiled, and she stood up and led me out the door and patted me on the back, leading me through the summer and into high school.

In the meantime, things were getting more complicated at home. Her poorly developed sense of self-worth and history of abuse made it impossible to be dropped into a healthy environment and consider everything fixed.

Cjet watched Abbie and her brother playing games and having fun, but she couldn't join in with childish abandon. Forced to grow up so fast and being exposed to such unsavory behavior at a young age made it hard for her to have fun.

"I didn't know how to just jump right in. I don't think anyone can. I think it's supposed to be gradual and I guess nobody realized. I didn't realize how hard it would be.

"Being on my own with my parents, I had control over my independence. Moving into Abbie's house, where it was a traditional setting with a nice Mom and Dad and kids who respected them, where everybody's loving and open and kind – I didn't have any of that."

Cjet's loss of independence felt like a loss of control. In an unconscious effort to regain her control, she changed her eating habits by drastically reducing her intake of food, sometimes to the point of nearly starving herself.

Abbie's mother noticed the change early and tried to address the problem by asking her to eat more. In response, Cjet insisted she was "disgustingly full" and denied having an eating disorder.

This constant conflict caused significant strain between the two women. The more Mrs. Jones tried to get her to eat, the more combative she became. The Jones' knack for clear communication became muddled and ineffective.

Cjet talked about the problem with her social worker. She complained that Mrs. Jones was always trying to get her to express her feelings, but she couldn't.

This prompted the social worker to tell Mrs. Jones to leave Cjet alone and stop initiating conversations with her. So, Mrs. Jones left her alone – which was the complete opposite of what Cjet really wanted.

Cjet's eating disorder was a cry for help – her way of saying she needed for extra attention. When Mrs. Jones stopped communicating, she felt abandoned, again. She then started looking for a new place to live.

She was now 15 years old, 5'8" and 125 pounds. She was lost, wracked with guilt and fear. She believed a fresh start would be best.

After 15 months with the Jones family, She moved in with a new foster mother named Lynn. Lynn didn't bother her about what to eat. "Just don't starve yourself," was her best advice. Left to her own devices, she obsessed even more about food and exercise, hoping to lose 20-30 pounds. Some days she ingested only 500 calories.

She lived at Lynn's for a month or two before moving on to her next foster home with a woman named Marina.

Her emotions, thoughts and memories were tangled and chaotic. To ease the pain, she began harming herself.

It started with burning. A friend told her she burned out the face of a dollar bill onto her hand, leaving a giant scar. The idea was appealing, so she tried it too.

I liked how the pain was. I know it sounds dumb, but I felt kind of alive. And, it's like I'm making a scar for later. Like, I can burn myself now, and have a story later; a story that will make all this pain more worth it somehow. The emotions inside me that seem to have nowhere to go, and seem to make no sense, can be expressed on my skin.

Things were going okay in her new home, but not great. She had been speaking with her birth mother intermittently, mostly during joint therapy sessions. Marina hit a nerve when she encouraged Cjet to make peace with her mother. During the discussion, Cjet mentioned she was thinking about looking for another place to live. Marina's response eerily echoed her father's words when she left home.

"If you think you have that many problems with us, all right."

Once again, she felt alone and dejected. By this point she had moved from burning herself to cutting. That evening, she wrote:

I cut myself on my leg; I'm not too sure why. I cut in the same place I had cut once before. A straight line down the side, deeper than the first time... once I realized I could cut like this, and it didn't hurt, I wanted to try something more dangerous. I cut along the inside of my wrist. I made a deep cut. For a moment, I had to stop and wait, because I was seeing stars and even felt woozy. That passed, and I kept going. But, all it did was fill a paper towel with blood. I cut along the length of my arm, whereas before, I had cut across my wrist. Before, it was definitely only for attention. Last time, I cut so that I had something to show; something to prove that I really was in pain. This time though, I'm just an idiot. I scared myself.

She soon met a young man named Don, through church. She became close to Don and his family, particularly his father Ken, a police officer. Ken was attentive, kind, and offered thought-provoking advice. Ken drew her out of her shell and helped her to open up. She even admitted something extremely private: having homosexual thoughts.

Ken and his wife had been foster parents before, so it wasn't long before she moved in with them. At first, it was good. Really good. She had a great relationship with the entire family. She was eating well, stopped cutting, and felt happy.

Regrettably, before long the bond between Cjet and Ken turned into an unhealthy relationship.

"I was like this little wounded thing that came flapping to him and he was the wrong person to find me."

She wrote about everything that had happened in her diary, which was found by her foster mother. Soon thereafter, she was swiftly whisked away and placed into a group home.

Cjet knew she had to change if she wanted to be happy. No more chaos. No more escapism. No more being a victim. "This is your last chance, figure it out," she told herself.

She finished high school, and did well academically. She held a job and stayed out of trouble as best she could.

With a palpable sense of relief, she says of this time, "It was so uneventful, which was nice. No more drama."

Cjet made slow but bumpy progress through the ages of 18 to 24. A few symbolic decisions illustrate her process of rebirth, starting with

Cjet

her name.

Cjet isn't her given name – it's one she invented. At 18 she had it legally changed. Next came the tattoo.

She came across a symbol called a Sankofa. Sankofa is an African word and symbol that translates to "reach back and get it." It is associated with a proverb that says, "It is not wrong to go back for that which you have forgotten." The symbol looks like the touching heads of two long-necked birds, fashioned in a swirling heart shape that curls at both the top and bottom.

"The point is you need to look back and bring with you what you've learned in order to move forward." She had the symbol tattooed in the middle of her lower back, colored with many bright hues for a special purpose – Cjet officially came out as gay.

"That was really important to me. I was just turning 18 and I was like, 'I'm done with all this childhood stuff and I'm going to bring the best with me and look forward.' I cut off my hair and I got this tattoo, I sported all my rainbows and I went to all the pride parades. I was a new me. I was much stronger in knowing who I was and I didn't have to keep hiding that I liked girls."

The Sankofa tattoo was a starting point for a larger design. "It just spread out from there and now it's my whole back. It turned into grass and flames and a dragonfly coming out of it. So it was something beautiful coming out of a mess."

She refers to a line from the Bible that reflects what she was experiencing at that time.

When you've taken the city, set it on fire. (Joshua 8:8)

"That's a scripture from way back when some dude had to walk around the city walls for a while, to scout it out because he was going to attack the city. God let him and his people know, once you've taken the city, set it on fire so they can't come back. It's burned. It's done. I felt that was also what I was doing. I was done with the sin and the evil and the grudges and the pain and everything."

After graduating from college with a double major in Art Therapy and Psychology, she found a life-changing opportunity. She went to a fundraiser for Justice for Children International, a non-profit headquartered in New Haven, Connecticut, now operating under the name Love146. Love146's mission is in helping women and children affected by the horrors of sex trafficking, exploitation, and other abuses.

"When I met them, things changed. Like my heart took a deep breath and I realized I can do something with myself."

She struck up a conversation with a woman representing the organization. "We met up at their office in New Haven. She and I are still good friends. I jumped right in and went with them and saw firsthand these issues with trafficking. You hear about it, but to see it is really different. And that just turned my heart, like – this is something I could be a part of."

A passage in *Dear Diary* notes:

Something changed in me that night. I stopped crying about me and started feeling for someone else. This was a turning point. From that moment on, I had some purpose. I could help others.

She traveled to Sri Lanka and educated therapists on child exploitation. She trained social workers on how to use art in their counseling sessions. Her passion for art therapy comes through in her voice as she describes the process.

"For me it's about expressing whatever it is you need to, whatever you're working through, without having to put it into words. That's hard for so many people. You can play, you can draw, you can squiggle in the sand, or just sit with things and manipulate them. You develop a trust with the person that you're working with. Art therapy specifically focuses on not having to pull words out of somebody.

"You have to meet a person where they're at, with regards to art. Some people haven't used paint, so they won't want to paint. And you don't have to. You can doodle with pens."

Cjet helped during the aftermath of the devastating 2004 tsunami that killed almost 300,000 people in the region. The disaster forced parents to sell their own children, believing that was their only option.

"They were working with children whose homes had been destroyed, so their families had gone off and sold them. Like a 10-year-old boy who they can't feed or house anymore, so they've given him away. We were working with the families to show them, here's something that your son can do: polish shoes. He can go to this school and he can learn how to build. He can help rebuild your home or your community.

"Also, there was a refugee camp I went to. I had them working on this fabric banner to decorate their area just to make it prettier. We did some things that helped them work together and know that they each had their own part and their own voice. They weren't just helpless. They could do something for themselves and their community."

She returned home for a few months, only to head back out to the Philippines and Cambodia.

"There was a 9-month training program on how to work with women and children who have been exploited. The focus of it was the aftercare of these people once they've been rescued from somewhere, once they've been reintegrated back into their families. I did four months of class work in the Philippines and a three-month internship in Cambodia. I lived in an orphanage. I worked on the reintegration of girls once they've aged out of an orphanage or care facility to get them back into the community, and then went back to the Philippines to finish the thesis work."

Cjet

Another facet of her rebirth was when she attended a conference in India. The event was headlined by the popular no-nonsense Christian lecturer and incest survivor Joyce Meyer. Always the prolific writer, she penned a multi-page confession addressed to Meyer herself.

"What I felt was I have to stop lying to anybody and everybody and myself. I confessed to her. I wrote a letter and I gave it to a guard. I don't know if she ever got it and it doesn't even matter, but it was about getting it out of me. I wrote four or five pages of the things that I've been doing with myself and not telling people, the things that I've told somebody that are an exaggeration because I don't feel good enough, having been abused. I confessed, cleaned up my brain and cleared out my heart from all of these little things."

Cjet regards this purification-by-ink as another pivotal point cleaving a line of demarcation between "then" and "now." She returned home fully rejuvenated.

Before she had left for Southeast Asia, she became friendly with another teacher at her school. Her friend's class helped raise money for her humanitarian mission abroad.

"When I came back home, our friendship suddenly changed, which is really nice."

She says a change inside of her occurred "almost magically. I look at it as my heart was healed enough and I was now able to feel like I could be loved."

The two have been married for six years and Cjet has adopted her wife's two teenage daughters as her own. Cjet was given away at their wedding by none other than Mrs. Lobo, who sadly passed away a few years later.

Cjet's parents moved out of state many years ago, and were not a part of her wedding. She kept minimal contact with her mother for a long time before she stopped communicating with her altogether. The separation works for her. The lack of reminders, questions and lingering resentments has helped her move on.

She is still involved in charitable activities. She's been a member on panels and a keynote speaker for several organizations, including the Department of Children and Families, Hands of Love and Take Back the Night.

She believes an important element in surviving an abusive childhood is to connect with at least one other person and to avoid isolating.

"I know this sounds hard to do, but you've got to find that one person. You've got to have one connection or one person who believes in you."

Cjet knows that she deserves to live a happy life, but that wasn't always the case. For those who have gone through a traumatic childhood, finding self-worth can be a lifelong challenge. Her mantra is, "I'm okay. It's okay to be okay." It's a sentiment she believes "you have to own."

"No matter what you've been through, you can overcome it and either become someone different or a better person."

Today, Cjet is the beautiful, kind, intelligent woman she always has been, but now no longer needs crutches like chaos and pain. By transforming her own grief into compassion for others who have suffered the same, she reminds those who have endured adversity that there is always a light at the end of the tunnel, and that light is love.

RESOURCES

After the Storm, Inc.
afterthestorminc.org
(860) 685-0698
88 Harvest Wood Road
Rockfall, CT 06481
afterthestorminc@yahoo.com

Alcoholics Anonymous:
aa.org
(866) 783-7712 (866-STEPS12)
(855) 377-2628 (en Espanol)
Connecticut site: www.ct-aa.org

American Cancer Society
cancer.org
(800) 227-2345
250 Williams Street, NW
Atlanta, GA 30303

Autism Speaks
autismspeaks.org
1 East 33rd Street, 4th Floor
New York, NY 10016
info@autismspeaks.org

Billy Smolinski Tip Line
www.justice4billy.com
(203) 530-9135
P.O. Box 123
Cheshire, CT 06410
info@justice4billy.com

Brain Injury Association of America
biausa.org
(800) 444-6443
1608 Spring Hill Road, Suite 110
Vienna, VA 22182
info@biausa.org

Brian T. Dagle Memorial Foundation
brianshealinghearts.org
(860) 625-5280
ann@brianshealinghearts.org

Foundation for Sarcoidosis Research
stopsarcoidosis.org
(866) 358-5477
1820 W. Webster Ave., Suite 304
Chicago, IL 60614
info@stopsarcoidosis.org

Histiocytosis Association
Histio.org
(856) 589-6606
332 North Broadway
Pitman, NJ 08071
info@histio.org

Innocence Project
innocenceproject.org
 (212) 364-5340
40 Worth Street, Suite 701
New York, NY 10013
info@innocenceproject.org

Love146:
love146.org
(203) 772-4420
P.O. Box 8266
New Haven, CT 06530
info@love146.org

My Child™ - the Ultimate Resource for Everything Cerebral Palsy
cerebralpalsy.org
(800) 692-4453
c/o Stern Law Group, PLLC
41850 West Eleven Mile Road, Suite 121
Novi, MI 48375
contactus@mychildwithcp.com

Narcotics Anonymous
na.org
(818) 773-9999
PO Box 9999
Van Nuys, CA 91409
fsmail@na.org

The National Domestic Abuse Hotline
thehotline.org
(800) 799-7233
P.O. Box 161810
Austin, TX 78716

National Missing and Unidentified Persons System (NamUs)
findthemissing.org
(855) 626-7600
questions@findthemissing.org

National Multiple Sclerosis Society (Northeast Chapter)
nationalmssociety.org
(800) 344-4867
101A First Avenue, Suite 6
Waltham, MA 02451-1115
nationalmssocietyGNE@nmss.org

National Suicide Prevention Hotline
suicidepreventionlifeline.org
(800) 273-8255
50 Broadway, 19th Floor
New York, NY 10004

PTSD Foundation of America
ptsdusa.org
(832) 912-4429
P.O. Box 690748
Houston, TX 77269
info@ptsdusa.org

Rape, Abuse & Incest National Network (RAINN)
rainn.org
(800) 656-4673
1200 L Street NW, Suite 505
Washington, DC 20005
info@rainn.org

The Transverse Myelitis Association
myelitis.org
(855) 380-3330
1787 Sutter Parkway
Powell, OH 43065-8806
info@myelitis.org

Connect.

info@outfoxbooks.com

www.outfoxbooks.com

facebook.com/outfoxbooks

twitter.com/OutfoxBooks

www.ingramcontent.com/pod-product-compliance
Lightning Source LLC
Chambersburg PA
CBHW051750040426
42446CB00007B/293